Calexico

꒰ ꒰ ꒰

Calexico

True Lives of the Borderlands

Peter Laufer

The University of Arizona Press
Tucson

The University of Arizona Press
© 2011 Peter Laufer
All rights reserved

www.uapress.arizona.edu

Library of Congress Cataloging-in-Publication Data

Laufer, Peter.
Calexico : true lives of the borderlands / Peter Laufer.
p. cm.
ISBN 978-0-8165-2951-3 (pbk. : alk. paper)   1. Calexico
(Calif.)—History.   2. Calexico (Calif.)—Social
conditions.   3. Borderlands—California—Calexico.   I. Title.
F869.C14L38 2011
979.4'99—dc22
2011007156

Publication of this book is made possible in part by the proceeds of a permanent
endowment created with the assistance of a Challenge Grant from the National
Endowment for the Humanities, a federal agency.

Manufactured in the United States of America on acid-free, archival-quality paper
containing a minimum of 30% post-consumer waste and processed chlorine free.

16   15   14   13   12   11   6   5   4   3   2   1

Photographs by Peter Laufer and Markos Kounalakis

Para ti, Sheilita, con el amor de siempre

Contents

※   ※   ※

Foreword

We can all learn from Calexico. You may know where Calexico is on the map, located on the border with Mexico about a two-hour drive east of San Diego. But Calexico is more than a dot on the map; it is a city that draws into sharp focus the often blurred images of what immigration means to our country. It does this by giving concrete images of lives lived and ideas born where cultures meet, conflict, and merge. Calexico is a city filled with stories reflecting fundamental questions about who we are as Americans, what our values are, and how our democracy works.

Growing up in San Diego, I was introduced to Calexico by my mother, who took us on drives to that town and into northern Baja California. I remember sitting in the backseat of our 1968 Dodge Dart, poking my head out the window and being struck by the contrasts and poetry of the place: stretches of desert broken by long green strips of agriculture and canals flowing next to the roads and highways near Calexico that people told me were filled with catfish the size of my little brother. I remember, also, whispering over and over the names Calexico and Mexicali, its sister city, and thinking that the people who came up with those names must have had a magical familiarity with the borderland where Mexico and California merge. A place, as one person interviewed in this book points out, that was not quite United States and not quite Mexico, but something else. The sister names well fit the meeting place of the two nation-families.

Wallace Stegner wrote that California is America—only more. Something similar could be said about Calexico: "Calexico is California—only more." The issues of water, environment, language, education, immigration, and the relations with the nation of Mexico are all ones that Calexico experiences more deeply than do places in California less critically situated. In my work at the California Council for the Humanities, I hear stories from across California that describe the beauty, sorrow, and joy that create the complex tapestry of life in our state. I hear stories that retell our past and provide clues as to how we can shape our future. Unfortunately, so far, few of those stories have come out of the southeast corner of our state—but it is to exactly this region and its unique combination of society and geography that we should be paying attention. Stories from this region are under-reported, yet they can vitally educate us about critical issues facing our state and nation.

In the spirit of John Steinbeck's *Travels with Charley* and Alexis de Tocqueville's *Democracy in America,* Peter Laufer and his longtime journalism colleague Markos Kounalakis went on a journey to uncover what was on the minds of the people of Calexico, to better understand the complexities of life on the border. The people that they encountered and spoke with on this journey revealed compassion, humor, concern, and curiosity about the world around them. Through Laufer's writing, the curtains are pulled back to reveal a people and a place that tell us as much about who we are as they do about who they are.

Ralph Lewin
President
California Council for the Humanities

≳　≳　≳

Preface

Why Calexico?

As a journalist and a Californian, I can't help but be drawn to the United States–Mexico Borderlands, the consequential border problems, and the migration crises affecting both sides of our southern national frontier. How can I not be? The border is an ongoing spectacular news story in the best *Front Page* tradition, and we Californians live that story—its tragedies and its joys—daily.

In this book, I seek to transcend the rhetoric of the stalled and vitriolic national immigration debate by bringing to life the realities of the people immediately involved with it on a day-to-day basis: those who live, work, and transit the California–Mexico border. The backdrop of the California–Mexico Borderlands provides a Hollywood-like setting to begin to understand the often dire circumstances along the entire southern front of the United States of America.

Calexico, as its name implies, is a city just on the California side of the California–Mexico border. This little-known community—along with its sister city of Mexicali, located just on the Mexican side of the divide—is a perfect place to contemplate the border, borderlands culture, and illegal Mexican migration, because it is far from the spotlighted Tijuana–San Diego or El Paso–Juárez type of border twin cities.

Today, downtown Calexico is a dusty shell of its vibrant past, many of its customers discouraged by the increased border security that appeared in the wake of 9/11. The malls that sprawl to the north took some of downtown's customers, many of them Mexicans crossing north to shop. But post-9/11 border security discouraged those Mexicans from bothering with the long wait to cross into the States, souring business both downtown and at the sprawling shopping centers.

The pace of life is slow in Calexico. The mood is much like the stereotype of a 1950s America. Yet it is jammed up against a wall, and on the other side of that wall is vibrant and cosmopolitan Mexicali.

A sign missed by freeway travelers hurtling nonstop along The Eight between San Diego and Yuma.

The small-town character of Calexico, with its warm, open populace, makes the border crises accessible and understandable in a person-to-person manner that is quick and easy to fathom. I used Calexico as a jumping-off point and a reference point. The stories I encountered in Calexico sent me to people and places all along the border and throughout North America.

This work revolves around a central claim: the border has become a new type of geopolitical fraud. That fraud results in no less than the criminalization of Mexican and other migrants, the bloating of the mismanaged Immigration and Customs Enforcement sector of the Homeland Security Department, the deterioration of living standards along the frontier, and the enrichment of American employers. I look at specific examples of the border crises and try to humanize them by showing, through experiential reporting and intimate interviewing, how they affect individuals and our body politic.

I take on the immigration issue with an explicit California focus. Throughout our nation's history, Californian innovations have driven the national experience and influenced the national culture. In the case of immigration, what seems to be a California problem is shared by the other forty-nine states, and I profess with the conceit of a Californian that they can learn from our examples. With typical California optimism, I examine the border in the context of its problems, but I also celebrate the vibrant borderlands culture.

The overarching problems of the borderlands now extend throughout Mexico and up through all fifty of the United States. The voices I encounter on the border bring to the policy-making corridors of Sacramento and Washington (and Mexico City) potential solutions to the problems we face on our southern frontier, grassroots-originated solutions from those who know the border and its challenges better than most bureaucrats and lawmakers. My desire is to contextualize the region as emblematic of the immigration crises facing California and the nation even as I spotlight the too-little-known individuality of the borderlands, via an intensive look at Calexico and a lifetime of living on the extended California border.

With an understanding of what makes the borderlands and its people unique, it may be easier to begin the process of fixing one of the most broken aspects of our nation's internal and international scenes: the Mexican border, and the immigration and security problems that come with it.

≋ ≋ ≋
Acknowledgments

As the text for *Calexico* was—to use the old newspaper jargon—being put to bed, I asked my border road trips partner Markos Kounalakis to help make sure I missed nobody here on the acknowledgments page. From his home away from home in Budapest he dispatched an e-mail to me that covers—to use an all-American metaphor—all the bases. Ever the diplomat, he suggested I thank "the hundreds of people you and I have met with, interviewed, broken bread with, and experienced genuine human kindness from in the many years of this lifelong learning profession to whom we are grateful, but who may never receive specific acknowledgement because the encounters were fleeting or respectfully anonymous."

I can't argue with those sentiments, but there are specific friends and colleagues appropriate to pick out of the crowd by name.

Some of the observations and ideas expressed in *Calexico* germinated from interviews and events I experienced while reporting on borders for previous assignments. Heartfelt thanks go to Ivan R. Dee, the editor and publisher of *Wetback Nation: The Case for Opening the Mexican–American Border;* Tom Christensen, the editor of *Iron Curtain Rising: A Personal Journey through the Changing Landscape of Eastern Europe; Penthouse* editor Peter Bloch; *Washington Monthly* editor-in-chief Paul Glastris; and Jim Farley, who, when he was a vice president at NBC News, sent me off as an NBC News correspondent to borders worldwide.

The *Calexico* project was made possible with support from the California Council for the Humanities in partnership with the Skirball Foundation. The council is an independent nonprofit organization and a partner of the National Endowment for the Humanities. For more information on the council, visit www.calhum.org. The initial research for *Calexico* fueled a radio documentary series that was broadcast as a special report of *Washington Monthly on the Radio,* a program (on hiatus) that I anchor with fellow traveler Kounalakis. The program's sound designer and technical director is Jim McKee. When they served as producers for *Washington Monthly on the Radio,* Ingalisa Schrobsdorff and Dan Zoll secured some of the most extraordinary interview "gets" who populate *Calexico.* Thanks also to Jay Harris, who, during his tenure as *Mother Jones* publisher, created the collegial atmosphere we found at his magazine's radio studio.

I'm lucky to enjoy a coterie of colleagues gracious enough to look at my works in progress: a special tip of the Stetson straw to George Papagiannis, Ira Kahn, Terry Phillips, Alex Roth, and Jeff Kamen. And I appreciate the three anonymous-to-me peer reviewers whom the University of Arizona Press asked to review the manuscript; their critiques were of consequential value to this book. Patti Hartmann, the senior editor at the press, embraced the print version of the *Calexico* project soon after we aired the radio series. *Gracías* to her, border studies editor Kristen Buckles, editor-in-chief Allyson Carter, and the entire University of Arizona Press team for their fine and important work.

As always, *abrazos y besos* to my wife, Sheila—the harsh first reader of all my works and an early champion of this one—who continues to save me from myself with great editorial skill, phenomenal personal patience, and stoic good humor.

≈   ≈   ≈

Introduction

Interviews and Borders

Interviews and borders fascinate me. All types of borders: personal and political, local and distant. I enjoy crossing most borders, experiencing what's on the other side, meeting other people and cultures I would otherwise never know.

That compunction to embrace and transit borders coexists well with my habitual delight in hearing personal narratives. I love to interview. By definition, a good interview crosses borders both for the interviewee and the interviewer. The interviewee, under circumstances ideal for the interviewer, reveals more than he or she expected or intended when the conversation started, and the interviewer—me in the case of this book—learns about himself as he asks questions and hears the answers. The key to turning a simple question-and-answer session into a gripping and revealing interview is active listening. And constructive active listening is hard work.

After over four decades of asking questions for a living, I have come to prefer the term *conversation* to the word *interview*. A consequential and intriguing interview stars both players; it is a theatrical give-and-take. The German word for it works perfectly: *Unterhalten* means both conversation and entertainment. As a journalist, I'm convinced story-telling success requires that the tale both entertain and inform.

I've studied and reported on lives lived on both sides of the Mexican–American border since the 1960s. Before I began asking questions professionally, I made the all-but-mandatory California coming-of-age high school summer vacation trip across the border to Rosarita with a couple of classmates; and the Mexican authorities turned us back when we tried to travel south from Ensenada, because we were underage and lacked written parental permission. That event started me thinking seriously about border politics and the idea that a state authority could curtail my wanderings.

Later, as a correspondent for NBC News, I reported extensively on the spectrum of drama around our southwest border and then wrote a book analyzing Mexican migration north. I gave it the deliberately unsettling title *Wetback Nation* because I came to believe we Americans needed a fresh look at a rapidly worsening national tragedy. I've also examined the southern border from an academic perspective, studying the Mexican diaspora living and working in the United States, and as an element of my Cultural Studies PhD I've crossed and come up against plenty of other national borders: the DMZ and its barbed wire separating North and South Korea, the Iron Curtain, Mexico's southern border luring undocumented Central Americans north, the nominally passive Canadian–U.S. line, Pakistan's wild North-West Frontier Province and Afghanistan at the Khyber Pass, refugee camps in Jordan just the other side of Iraq, and post-Wall Europe, with its borders passport-free once you're inside the Schengen zone.

We all cross lines—political, cultural, social, familial, personal—continually. We're not static and in one place, ever.

Get up in the morning and stumble to the bathroom. There is probably a door on that bathroom. Do you close it? That probably depends on who is in the house with you. If you've been sleeping with a friend or a lover, or just sharing a bed for convenience, you've faced a border before the bathroom. "Get back on your side of the bed," you may have mumbled if your companion disturbed your sleep. Or, "You've got all the covers!"

We are surrounded by borders. They provide us with security and comfort, limits and definitions. Crossed, some borderlines generate fear, hate, rage, and war.

Once in the bathroom, perhaps you decide to close the door. You might want some privacy while you go about your morning routine. Or maybe you don't want to disturb your companion with the noise you make, and closing the door creates some sound barrier. If the door is equipped with a lock, you face another decision: create complete privacy by pushing on the button on the knob or allow your companion(s) to choose whether to respect the indication that you made when you shut the door that you wish privacy. Of course, in most modern American houses, you can defeat the bathroom door lock by sticking a bobby pin or a nail into the hole in the knob on the outside of the door. So the security of your privacy in the bathroom depends on an expectation that your companions will respect the message of the locked door and not intrude on you unless they face a bathroom emergency or hear you calling for help.

There are plenty of other borders in your home. "Stay out of my room," you may instruct your kids. Perhaps you've got some secrets in the dresser, or you just don't want the kids sitting on your clean sheets with their dirty jeans. The kids may want to keep you out of their rooms, too. House rules also create borders without walls and doors. You may not allow food in the living room, or you may forbid roller skates on the rugs. A particularly unruly friend of one of your kids might be barred from spending the night in the family home, or even forbidden from visiting under any circumstances.

Of course if your own child is a tad mischievous, he may let that blacklisted friend in through his bedroom window in the middle of the night and shove him out at dawn. You might never know that the troublemaker was in your house. And while you're at work, someone might be watching TV in the living room, eating a peanut-butter-and-grape-jelly sandwich, in violation of your house rules. As long as there are no crumbs on the floor, or purple stains on the carpet, you might never know that it was transformed into an after-school snack room.

Is there a fence around your house? If so, why is it there? Perhaps it keeps your dog in your yard. Perhaps it keeps other dogs out of your yard. Maybe you built it just to define the border of your property, to give you a sense of what is yours and how far into the distance that legal ownership extends. Or your fence may block a view you don't want to look at: the neighbors' turquoise house, or their '67 Dodge Charger up on blocks. Your fence may provide a sequestered playground for your children, a safety zone from which they can't escape if they're still toddlers.

Is there a lock on your gate? Is there a lock on your front door? If you live in a metropolis, there are probably several different types of locks on your door: a spring lock, a couple of deadbolts, and a chain to allow for some restricted communication or exchange of goods without actual entry. This crucial border between your sanctuary and the rest of the world may well be equipped with a peephole to check on the identity of visitors, in an attempt to ensure, along with all the locks, that no one violates your person or property. Inner-city apartments in rough neighborhoods now often are equipped with a steel bar that fits into a hole in the floor and braces against the front door, creating an obstacle to those who, frustrated by the locks, may attempt to break down the door and cross the border—uninvited—into your house.

We create borders to define our personal space, and we devise techniques to patrol and enforce them. How close do we stand to others in a line? Where do we keep our hands in a crowded subway car? Do we kiss, or shake hands, or bow upon meeting someone? All these decisions mark borders.

Worldwide, national borders allow states and their employed minions to exert power over those of us who wish to cross them. One of my lasting favorite examples dates from late 1990, at the Hungarian–Romanian border. It was almost winter and I was driving from Szeged toward Arad almost a year after the revolution that overthrew the brutal dictator Nicolae Ceauşescu. Great change had occurred, but many of the irritations and oddities that had accompanied border crossings along the former Iron Curtain were still in place.

The crossing was slow. A line of cars sat, engines off, drivers and passengers wandering around looking at the meager pickings available at the border kiosk: cigarettes and candy. The entrance visa still cost thirty U.S. dollars, even though other liberated Eastern bloc countries dumped border-crossing fees months before.

Inside the concrete customs building, the lighting was dim. The lobby was stacked full of tires, and the smell of rubber was strong. One aging customs woman, a thick-waisted, stolid relic of the old Stalinist regime, stood with the tires. There was no other sign of business in the building, no explanation for the tire warehouse.

After a routine passport check, there was a customs inspection. The chief inspector was wearing jeans, a civilian jacket—like a ski parka—dark glasses, and a beard. He looked as though he was in his thirties.

"Do you have any guns?"

"No."

"Or roses?" He laughed and asked, "Do you know the band Guns 'n' Roses?"

"Yes," I answered tentatively. "Do you like them?"

He smiled his approval of the band.

But we were still not through the gate, not yet in the country. My colleague Markos offered the guard a package of American cigarettes as he was searching the car. We had come with plenty of Kents; at the time Romanians were famous for loving them. That brand, for some inexplicable reason, was the most-sought-after cigarette; Kents were used as second currency. But a border guard can afford to be fussy. He dismissed the offered cigarettes with disdain and reverse snobbery.

"I only smoke Camels."

The paperwork continued, delayed and slow. Markos was equipped with a valid visa, but the passport checker refused to accept it. Markos was forced back to the visa hut to get another thirty-dollar stamp. While he was buying the new visa, the guard that refused to accept his valid old one was kissing the visa lady on the back of the neck. It was hard to imagine that they wouldn't be splitting that extra thirty dollars when their shift ended.

The covered drive through the inspection zone was decorated with faded tourist signs that suffered from poor color reproduction—like bad Technicolor—advertising hotels and campgrounds. The result was a failed attempt to intrigue visitors with Romania as an appealing ski resort or health spa destination. Instead, these deteriorating posters worked as statements of reality, making it clear that ahead lay a failed system, a system that could not even promote itself without drawing attention to its historic corruption and continuing internal decay.

The last passport check came at a window marked: SKON RO L. It used to say PASSKONTROLL; the plastic letters had dropped off, and no one cared enough to replace them. Above the SKON RO L sign was a rusting fluorescent light fixture with no tube in it. Finally, the guard lifted the red-and-white metal gate, and we were in Romania, driving toward Arad.

The Mexican–American border is one of the most thoroughly examined in the world. Yet it continues to lure me as both a news reporter and as a social scientist. In part, I'm sure, that's because it's in my own backyard and I grew up with it. It extends north to San Francisco and on to the fishing village where I live, north of the Golden Gate Bridge on the Pacific coast. Mexicans, most of them from Jalisco, live and work in this village with a name that combines Spanish and English—Bodega Bay—many of them unequipped with the documents required for legal residency.

Much of the journalistic and academic focus on the Mexican–American border has been—understandably—at two types of places. One is the metropolitan crossing points such as Tijuana–San Diego and Juárez–El Paso. There the austere and severe border wall on the American side is a memorial to failed U.S. government policies. The other is the cruel, wild Sonoran desert, where desperate Mexicans hurl themselves north in hopes of making it alive to a job in the States.

Attracting much less attention are places such as Calexico, little-known border points spotted along the two-thousand-mile line separating the United States and Mexico. I've always been attracted to places like Calexico that are off the beaten track. And I've been drawn to the types of people who make a life in such places, especially those who root themselves and live happily ever after in locales most of us never even heard of and just fly over or speed past.

The legendary and best-selling documentary author Studs Terkel is one of my heroes. Long ago he recognized the value of the modern American Everyman story and immortalized hundreds of them from the otherwise anonymous neighborhoods of, first, Chicago and ultimately across the country. "A tape recorder," he wrote in the introduction to his masterpiece *Working*, "with microphone in hand, on the table or the arm of the chair or on the grass, can transform both the visitor and the host. On one occasion, during the play-back, my companion murmured in wonder, 'I never realized I felt that way.' And I was filled with wonder, too." I, too, am filled with wonder during conversations with interviewees. Today the technology is changed. My digital recorder is the size of a pack of Kents and fits undetected in my shirt pocket. At times, such as during the revealing conversation with Border patrolman Martino, conducted as I was leaving the Imperial Valley to return to San Francisco, I'm convinced the candor expressed would be muted were a microphone between us and a recording device in evidence. I never hide my role as a journalist if asked, but I often feel no need to advertise it.

Calexico and, to a lesser extent, its twin city Mexicali on the other side of the border, suffer quietly the failures of public policy makers in Washington and Mexico City to solve the perpetual crises on the frontier that divides the two nations. Calexico was founded in 1908, a city made possible because Colorado River water was rerouted to irrigate the desert. When my traveling companion Markos Kounalakis and I were flying over the desert en route to the border, the line between the barren and the bountiful was clean, stark, and defined by the wending waterway that brings the Colorado water west. Calexico is just south of the airport. Its shabby downtown sits smack against the border. Strip malls extend north toward El Centro, filled with chain stores sucking commerce from the local shops along First Street.

Over the last twenty-plus years, Markos and I have found ourselves on several occasions on the road together on reporting trips. We travel borders well together—along borders and across borders. As journalists we share the lure of perpetual news that breaks on borders, passive and disputed. As Americans born of immigrant parents, we share a stark personal awareness of the role of borders in our own lives. And as adventurers, we both enjoy the unknowns and the unexpected that define borders. We're drawn to the clash borders create—a point so many travelers seek to avoid or to transit as fast as possible.

Prior to this trip, I last passed through Calexico when I spoke at a book fair in Mexicali. The literary event's organizers gave me a ride back to the El Centro airport for my flight home, and as we waited to cross into California the driver told me that since 9/11 the wait can be up to two hours to get through the recently hardened border; it's a wait that is nasty in the summer sun, which burns in the triple digits through July and August. "I don't like coming here," he told me, "because I don't like to give them the pleasure of making me wait. But merchandise is cheaper up here, so we come." He told me that he and his friends joke about the U.S. immigration officers and what they ask Mexicans as they try to verify the likelihood that a traveler will return to Mexico after a day's shopping. But his best story was about himself. "When I was a child I believed that as soon as you crossed the border you were able to speak English!"

It's important for gringos to remember that not every Mexican wants to invade the United States. When I was at the Guadalajara book fair, one of my taxi drivers proudly showed off his car as he told me how happy he was to be back in Mexico. "I stayed in California," he said, "just long enough to learn English and earn enough money to buy this cab."

I joined a colleague on her Guadalajara radio talk show, and we asked the audience to call if they did not want to migrate north and to tell us why they wished instead to stay in Mexico. The factors were fascinating. Predictably high on the list were family and a desire to live in the Mexican culture. Less expected: *el otro lado* is dangerous and packed with prejudice against Mexicans. Additionally, we were told that the land north of the border is too money-oriented and its culture too fast for properly enjoying life.

My journey to Calexico documented in these pages was an opportunity to experience its people, to learn about their lives. There's a wise old saying in the news business, and it's one of my favorites: "There are no slow news days, only slow news reporters." No life is mundane; we all live a real-life drama, and that drama includes unique observations and experiences. The Calexico conversations I enjoyed are those of lives lived in a sleepy crossroads that exists at a global flashpoint: America's southern border. Consequently, the stories I collected are both of human interest and of international concern. Chronicled here is the week I spent in Calexico engaged in one intensive interview after another with its stoic citizens.

Waitress Bonnie Peterson introduced me to what draws many of her neighbors to Calexico. "The slow pace, the people, the friendly atmosphere. They're different," she said about those who live in big cities. "It's not that they're bad people up there; it's just the city has a different kind of people."

Political consultant Frank Salazar came home to Calexico from a stint in Washington working for the Clinton administration, "because I love my Valley. It's me. I like it. It's different. It's not the same hobnob like at the Capital Grille in D.C. You focus on your family, you work hard, you sweat hard."

Radio station owner Carroll Buckley thrives in the melting pot of Imperial County. "You will be sitting in the Owl Café . . . and see two people sitting, one eating ham and eggs, the other eating *chorizo y huevos*. One speaking in English, and the other in Spanish, the two of them conversing."

Ninety-something Virginia Munger shared her memories of pioneer Calexico days. "I can't figure out why we were all so happy. We didn't have air-conditioning, and we didn't have a fan. At the library they had a big tub of water and a fan that would hit the water to cool things out. But I can't remember ever really being uncomfortable."

Dual national Gustavo Yee, busy trying to sell Calexico tract houses in a down market, and taking advantage of the best of both worlds, told me, "I always joke that if I'm flying and the plane gets, like, kidnapped, I'll just throw away my U.S. passport and keep the Mexican, because they always take the U.S. citizens as hostages."

These Calexico conversations led me to adjacent Imperial Valley communities and characters, both of which helped me understand and enjoy the quiet richness of this little-known scene, and they motivated me to connect with relevant personalities who were far from Calexico, yet intimately involved in Calexican affairs, from the famous and the infamous to the previously unknown to me. Former CNN commentator Lou Dobbs and his jingoist nativism became a running theme during my time in Calexico. Celebrities ranging in style and influence from poet Rod McKuen to Fox News actor Geraldo Rivera played critical cameo roles. I talked with a Texas property owner whose family has lived directly on the border for generations; she put the border wall into perspective as she described the scene outside her kitchen window. My chat with a Canadian border city mayor made it clear that the problems that Washington was causing Calexico are the same ones it was causing from sea to shining sea on both our northern and southern frontiers.

I come away from this project educated and impressed by the California (and other) voices I've been privileged to record. I've learned to appreciate a desperate little city where I would never wish to live but hope to visit often. And I'm more convinced than ever that the solution to the immediate crises on our southern border is to open it to Mexicans who wish to come north—just as their border is open to those of us gringos who wish to travel south.

Calexico

Monday

"Where California and Mexico Meet!"

Growing up in and around San Francisco, as I did, is both a delight and a burden. The burden comes from the inbred chauvinism that comes with being a San Franciscan. We're a pretentious crowd—elitist and self-centered—convinced we're hipper than thou. We eat better food, our weather is nicer, our fashions are more dashing, and our innovations are much more creative. Than what? Than whose? Ah, that's another example of our San Francisco pretentiousness. We don't need to complete no stinking comparisons. We think we're better than anyplace else and anybody else. That's part of our charm, or so we like to imagine. And it also can make us insufferable to be around. We're in love with ourselves and our city.

As I headed south for another trip to the California border, I couldn't help but travel with that attitude. As noted, it's inbred. I was off to the border to report another chapter of the never-ending story of the American standoff with Mexico, but I was also slumming. I was en route to check out how my poor brothers and sisters survived far from my cosmopolitan home.

I picked Calexico as a base camp because it defies the stereotypes most of us rely on when we think about the Mexican border. Calexico is not another example of the Tijuana–San Diego type of dichotomy: a teeming megalopolis of contrasts, with extreme poverty punctuated by lawlessness on the south side of the line and pristine affluence to the north. Instead, Calexico is another dusty stop along the brutal desert border, one of those places where the *coyotes* and drug traffickers drop their loads before disappearing again south of the border. Calexico, my preliminary research suggested to me, was also a struggling Mayberry RFD of the border, with unique twists on the theme of a Norman Rockwell–type America.

Calexico is poor, undereducated, and polluted. It is within Imperial County, which suffers last place among California counties in water and air quality, schooling, and income. Calexico is a struggling market city of fewer than fifty thousand citizens. It can claim few cultural amenities. Cosmopolitan sophistication is across the border in Mexicali, a twenty-four-hour-a-day cornucopia of dining and nightclubs, theater and concerts. It is the state capital of Baja California and home to the Universidad Autónoma de Baja California. Calexico was an unknown place for me; I'd only passed through it en route elsewhere. Much like naive anthropologists searching for an undiscovered (by them) indigenous population to study, I was off to tell the tales of what I figured would be a colorful—but underprivileged—collection of Californians.

I knew I would find a unique culture to celebrate, and one that could help us all better understand our border wars with Mexico and Mexicans. Over many years of studying borders I've learned that frontier dwellers experience a transnational lifestyle that often transcends the prejudices of fellow citizens living distant from the Other. It's a rite of passage for most Californians to make a trip to the border and cross over into a few blocks of Mexico, the legendary land of (for a teenager) easy underage booze, Wolfman Jack, and the donkey act—experiences that tend to reinforce, not dash, those prejudices. California and Mexico come together at the only place where the first and third worlds meet. For Calexico, far from the spotlight of Tijuana, that clash creates frustration and opportunity, in the midst of daily routines. The border-straddling Calexico lifestyle is one the rest of us can learn from, and we can use the lessons of our border's Calexicos—with luck—to move the immigration debate in Washington and Mexico City from hype and hysteria to hope.

I am fortunate enough to have lived on and reported from all sorts of borders, political and social. Berlin before the Wall came down. The Greece–Turkey crises. Afghanistan–Pakistan. The Iraq–Jordan line. North and South Korea. I've heard the Montana jokes Minnesotans make. Along any borders cultures exchange with each other and thrive, even as the artificiality of what we call a political border inevitably creates strains. As I was preparing for my trip south to Calexico, I met my friend Markos for lunch in Fairfax, a village on the north side of Mt. Tamalpais in Marin County, across the Golden Gate Bridge from San Francisco. I had convinced Markos to join me for a week in Calexico. We ate at Fradelizio's ("Ristorante Italiano" it makes clear on its business card, in another example of a drawn border). While we were eating, owner Paul Fradelizio showed up and, as is his style, stopped by our table to say hello.

"How are you?" I asked him.

"Fine, now that I'm back home in Fairfax," was his answer.

The obvious follow-up question was to find out about his travels; it sounded as if he had just returned from distant lands. "Where were you?" we asked.

"San Rafael," he said. "And I always feel so much better as soon as I cross the line."

San Rafael is the county seat, just three miles east of Fairfax.

Borders help us define ourselves, and Mr. Fradelizio made it clear he does not identify with San Rafael. Borders don't just meet, they conflict, they abut, they crash into each other, and they create a mélange that is that uniqueness of the California borderlands that I looked forward—on the eve of my departure—to celebrating.

Markos and I were off on what I thought could be another classic road trip; perhaps we would stray from Calexico and run the length of the border. We sat around and thought about our famous highway-wandering predecessors. We considered our ride: what should we be driving? It was a question posed to me by my friend the author Jonah Raskin.

"What kind of car are you going to use?" he queried.

"Why do you ask that?"

"It's an important question," was his response. "This is America. You'll be spending a lot of time in the car. It needs to be comfortable. It can't break down. It must be air-conditioned. It needs a good radio."

But that was just the practical list.

"Your identity is connected with the car." He was explaining what most Californians know all but intuitively. "People will form opinions based on what kind of car you drive." And Raskin advised me to buy the car, not rent it, suggesting it would have intrinsic value after the trip because it would be a character in this book.

The genre includes some impressive classics, of course. *Travels with Charley* stars both John Steinbeck and his pickup truck camper (and of course the dog). *On the Road*, the Jack Kerouac bible for road trips, makes it clear that the choice of the vehicle is critical. The same goes for *Blue Highways* and William Least Heat Moon's vehicle of choice.

The van, embraced with the moniker Ghost Dancing, became a character. Add to the list André Codrescu and his *Road Scholar* quest, looking for America in a sharp Cadillac.

I considered an early sixties Chevy in immaculate condition as a candidate, a classic that I'd seen in front of a California body shop, although it sported no "for sale" sign. But as Markos and I ate lunch in Fairfax, we agreed we would want something a bit funky, not a perfectly restored machine that would be a likely target for thieves.

"We could take it across the border. We could get hydraulics to make it jump, and a tuck and roll job."

"I like the lights underneath the fender wells."

"The blue neon?"

"Yeah, that's really very appealing."

"Or maybe too stereotypical."

"I think it might be."

"So maybe we should have a Lexus!"

"No, no. An Audi A4."

"Yeah. That would be interesting, taking a German car to the California border."

"Why not?"

We were enjoying ourselves, a couple of Californians planning a road trip. Twenty years before, the two of us were living in Europe when—as some Mexicans living in California like to say—we didn't cross the border, the border crossed us. With shocking suddenness the Iron Curtain collapsed, and we headed east from Berlin, following the revolutions cascading across Eastern Europe.

Driving across the Magyar plains, we were figuring out our route from Budapest to Sofia. At the time, Markos was considering a teaching job in Ohio. He studied the road map labeled *Mitteleuropa*, checking highways and places by now so familiar to us both. Suddenly he looked up and said, "I'd better take this job in Ohio. I'm getting to know Europe better than America. I know how to get to Sofia, but I don't know my way from Cleveland to Columbus."

Since that road trip across Europe, I've exerted considerable effort studying and coming to terms with the crises on the Mexican border. In my book *Wetback Nation* I called for opening that border to Mexicans who want to come north, since most Mexicans who do want to make the trip manage to get across *la línea* eventually. I find myself caught up in border debates in my backyard, far north of the political border, yet it's still a borderland with Mexico.

Take, for example, a neighborhood e-mail list I subscribed to for a while in Bodega Bay. I opened my inbox to find this note: "A few minutes ago, I and another neighbor witnessed a Mexican family of three cutting and stealing arm loads of Calla lilies from the yard of a house located at Sierra Grande and Calle del Sol. They were tossing loads of the flowers into their older model red Toyota Camry—license plate number escaped me except for the last three numbers (929). Maybe stealing flowers is not a big deal, but what is next?" It was signed Barbara Makris.

Maybe because I'm the son of an immigrant, I'm overly sensitive. I responded immediately with this screed:

Why, pray tell, do you use the modifier Mexican, Barbara Makris? What is the ethnicity of the neighbor who witnessed these events with you? What is your ethnicity?

And if being Mexican somehow is germane, other questions arise. How do you know this family was Mexican? Are you able to discern the difference between a Mexican family and a Guatemalan family? Can you differentiate between a family who crossed the border yesterday (presumably Mexican) and one whose roots in Sonoma County predate yours and even California statehood (presumably local U.S. citizens, but of Mexican descent)?

Should one, from your name, assume that you are Greek, or of Greek origin? If so, should one presume anything about your report based on that lineage?

Stealing is stealing, and a thief is a thief. Mexican in this case is as moot as Greek. It would not even help a sheriff's deputy identify suspects. Note you did not describe their physicality in any detail—just your presumption of a nationality that encompasses an endless variety of ethnicity and race (Frida Kahlo's daddy was a Hungarian Jew, for example. The family of Mexican Carlos Slim, the compañero currently rated by Forbes as the richest man in the world, came from Lebanon). Better, if we are all unfortunate enough to experience another crime in our midst, that we do an efficient job of collecting license plate data and physical descriptions than burden ourselves casting not-so-veiled aspersions on those amongst us with no connections to the criminals other than prejudice.

As long as you bring this up, did you ask the family if they had permission to take the flowers? If you knew they did not have permission, did you ask them to stop cutting the flowers? Neighborhood watch includes engagement, does it not? I am not suggesting you endanger yourself if you witness a crime, but querying a family of flower gatherers would likely be a safe proposition on a sunny spring weekend day. Perhaps, in fact, they were licensed to gather the Calla lilies (Calla, likely from the Greek for cock wattle, as you may know) by the property owners.

Perhaps the property owners are Mexicans. All food for thought, at least so I think, on this sunny spring afternoon.

And I signed it: "Peter (for the saint? or the Russian tsar? or the Greek rock?) David (must be for the king, yeah?) Laufer (is he German? a good runner?)."

Within minutes the list was alive with debate, and I was pleased to see a decent number of correspondents agreeing with me, reinforcing my faith in the melting pot.

Journalist Chuck Bowden has spent a couple of decades focusing on border issues. I caught up with him just as his book *Down by the River: Drugs, Money, Murder and Family* was published, and as I was continuing my research prior to traveling south to Calexico. He works in an isolated house about twenty miles from the border, a place he identified as one "with illegals streaming by all of the time." Gaining an update on the border from Bowden provided an ideal primer for my trip south.

I suggested to him that since Operation Gatekeeper pushed migrants into the Arizona desert, it's more of a river than a stream.

"Probably the largest human migration on planet Earth is occurring on the United States–Mexican border as poor Mexicans stream north to make a living," is how Bowden put it. He considered the illicit commerce heading north at the same time a part of the border equation that should not be viewed in isolation from the migrants. "The second thing going on is a massive shipment of drugs from Mexico to the United States as Americans seek some solace, apparently. What most people think," he said about the American electorate, "is let's seal the border. But people that think that have not had to go look at it. It's almost nineteen hundred miles long, it's largely unpopulated, it's very rugged terrain, and there is no known technology that would 'seal the border.'"

It was a succinct summary of reality: the border cannot be sealed. Again, all one need do is look at the Berlin Wall for a recent historical example of such failure. Bowden saw the irony of the billions of dollars budgeted for the so-called border fence. "These metal fences they're putting up are destined to become roofing material on Mexican homes. The electronic virtual border they're testing about forty miles from my house is already proving to be a failure. Even Michael Chertoff [Homeland Security secretary under George W. Bush] is starting to back off from it."

Despite his attack on U.S. border policy, Chuck Bowden is not an open-borders advocate, not one of those border critics who reactively says to open up the border and let anybody come north who wants to come north.

Bowden is 100 percent against an open border. He ridicules those who propose such a solution to the crises on the Mexico–U.S. line, suggesting they take the doors off their own homes. Nonetheless, the U.S. government has neither the political will nor the physical ability to seal the border against people smugglers and drug traffickers. "You can't stop the migration of human beings by physical barriers."

There is a logical solution to that reality: if the States want to end illegal Mexican migration, stop employers from hiring workers without proper papers, and if the States want to stop the trafficking of illegal drugs, either make those drugs legal or somehow eliminate the demand.

"You have to define what the problem is," Bowden suggested. "If you say the problem is you don't want any human being entering the United States illegally, you can't stop them with physical barriers. You cannot search every ship coming from China, for example, and every container. You can't afford what it would take to put enough human beings on the Mexican border to stop them. If you were serious about stopping them, you would make them unemployable. Of course, the only way to do that would be some variation of either a national database or a national identity card."

But to stop the desperate push north, no matter the changes in the States, Mexico must create job opportunities to address the fact that work paying five dollars a day south of the border pays twenty dollars an hour on the north side. Were undocumented immigration to cease, not only would U.S. employers find themselves without needed workers, the Mexican economy would lose the billions and billions of dollars that flow south to support the families workers leave behind. Such remittances, along with tourism and oil income, sustain Mexico.

Nothing the Republicans or the Democrats suggest as policy changes made sense to Chuck Bowden as practical responses to the ever-worsening crises.

Policing the border is no solution, Bowden knows, and neither is the political sop of allowing a few hundred thousand more Mexicans to come to the United States as guest workers—not when millions are north without legal documents. "Well, we'll just lock them up, I guess, in concentration camps," he said, mocking the "just what part of 'illegal' don't you understand" crowd. "That's the nonsense of people like Representative [Tom] Tancredo; nobody really thinks that's going to happen. Nobody really thinks you can convert the United States into a mind-set like Nazi Germany where we have huge raids and drag people who have lived here for years and own homes out of their homes and put them on cattle cars or something, or in camps, and then ship them home." U.S. politicians have yet to acknowledge the realpolitik of this massive migration. "I don't think either party can face the fact that they're looking at an economic policy they believe in, which they call free trade or global trade, and in the case of Mexico and Central America specifically, it isn't working. People are fleeing and going to where they can survive. Until you admit that, you can't even begin to look at a solution."

I asked Chuck Bowden to describe what the view out his window looks like. He was correct when he charged that most Americans fail to understand the reality of the border. It was the same complaint I was to hear repeatedly in Calexico.

"I'm seeing my yard, praise the Lord, which is full of desert plants and birds. This is my solace," he said about his Tucson residence, where I found him that day. But he maintains another place just north of the international line. Bowden summers in a cabin just a few miles north of the border where border jumpers routinely plead with him for help in the form of the most basic human needs: food and water. He regularly provides the life-sustaining supplies.

Again he pointed to the irony and the contradictions. "One, my house is two hundred yards from a Border Patrol checkpoint, which doesn't bother these people at all. I'll tell them that, and they say, 'Ah, no problem.' The second thing is, I've had Border Patrol helicopters right overhead while I've been dealing with them; that doesn't seem to bother them, or have any effect. But the most telling thing was when these guys came up, ten of them, who were just crushed. This was in June, the heat then runs well over a hundred degrees. They needed food and water. I could look in their eyes and see that glaze you get when your body's shutting down.

"So I handed out all these cans of food—I keep cases of them outside so even if I'm gone they can just take them—and I said, 'Look, I apologize, but I don't have a can opener.' The guys says, 'Not a problem.' And I said, 'What do you mean?' He reached down and picked up a rock, and then they all walked off.'" Bowden ended the story with a question that all Americans should ponder: "How do you stop people with that much grit?"

The answer is that you *don't* stop people with that much grit. Plus, there's a valid argument to be made that we want people with that much grit in our society. I asked Bowden, before I said good-bye to him, to imagine a phone call from the White House, with a voice on the other end of the line saying, "Help us with this, what's the solution?" What would he answer?

"I'm going to tell them that they'll never solve this problem until they face the economic realities of Mexico, where 50 percent of the population lives in poverty, meaning two or three dollars a day. And 50 percent of the population is underemployed. Unless they are going to face that they have a neighbor in deep distress, unless you look at that reality, you're just postponing an explosion that is going to blow this way. If you want a good neighbor, you have to help your neighbor out, okay?"

Okay. Makes sense. I was headed south to check out the neighborhood again.

I dragged out detailed maps of the routes along the border that connect with Calexico. Interstate 8—known in these parts, I'll learn, as The Eight—shoots due east out of San Diego and then dips down to El Centro and skirts the border as it sprints to the state line at Winterhaven. State Route 94 drops down to the border as soon as it leaves San Diego, connects with Mexico in the twin cities of Tecate, California, and Tecate, Baja California, and meets up with The Eight on the west side of Mountain Spring Pass. State Route 98 hugs the border from the east side of Mountain Spring Pass and Devil's Canyon through Calexico and continues east adjacent to the route of the Old Plank Road. Great names: the Old Plank Road, Mountain Spring, Devil's Canyon, and of course Tecate, famous for the beer and for tunnels dug under the international border by industrious workers on the south side seeking unofficial routes north for people and cargo.

Calexico, next exit.

The Old Plank Road was the first route over the Imperial Sand Dunes. Traffic ran on planks of wood placed directly on the desert floor. Not far from the plank road is Felicity, self-described as "The Center of the World." Pilot Knob is out there, where General Patton trained troops for World War II, under skies where the Blue Angels now practice their aerobatics. Further east is the Quechan Indian Reservation; I found a recent newspaper clipping quoting Tribal Elder Milton Jefferson Sr., lamenting the loss of Quechan tradition.

"We are talking, but nobody is listening," warned Jefferson. "That really makes me mad."

And I discovered Barbara Worth. *The Winning of Barbara Worth* was published in 1911, just a few years after the Colorado River was diverted by the engineers and businessmen who must be credited with turning California desert into some of the most productive farmland anywhere in the world (albeit at the water expense of those downriver, on the Mexican side of the border). The book was another bestseller for Harold Bell Wright, and it was Gary Cooper's first film, a silent.

"While this story is not in any way a history of this part of the Colorado Desert now known as the Imperial Valley," wrote Wright in his acknowledgment, "nor a biography of anyone connected with this splendid achievement, I must in honesty admit that this work which in the past ten years has transformed a vast desolate waste into a beautiful land of homes, cities, and farms, has been my inspiration." In fact, the book is filled with real people, actual places, and the radical metamorphosis of the Valley, all just slightly fictionalized. The mythical Barbara Worth, a dashing and gorgeous woman, remains iconic in the Valley, her name fixed on old produce labels, on the long-gone Barbara Worth Hotel and the Barbara Worth Café, and on the Barbara Worth Resort—which became my Imperial Valley home.

Harold Bell Wright made the orphaned Barbara Worth liberated: "Look, George," a tourist from the East says to another "stranger" as the two see her early in the novel, "she is wearing a divided skirt and riding a man's saddle! And look! Quick! Where's your camera? She has a revolver!" He made her a looker: "The khaki-clad figure was so richly alive—there was such a wealth of vitality; such an abundance of young woman's strength; such a glow of red blood expressed in every curved line and revealed in every graceful movement—that the attraction was irresistible. To look at Barbara Worth was a pleasure; to be near her a delight." And he made her bilingual and charitable, as evidenced when she solicited cash from her adoptive banker father: "I want it for that poor Mexican family down by the wagon yard—the Garcias. Pablo's leg was broken in the mines, you know, and there is no one to look after his mother and the children. Someone must care for them." What's not to like about this character Barbara Worth?

Markos and I decided to jettison the idea of a long road trip on the border, and instead we chose to headquarter near Barbara Worth's homestead in the Imperial Valley. As a foreign correspondent, too often I've been forced to jump into a locale, grab the headlines, and, just as I was beginning to get to know the people and the places, be sent by a voracious assignment editor on to the next breaking story. This time I was my own assignment editor, and I wanted to stay in one place for a while, use it as a base to consider borders and identity, nationalism and transnationalism. I wanted a chance to get to know Ms. Barbara Worth and her friends and neighbors on a first-name basis.

Calexico became my destination, my home away from home—what the Chamber of Commerce calls "Where California and Mexico Meet!" United flight 5778 touched down in El Centro; my Skywest Fokker 50 taxied to a stop at the terminal building, the only commercial plane

Barbara Worth
Citrus Crate Labels

The mythical, omnipresent Barbara Worth, icon of the Imperial Valley.

on the tarmac this Monday afternoon. Coming across the desert, as the propellers were beating me south and east, I could see the desert turn green and fertile as we crossed into Imperial County. And as the pilot made a first pass over the airfield to confirm our approach, I could see housing subdivisions marching out from El Centro, replacing irrigated farmland with instant neighborhoods.

"Welcome to the Imperial Valley Airport," announced the stewardess. "Please close the window shades to help us keep the aircraft cool." The door opened and it was *hot*. I was far from my San Francisco fog, but as the temperature soared toward three digits, I learned from the natives that this was temperate. They don't complain until they see their mercury climb to around 117, and even then, they speak of the high numbers with the sound of scorched pride.

The terminal building was all but deserted. Congressman Bob Filner's field office was closed; a note on the door offered a phone number. Posters advertised the Sonny Bono Salton Sea National Wildlife Refuge. And at the Hertz counter, the clerks laughed at our talk about the heat.

"My brother is in Saudi Arabia," said one. "He feels right at home."

The other had just finished his lunch and was sneezing.

"Gesundheit," I responded.

"That's German, isn't it?" he said. "Are you Germans? Ten minutes after I eat, I always sneeze."

Of course I asked him why.

"I have no idea," he said, and he sneezed again.

They picked out a sleek, black Mazda, promising it was fast, with a magnificent air conditioner.

"Are you going to Mexico with it?" If so, I would be required to buy extra insurance.

"Yeah, I'm taking it over there to sell the engine and the tires. Then I'll report it to you as stolen."

They laughed, but it seemed they'd heard a variation on my attempted joke plenty of times. With their directions to the Barbara Worth Resort in hand, we threw the baggage in the Mazda and headed farther south. It wasn't a 1961 Impala, but the air conditioner was, in fact, killer.

"Welcome to our desert oasis!" said the Barbara Worth Resort motto. And a slightly tattered one it proved to be. Not quite threadbare, but "a little worse for the wear and tear since the National Guard was billeted there," more than one local suggested. The architecture is pure California roadside motel, the golf course greens show spots of brown,

The corporate border that Hertz tries to enforce at its El Centro airport car rental counter.

and eight-by-ten glossies adorn the restaurant wall: from Bob Crosby and His Bobcats to Carol Channing, Count Basie, and Ronald Reagan. At one time, this place clearly swung.

Waitress Bonnie Peterson welcomed us for a late lunch with the kind of "Hi, honey!" that defines the American diner experience. Her uniform was a white blouse that looked like a tuxedo shirt with a high collar, and wrapped around the collar was a short black tie, loosely tied with a jaunty bow. Her salt-and-pepper hair was brushed back to reveal an olive-skinned, serious look.

Bonnie slings hash, but that's not fair to the Barbara Worth menu. Before the week was out, I ate a fine halibut dinner in the old resort, washed down with a superb California wine. Bonnie seems to know every customer, and if they're new in town, as we were, she gets to know them fast. The Valley is her home, try as she did to leave it behind.

"I left lots of times," she told me and laughed. She laughs easily. "I went to San Diego. I went to Bakersfield. I went all over and came back."

I looked out the dining room window at the sprinklers trying to keep the golf course greens green. What brought her back?

Ronald Reagan was one of the scores of movers and shakers who once stopped off at the now-threadbare Barbara Worth Resort.

She knew. It's natural to want to go off to the big city when you grow up in the little towns of the Imperial Valley, she said. "But when you get to the big city, it isn't what you think it is, and you really miss the slow pace, the people, the friendly atmosphere. They're different," she said about the people in big cities. "It's not that they're bad people up there; it's just the city has a different kind of people."

She missed that good old hometown feeling.

"Yeah, it's the hometown and the people. Because since you were little you've known all these people. You've been around. Me more, because I started to waitress since I was fifteen. I got to know a lot of people. That's the good thing about being a waitress."

True enough. Whenever I mentioned "my waitress Bonnie" around the Valley, I heard back, "I know Bonnie."

Bonnie wanted to make sure I took note that each of the Imperial Valley communities has its own personality. Right. Although I was focusing on Calexico because it is directly on the border, I already knew

Longtime Barbara Worth resort waitress Bonnie Peterson, a woman who knows that, in fact, you can go home again.

from my studies back at home that the Valley—as it is known to the locals—is sprinkled with cities proud of their separate identities. I started reciting the places on my list: Calexico, Holtville, Brawley, El Centro . . .

"Niland," she interrupted. "Yeah, they're all different. You can even go to Niland, but they're still friendly. But there are different lifestyles in each. Niland," she said again. "You been to Niland?"

Not yet.

"You go to Niland," she instructed, "and on your way to Niland, stop in Brawley at a place called Brownie's, it's a restaurant. Go there and then go on to Calipat, that's where the prison is. Then you go a little farther—it's going to take like an hour or so—into Niland, and it's like you went from the city into a smaller town into a *small* town. There's a lot to learn, a lot in the Valley that we never saw when we were young."

Her tutorial travelogue continued.

"Calexico is like Mexicali, really, because they're," she slapped her hands with a loud clap, "right together. And there's a lot of Spanish,

Mexican people. Spanish and Mexico. When you go to Holtville there's people from Oklahoma, Tennessee, Texas. It's a different mixture. I was raised on cornbread and black-eyed peas in Holtville. You come to El Centro and you have a mixture of everybody. They're good, you know, and bad," she said about the people in the Valley. "Like anyplace else, but there's a lot of different people in Imperial Valley. You'd be surprised."

But there must be some common denominator to the types of people who call home to what looked to me bleak and harsh and isolated.

"You have to like the desert, and you have to like the heat, and you just have to like this kind of lifestyle." Quiet, she meant. "To us it's getting more hectic, because there's more people, but that's progress. We can't stop progress. I can look at the sun here and look at the sun in San Diego and see the difference. There's a beauty when it goes up or comes down in San Diego, and there is a beauty when it goes up or comes down here. But there's difference. Sometimes it's so pretty here that you can't believe it, this desert. But if you really stop and look, there's beauty wherever you are. It's up to you to see it. Me, I'm nosy, I look everywhere. I even see beauty in people. Even in some of them that I don't like, I see it."

Time for a waitress joke.

"I've been to Texas, you know, and there's to me just two type of people there."

"Yeah?" I bit. "What are those two types?"

"Hillbillies and hillbillies." That made her laugh. "Here they're just a mixture and they blend together. If you go to a city, there's Chinatown, there's Little Italy. Different cultures have their different little community. Here if you live on the eastside—they call the eastside "eastside" because they're poor people—they're mostly Spanish and your colored; we've lived that way all our lives here." But she viewed that as an economic line. "I don't think a lot of us see difference in races. I don't see it."

I heard Bonnie take orders and banter with customers in Spanish.

"Yeah, my momma is Indian and Spanish and Mexican. My mother spoke good English, but her language in the home was Spanish."

Nonetheless, Bonnie Peterson insisted to me that a real social problem in the Valley is that too many native Spanish-speakers are not learning English, the tongue that she called "the language of this country."

I changed the subject. Where does she go on vacation, this Valley lover?

She laughed, "I don't go on vacation."

She hesitated. I pushed her. "To me vacation is driving over to San Diego. In the summertime nobody wants to be here. The people that are here are the diehards. I stay here because I have a year-round job. But I have a daughter who works at the schools, the high schools. She's off for three months. She don't go nowhere."

She stays in the Valley through 117-degree summers?

"She stays here. If she goes anywhere, she goes to San Diego."

I asked her to describe a typical day in that heat.

"We become bears," she laughed. "We hibernate. We'll go to work. You won't see us out from two to six in the summertime; it's dead because that's the hottest time of the day. If we're working, we're in an air-conditioned place."

I asked her why the restaurants were all closed so early on the California side in evening, while in Mexicali you can eat as late as you wish.

"Different lifestyles. You have to remember that. Their lifestyle is different than our lifestyle. They're different people, their way of life, their laws, everything's different than ours. Over there the bars can stay open all night if they want."

What is it that creates that difference where people want to be out eating, drinking, dancing late at night on the south side of the border, and on the north side of the border they don't?

"I think it's just the way we're brought up. Don't you?"

"Bonnie," I said to her, "this is the Barbara Worth Resort. Does Barbara Worth play any role in your life? Is there any mystique to the Barbara Worth story for you?" That turned her all but religious.

"Oh, Barbara Worth. There's a lot to the Barbara Worth name. When I was growing up, this was a society place. We didn't even think about coming here. The stories that you hear. There was a man in the bar who said he remembers his father telling him about the song 'Mexicali Rose.' The man who wrote that song, he said, wrote it somewhere around here because he had a girl named Rose and she lived in Mexicali, as a matter of fact. They broke up and he had a broken heart and he wrote that song."

Not quite. The man who wrote the music was Jack Tenney, later to become a California state senator. At the time he wrote the tune, claims local legend, he was playing piano at the Imperial Cabaret in Mexicali. He called the song simply "The Waltz" and later debunked any suggestion that it was about an old flame, according to the English-language

Mexican newspaper *El Ojo del lago.* "There was an old lady who ran a boarding house in Brawley," the paper quotes Tenney as recalling. "Every 30 days when the railroad men were paid, she came to Mexicali. We'd play the waltz for her, and she'd sit around drinking and crying. She must have been 50 or 60 years old and weighed 200 pounds. I don't know what her name was but Jack Hazelip, my saxophone player, called her Mexicali Rose. I already had the tune and we started fiddling around with the words as a result of watching her cry." The lyrics, credited to Helen Stone, conclude with a sorrowful, "Dry those big brown eyes and smile, dear/Banish all those tears and please don't sigh/Kiss me once again and hold me;/Mexicali Rose good-bye."

Over a decade later, Senator Tenney was sitting in the state senate, busy not with tear-jerking waltzes but red-baiting his opponents as chairman of the legislature's Un-American Activities Committee, particularly targeting individuals and organizations working to protect the rights and interests of Mexicans living and working in California, and Mexican American California citizens. "Mexicali Rose, good-bye," indeed.

What about the author who wrote the Barbara Worth story? I asked Bonnie Peterson if she knew him.

"No. But I have a picture of him in here."

Okay.

"Yeah. And I believe that there is a lady named Barbara Worth."

She believes there was a real lady named Barbara Worth, not just a fictional character in the Harold Bell Wright novel?

"Yes." She was no longer laughing. "It's not a fiction. I think there is a woman named Barbara Worth."

"And what makes you think that, Bonnie?"

"I think there was more to it than people will say. She was very pretty and she was like a man. In those days she wore pants and a hat. And she was beautiful. There's a picture of her. They don't say it's her, but you know it's her. This man, I think, is the man that liked her. There were probably a lot of men that liked her."

"Which man was the man who liked her?"

"The man who wrote the book, the story of this lady, Barbara. I don't think she was fictional. I think she was someone who was here at one time, and she was so pretty she turned a lot of people's heads and left a lot of memories here. Or she could have lived here all of her life. We don't know. I don't know. I'll have to read the book one of these days. But she had to have left a mark, because there is this place here, there is a road called Barbara Worth. The Barbara Worth Hotel in downtown El Centro burnt to the ground. It was beautiful. It was gorgeous. And it was called the Barbara Worth. It wasn't a motel; it was a hotel. Why are there so many things called Barbara Worth? Why is it keeping going?" Her rhapsody was contagious, but I was not prepared for what came next.

"It's like, why does Jesus's name still continue on and on? Yeah?"

Barbara Worth as a Christlike figure?

"There is a difference between Christ and Barbara Worth," she acknowledged. "But not that much. He is not a fiction, but yet a lot of people believe he is. She, they say, is a fiction. But I don't think she is. You know, it's what you believe in. And what I believe in. I believe that she is a lady that was here. And probably on this property at one time. This place has been here quite a while. And it has some stories, a lot of stories."

I pointed to the celebrity glossies lining the walls. Had Bonnie met them all?

"Only a few," because in the glory days, "I worked more at the Brunner's in El Centro, and I met Rock Hudson. This place would be packed with people. A lot of movie stars came down."

"Is it ever packed anymore?"

"Not like it used to be." But still there is plenty going on, Bonnie made clear to me. "There's a TB sanitarium over in Holtville, and it was at one time a base. As a matter of fact, years and years and years ago some kid dug up a bomb, and it blew him up and killed him. There is history everywhere you go." The Blue Angels winter in the Valley. "Every year they have a golf tournament. It's the Blue Angels Golf Tournament, and they of course put on their show out here too. There's a lot to see. Holtville's got the Carrot Carnival. Niland's got the Tomato Festival. Westmorland's got the Honey Bee Festival. El Centro has the Christmas parade; Calexico has a Christmas parade, too."

Bonnie Peterson had tables to wait. I'd kept her long enough with my questions, but I couldn't let her go without her opinion about the changed border, the fence/wall separating California from Mexico. No surprise: an opinion she certainly had for me.

"There's always something separating something. I don't think there should be a wall nowhere, because this earth doesn't belong to nobody. This earth and the ground we walk on, the air we breathe in, everything, is not owned. We might think we own something, but we don't own nothing, because we came in here with nothing, we're going to leave with nothing. So I don't think that we should have walls. That's my opinion. I don't think we should have walls. Because we're all people. Only thing different is our skin colors or, you know, the Chinese have slanted eyes. But inside we're all the same. We have the same heart. Same blood. Everything. But that's the way it is," she said about the border, "people put barriers around everything. I don't even look at the wall there, but I know it's a different town, and I don't go there."

Not that she wants the Valley to fill up with Mexican migrants.

"I'd be lying if I sat here and said that I want all those people to come here, because I don't. That's only, you know, because we have to take care of ourselves. But they have the right to want what they can't find there, and that's a life. Some of them come over here and they're ornery and mean, and they destroy. If they come over here and appreciate it and enjoy it, there's nothing wrong with that. To me the United States is . . . how do they call it? A melting pot? Because there are people here of every race, every country, everything. They're here. They're here. Promised Land. Right here."

It was cocktail hour. Markos and I had been in the air and on the road since early in the morning. An old San Francisco high school friend of Markos lived close by, and we invited him to join us at our resort for a drink.

"George and I were best friends in high school, but our paths diverged." Markos told me about the pal he was about to see for the first time in a generation. "He married Maria in San Diego, and I thought that he would work in the Valley and commute to the urbane reality of San Diego. The opposite happened. He chose to live in the Valley and farms with a zeal for the land and its productivity, along with an embrace of the early rhythms of pre-sunrise awakening and pre-evening-newscast slumber."

When George married Valley girl Maria they moved to her family's homestead, just a few miles south of our Valley headquarters on Barbara Worth Road. Now a big Valley grower (they call themselves growers, not farmers, in the Valley), selling his organic produce to Whole

Foods, George joined us for a beer, and summed up the Valley with a variation on Frank Sinatra's take on New York City. "You can make it here," George told us. Meaning: work hard and you'll do okay here. Just, "You can make it here," and not the conditional comparison of the Sinatra tune, "*If* you can make it here, you can make it *anywhere*" (of course the italics are mine; who would dare change the phrasing of Old Blue Eyes?).

George drove off in his pickup after a couple of beers, but not before inviting us to his farmhouse later in the week to join his family for an Imperial Valley dinner.

Was it a beacon or a warning sign? It glowed yellow and red, high on a stanchion, never blinking, always on, always open. Denny's. Just below the promise of something to eat was a sign for Mexican Auto Insurance.

We pulled up to the restaurant, hungry, tired, my head full of those first impressions of a place that can be refreshing and accurate or naive and absurd. Or both. But reporting eyes take a break when they are confronted with the familiar and routine. A Denny's is a Denny's is a Denny's, even on the border, or so we thought. The same restaurant construction, color scheme, counter at the double-door entry, plasticized menus, Formica-ed tables, Naugahyde-ed banquettes, fluorescent lighting, cake displays, and imperceptible music. We plopped ourselves down without much conscious thought and opened up the well-illustrated menu full of suggestive, if slightly misleading, food photos that showed unvarying fare. A couple of glasses of ice water landed in front of us without our having to look up or interact with anyone or anything other than the plate pictures and meal descriptions we held in our hands like prayer books.

It was a little after eight in the evening, and there was no other place we could find in Calexico that was open for dinner. George had warned us we would not find a place to eat, but we arrogantly assumed that he was reflecting his years of domesticity, and that he didn't get out much. As a grower, his days start at four-thirty in the morning, another reason we thought he might not be as well informed about life on the border and the teeming *taquerías* that we expected to find down in Calexico's midtown, near the twenty-four-hour border crossing for pedestrians. We drove down Highway 111, south of The Eight, past the few intersections with traffic lights, and toward the Mexican restaurant we were sure would be open, D Poly. It was exactly eight p.m., and there

Picture-postcard palms tower in bucolic contrast with the commercial strip
that stretches north from the Calexico border crossing.

Palm trees and roadside lodging: A typical Calexico border cityscape.

was no indication that the restaurant had ever been open that day. We drove down a commercial street to get to this house-turned-restaurant, a block away from a fence that shielded and dissipated the vibrant neon light flashing color from the other side, in Mexicali.

D Poly was recommended to us earlier in the day by a clerk at Sam Ellis, a haberdashery with some of the finest clothing at the bottom end of the United States. Walking in from the hot sidewalk to the air-conditioned and soothingly well-organized familiarity of a clothing store was a welcome respite from the heat of the day. There were few visual indicators that this shop was on the border; what made the locale clear was that everyone inside was speaking Spanish. We each needed an article of clothing: a Stetson hat to protect my pate and a pair of light-colored Calvin Klein pants for Markos to fend off the heat.

Once at the register, the question of food came up and where we could get a good bite to eat later in the day. Two suggestions were offered, one in Calexico (D Poly), the other in Mexicali, across the border: the Heidelberg. A German restaurant in a faux *fachwerk* structure that served rich food and cold beer seemed no stranger than going to

Las Vegas to eat in the Eiffel Tower, but Las Vegas is known as the capital of nowhere and impersonator of all. While Germany and Mexico have some shared history, it is pretty much reduced to beer and *Blasorchester* (the accordions of *ranchero* music can trace their origin directly to German immigrants) these days, so a recommendation for a place like the Heidelberg for fried schnitzel instead of staying on the north side of the border for homemade rice and beans was not intriguing. But that was before we found out about the unwritten eight o'clock rule.

No rice or beans at the closed D Poly and no Chinese food from what looked like a greasy spoon along the main drag—a place called the Yum Yum. We were cruising along the highway, up and down, from the north end of Calexico down toward the border. We made a U-turn at the checkpoint, not ready to face a two-hour wait on the borderline during the drive home to the Barbara Worth after a dinner in Mexicali. The Yum Yum had lights on, though the doors were shut and it looked closed for the night. We drove past it, past a hotel where a pack of Dutch bikers (flags and license plates were telltale identifiers) on Harleys were hanging out on the porch in front of the reception desk and the closed restaurant. They were drinking from 16-ounce Bud cans probably bought at a nearby convenience store because everything other than the ice machine, Coke machine, and (Free Coffee!) rooms in the hotel was closed.

So we returned to Denny's; the only other open Calexico option we could find was the Carrows on the other side of the highway. We already had an appointment in a couple of days for dinner at Carrows, chosen at our guest's request. We wanted to vary our cuisine.

Denny's is nothing if not familiar. Not appealing, but not strange.

Naturally, when the waiter came, we started speaking to him in Spanish. We had been listening. Everyone in the restaurant was chattering in that melodious idiom, so it seemed natural to do the same.

"You guys here doing business?" he queried. "You're not from around here, are you?" But he already knew the answer. We were gringos starting a Denny's conversation in Spanish, and we were eating late. Perhaps more telling, I ordered a Gardenburger.

He brought the food and stuck around to chat. Where might we find some real food, we asked him, and at a reasonable hour? His answer was predictable. "Go to Mexicali." He flipped over the placemat and took out his pen. He drew the border and added a grid showing a few key Mexicali streets. "Go to Las Villas," he instructed us, "or Sarape." He added his name and telephone number. "Call if you get lost," he said, with a Calexico friendliness we were beginning to recognize and appreciate.

"Here we were in the Imperial Valley, but there's not much sign of empire," noted Markos as the day waned. "It looks to be a colony at best, an outpost for refugees and dirt farmers."

Back at the Barbara Worth ("Welcome to Our Desert Oasis"), I started paging through the stack of newspapers I'd collected during the day; those and the Yellow Pages always serve as ideal CliffsNotes to speed acclimating to a new locale. At the cash registers along First Street, *La Voz de la Frontera,* the Mexicali newspaper, sits with its screaming headlines, waiting for the impulse buyer. The big news Monday: a Chevy Suburban packed with migrants crashed in Calexico while being chased by the Border Patrol. Two died, was the initial report on the Mexican side (the Americans reported one), there were serious injuries to others. Other front-page headlines teased details about traffic accidents in Mexicali and drug trafficker shootouts in the streets of Tijuana. It is a bloody front page. A couple of handcuffed Mexicans are shown being arrested on the south side of the border. Wearing T-shirts, jeans, and running shoes, they are identified in a perp-walk color photograph as people smugglers, using the term in common currency on the border for the hustlers who conduct wetbacks north: *polleros,* chicken handlers. The desperate migrants are known colloquially in the borderlands as *pollos,* chickens. And *La Voz* does not bother with any of the niceties or use the caution expected in papers north of the border. These two are not tagged "alleged traffickers," but definitively as polleros. Intriguing also is the word used for the U.S. Border Patrol officers tailing the Suburban that crashed. *La Migra* is the term, left over from the years that the Border Patrol was a unit of the defunct Immigration and Naturalization Service. The agency had become Immigration and Customs Enforcement, self-identified with the acronym ICE. "ICE" offers a creepy, 1984 Orwellian image but has yet to catch on in the streets on either side of the border. The Migra is the Migra.

La Voz is thick with local Mexicali and border news, the op-ed pages rich with opinion, and its pages packed with advertising. In case any readers need a reminder, there is a dramatic photograph of cars lining up at the border, waiting to cross into Calexico. The caption is simple: "The line of vehicles waiting to cross into the neighbor country is very long." It is a sweet term: *el vecino país,* the neighbor country. There is a page titled "Airport," which features color portraits of travelers coming and going from the Mexicali airport.

The national news section of *La Voz* features a long take on the increase in the cost of wheat and corn and the inflationary impact those commodities place on market prices for bread and tortillas. Raúl Castro and Hugo Chávez share equal space with Barack Obama and Pope Benedict.

And the society pages! Proud parents at baptisms holding what look like squirming babies dressed up in frilly whites. Parties for expectant mothers. *Un gran fiesta* to celebrate Ramón Talamantes Zamora's birthday. His brothers and sisters—Pablo, Francisco, Elena, Santa Ana, Gume, Ernesto, and Alfredo—got up early, reports *La Voz,* and decorated a local park with balloons and a sign reading "Happy Birthday." All invited enjoyed a good time and delicious food, reports the paper. Three fuzzy pictures of Ramón and the clan in the park with the birthday cake adorn the text. It's a full page of birthdays. Joel Andrés is five. Barbarita Ibarra is two. Lots of photographs document their parties.

The entertainment section is packed with news of Britney Spears, Jennifer Lopez, Paris Hilton, and Madonna. But there is Mexico-centric celebrity gossip, too. Gaby, the singer with Timbiriche, may be suffering from anorexia? Who knew? The singer Luis Miguel is out with a new video. Apparently the actress Edith González wants to have another child.

Need a job? *La Voz* is thick with want ads. Craigslist has yet to undermine the Mexicali newspaper's role of connecting jobs with workers. More cultural differences across the border are apparent in the ads. Andercraft, which makes injection molds, seeks a quality inspector. They announce they prefer a male for the job. Try getting away with that in Calexico. Bimbo Bread seeks sales help and says it offers a good working environment. Walmart needs cashiers. Gulfstream seeks mechanics. Eurocar wants cleaners. And the *La Voz* circulation department needs help to cover workers' vacations. Telling, too, are the ads in English. Amphenol de México needs a financial analyst and an automation engineer. You can apply via e-mail. But beware: "Candidates please send resume in English." The same holds true if you want to apply for the restaurant manager job open at the beachfront restaurant near La Paz. "Must speak English," warns the ad.

The sports section, of course, is jammed with soccer and bullfighting news and includes dramatic photographs of Mario Toledo and Jorge Guerrero being gored, along with a shot of Manolo Juárez gracefully

Bright neon beckons travelers to Calexico's Border Motel.

trying to perform the coup de grâce, a reminder of why Manolo is known as "El Poeta."

The Monday edition of *La Voz* totals a whopping ninety-six pages, but the *Imperial Valley News,* published in El Centro ("The Imperial Valley's Source for News"), is as anorexic as Gaby when compared with *La Voz.* Just two thin sections, reflecting the imbalance across the border. Mexicali boasts over one and a half million citizens, the Baja California state capital, and the Universidad Autónoma de Baja California, and it is packed with restaurants like the Heidelberg, Las Villas, and Sarape, serving sophisticated food late into the night. Mexicali is—to cite Paul Gilroy—where it's at for the Imperial Valley. Sociologist Gilroy famously analyzed identity with the line, "It ain't where you're from, it's where you're at."

Calexico and the Imperial Valley are the rural backwater to Mexicali's cosmopolitan dominance of the region.

There is a poignant story filling the Monday front page in the *Press* about a local Iraq War veteran now home and dealing with battlefield injuries that will last a lifetime. The paper also features the Migra chase on its front page, noting that the Suburban was chased by "U.S. Border

Patrol officers." The *Press* carefully calls the passengers in the car "suspected illegal immigrants" and says that Border Patrol agent Enrique Lozano will release information as the investigation continues. There's no mention in the *Press* story of the polleros in custody south of the border and announced by Mexicali police as connected to the rollover Suburban crash.

On the op-ed page, Karen Kelley takes the spotlight with her contribution to the feature "A Reader Writes." She tells the story of her family's move in 1948 from suburban Los Angeles to the Imperial Valley, and of the new life they started as pig farmers. She was twelve. After several years, the family returned to Los Angeles. Her brother and her mother "weren't all that broken up about leaving Imperial Valley," she reports, "but it was different for me, because I had made a number of friends, and had come to love the Valley." As an adult, she returned and made it her home once again, a place, she notes at the end of her story, that "may not have been heaven, as my grandmother . . . put it, but it was home. And that may have been close enough."

My first day in Calexico ended with me in complete agreement with Karen Kelley's grandmother, and wondering what Markos and I might discover Tuesday.

≥ ≥ ≥

Tuesday

Whither Calexico? Wither All of Us When It's 100 in the Shade!

Dawn at the Barbara Worth Resort. The empty parking lot reinforces the sense of a bygone heyday. But it is a precious and gorgeous dawn. The huge, bushy trees around the motel are alive with an orchestra of songbirds. The temperature is a perfect San Diego–like seventy degrees or so, without a hint of the scorcher to come. Looking south toward the sparse traffic about a mile distant on The Eight, the irrigated desert is green with crops, the adjacent access roads cracked and dusty from the perpetual baking of the irrepressible Imperial Valley sunshine.

"NO ANIMALS!" yells a sign posted on the field adjacent to Barbara Worth Road. "It's a food safety violation!" This was where Harold Bell Wright wrote *The Winning of Barbara Worth,* a place he called Tecolote Rancho at Meloland. "And the desert shall rejoice and blossom as the rose," Isaiah is quoted where Wright's ashes were buried in San Diego, a site marked with a book-shaped sculpture.

Breakfast in the Barbara Worth restaurant. The eight-by-ten glossy stars on the wall smile down at me as I pick from the roomful of empty tables for the continental breakfast. Packaged bagels. Individual containers of Philadelphia cream cheese. No lox. The 1960s-looking interior décor sits static in a state of arrested decay—water stains on the ceiling, a temperamental toaster for the self-service bagels. Orange juice, tea, and the *Imperial Valley Press.*

Time to start the day. What's happening here on the border? "Breezy and mostly sunny today." Okay. But the high temperature is forecast to be ninety-eight. More details about the crash Sunday morning on Drew Road, the Chevy Suburban filled with twenty-two passengers that rolled over while being followed by the Border Patrol. The driver is in jail, seventeen years old and expected to be charged with vehicular manslaughter. It wasn't a high-speed chase, Highway Patrol officer Wes Boerner reports. "From what I've heard from the Border

The Barbara Worth Resort: home away from home.

Patrol, they were tailing him and keeping an eye on him while they formulated a plan."

What else is border news? Controversy regarding the relining of the All-American Canal, the lifeline that diverts Colorado River water to the Valley. Should extra money be spent building ridges on the walls as a device to aid the escape of those who fall into the water, or are ladders placed every 250 feet adequate safety features? The Imperial Valley National Day of Prayer Task Force announces a service scheduled for Thursday. Barbara Worth Junior High in Brawley is hosting a "Family Fun Movie Night" featuring *Grease!* Free. Green's Jewelry ("Since 1952 The Jeweler You Can Trust"), mentioned in a display ad set in typography that looks like 1952, reminds us that Mother's Day is next Sunday. "Let us help you find a thoughtful and unique gift that's just right for your mom." It features an image of a diamond with cartoon-like lines representing its sparkle.

On the Opinion page "Stories of the Past" notes the good-old-boy atmosphere of those days, reporting that fifty years ago "John Andrew Demay, 37, an assistant superintendent at Imperial County Juvenile Hall, was arrested early Monday morning when El Centro police found him in an allegedly intoxicated condition. 'I work at Juvenile Hall. Doesn't that make a difference?' Demay asked officers, they said. Police reported Demay was caught trying to drive his car twice—once returning to it after police sent him home in a taxi. He was released without formal charges being filed. 'To prevent embarrassment to the juvenile court and their County Probation Office,' is the statement on Demay's police record, explaining why he was released." Ah, those innocent, naive, crony-filled days of 1958.

On that same page, a harsh editorial suggests just such contemporary cronyism, under the headline, "Pacheco Should Resign from Board." It attacks the Pacheco brothers: Salvador, the Calexico school board and city council member, for voting to hire, as an assistant school superintendent, Lewis, the mayor. "Nepotism and the '*compadre*' have been caught dead to rights in Calexico," screams the offended newspaper. "What is it about Calexico that the stench of it hangs thick in the air, a lingering scent that no matter how many years and elections and promises of change, it just won't go away?" The story in the El Centro–based paper about the border city south of The Eight continues relentlessly, calling Calexico a city "where backroom deals and collusion have taken on mythic proportions," and it ends with an arrogant personal attack and demand: "Salvador Pacheco, it's time to go, but we won't hold our breath, considering this kind of thing seems to happen all the time 'only in Calexico.'"

We finished breakfast intrigued with the Calexico news and anxious to meet politicians such as the Pacheco brothers, so vilified by the local newspaper editor. Only in Calexico! That suggested real promise. Not quite "What happens in Vegas stays in Vegas," but pretty good for a struggling border city, newly walled off from its cosmopolitan neighbor to the south and clearly despised by the establishment in its county seat, El Centro, just a few miles to the north. Markos and I set off to find out more about what happens only in Calexico—foreign correspondents in our home state—he summing up his premature impressions of the beat with a terse, "Heat and dust. Everywhere heat and dust."

In 1994, the U.S. government imposed what it called Operation Gatekeeper along the border at San Diego. A Berlin Wall–like barrier— a high gash of concrete—replaced ad hoc and sometimes minimal fencing, while the Border Patrol bloated with new hires. Operation Gatekeeper did not keep Mexicans out of the United States; it simply pushed them from the urban crossing points like Tijuana–San Diego to the rural

Borderlands wilderness. The Migra claimed it was not surprised that the migrants kept coming and just moved to the more dangerous deserts. "Our national strategy calls for shutting down the San Diego sector first, maintaining control there, then controlling the Tucson and South Texas corridors," explained the INS spokeswoman at the time, Virginia Kice. "We recognize that traffic will increase in other sectors, but we need to control the major corridors first." It was a failed policy. Traffic across the borderline only grew, with deadly results for migrants.

Equating the new all-American barrier that's growing ever higher and less pregnable on the U.S.–Mexico border with the Iron Curtain version is dead wrong, but it's impossible not to make the comparison. Wrong to equate because, of course, the Berlin Wall (and its extension separating East and West Germany) was designed to keep the citizens of East Germany inside their unfortunate Soviet-bloc country. The barricade thrown up between Calexico and Mexicali (and creeping along in places throughout California, Arizona, New Mexico, and Texas, to the applause of the Lou Dobbs–Bill O'Reilly–Pat Buchanan–type talk-show-host cheerleading cabal) is supposed to keep Mexicans (and OTMs, the Border Patrol euphemism for those nationals Other Than Mexicans) out of the good old United States of America. Nonetheless, the effects of the two monoliths are much the same. A hideous architectural intrusion. A grotesque division. A dehumanizing reminder of failed policy.

From my time living in Germany in the late 1980s, I have stacks of literature in my files analyzing and explaining the Berlin Wall and the fortifications along the East German–West German border, phenomena that were part of my daily life then, over there. The parallels with the American variant—what the U.S. government officially calls a "fence"—are creepy. An ever-increasing wall: higher, stouter, and its mission reinforced with watchtowers and technological gimmicks. On the East Berlin side of the Wall was a free-fire zone, land wiped clean of buildings and brush, offering a clear line of sight for snipers ordered to shoot-to-kill escaping countrymen and women. Floodlights made night into day. Mean German shepherd dogs patrolled the no-man's-land. And an ominous manifestation of German ingenuity and engineering augmented the death-strip: the *Selbstschußanlage* SM 70, automated guns that were triggered by tripwires if escapees managed to get past the multiple perimeters of the nation-prison.

East Germany erected what they called their "anti-imperialist" barrier in 1961. Too many Germans who ended up in what was Soviet-occupied territory after World War II were choosing to abandon their homeland and seek their fortunes in the capitalistic West. The brain-and-brawn drain was a crisis. In mid-August of that year, in the dark of night, what the East Germany government referred to as "fighting squads of the working class" along with units of the Volkspolizei—the People's Police—uncoiled the rolls of barbed wire that eventually metastasized into the Berlin Wall. The symbolism captured the essence of the cold war: communism of the type practiced by the Soviet Union and its clients was a failure. Or as President Ronald Reagan immortalized that reality in a 1987 Berlin speech, "Mr. Gorbachev, tear down this wall!" Tear it down Gorbachev did, just two years later, by signaling to the morally and financially bankrupt East German government that Soviet troops would stay in their barracks if the Volkspolizei and the Volksarmee were to use force in an attempt to stop the 1989 revolution.

Only months before the Wall fell, I was on an East German bus, talking with the driver about his confinement and his dreams, while making the trip from East Berlin to Potsdam. I looked out at the snaking length of Wall running parallel to the road. From the east side, without its colorful graffiti and artwork, the Wall almost looked less intimidating than it did from the west—just another slab of concrete in the dismal cityscape (if you avoided focusing on the watchtowers). The viewing platforms built on the west side, designed to allow tourists a vantage point to observe the Wall and the empty swath of separation, drew more attention to the restriction the Wall sliced through Berlin than did the bare concrete on the East side.

"There are advantages and disadvantages to everything," the bus driver said in a resigned voice. He offered a halfhearted endorsement of the government's recent further rationalization for the Wall as a blockade against terrorism and crime. He mused about the American television shows he watched "I see the beach and women and life." He gestured out the window at the gray drizzle and Stalinist architecture. "And here I am," he muttered.

In 1973, the Berlin artist Matthias Koeppel captured the bifurcated mentality of his hometown in a painting he titled *Potsdamer Platz*. Three figures are up on one of the observation platforms, looking out over the wall and a minimalistic East Berlin skyline. They are bundled up against the cold. The middle figure—a middle-aged man—is gesticulating east in a dismissive manner with a raised, clawlike hand. He is flanked by two jeering women, and he—his face almost apelike—is sticking his tongue out at the East.

America's "fence" is splitting the twin cities of Calexico and Mexicali with the same farcical and fatal type of barrier that divided Berlin.

I encountered a Border patrolman (*Chavez* read his nameplate) on the east side of Calexico, out past town. I pulled off Anza Road, just west of where it intersects with Barbara Worth Road and at the point it crosses a canal, to look at a historical marker identifying the place that is the site of the primal spigot. "At this historic spot," I read, "the first irrigation water from the Colorado River reached Imperial Valley in 1901, coming from Mexico. This waterway was replaced in 1942 by the All-American Canal. Water has made this once arid area into an agricultural paradise. Dedicated January 26, 1974, by the Native Sons of the Golden West." When we looked closer, we saw the edited version. In red marker "agricultural paradise" was crossed out and rewritten "toxic hellhole." Native Sons of the Golden West became Non-Native Sons of the Golden West.

The defaced plaque marking the canal that first brought water from the Colorado River to irrigate crops in the Imperial County desert.

The All-American Canal filled with Colorado River water that fuels Imperial Valley desert agriculture.

The editor remained anonymous, but the Native Sons do suffer from a sordid nativist history, actively opposing the immigration not just of Mexicans, but also of Chinese and Japanese.

Officer Chavez sat in his truck, engine idling (hey, you expect him to suffer his shift with no air-conditioning?), parked with a vista looking west along the wall, his eyes trained to spot border crossers coming over the fence even here, where it stretches higher than the Berlin Wall I remembered. He was a hired hand from San Diego, and with his blonde hair and deep, even tan he looked much more like a surfer than a guard. I asked him about the Native Sons marker, and he shrugged. He said he'd never left his truck to check it out.

I followed the wall west on Anza Road for a couple of miles; it turned into First Street when I got back to town. In places the wall was opaque, a harsh blind spot making it impossible to see activity on the Mexican side. Its more sophisticated components leave viewing spaces between upright posts that are spaced tightly enough together to keep out even the skinniest migrant. This allows Border Patrol agents to keep track of activities on the Mexican side, migrants preparing to make their move north. I could see the traffic backup on the Mexico side, cars and trucks idling for hours, spewing expensive gasoline as exhaust into the already polluted Imperial Valley air.

It looked so familiar: the wall, the cleared land, the floodlights. Of course this was no free-fire zone. Officer Chavez and his fellow officers often save lives, especially far from urban centers, as migrants struggle to survive a clandestine crossing. There's no Selbstschußanlage SM 70; here in America our wall is reinforced with humane automation— motion detectors and cameras designed to alert the Border Patrol and guide officers to make arrests. Still, consider this sobering reality: since 1993, when the nascent wall first appeared on the San Diego–Tijuana line and migrants started looking east into the murderous desert for easier crossing points, more border crossers have died making the trek north from Mexico than were killed by the Volkspolizei in the entire twenty-eight-year lifetime of the Berlin Wall.

In a 2006 column titled "Immigration 101 for Beginners and Non-Texans," the late Molly Ivins was typically succinct. "The Fence will not work," she announced. "No fence will work. The Great darn Wall of China will not work. Do not build a fence. It will not work. They will come anyway. Over, under or through." Ivins is often credited with the now-proved axiom, "If we build a 12-foot fence, they'll make a 13-foot ladder." (This realistic joke also is attributed to New Mexico governor Bill Richardson.)

Michael Chertoff didn't disagree, even as the former Department of Homeland Security secretary presided over the fence-building project. "I don't believe the fence is a cure-all," Chertoff told the *New York Times* in 2008, "nor do I believe it is a waste. Yes, you can get over it; yes, you can get under it. But it is a useful tool that makes it more difficult for people to cross. It is one of a number of tools we have, and you've got to use all of the tools."

Trouble is, this ugly tool is laying waste to the Calexicos of the borderlands. The cost/benefit ratio is absurd whether you measure in dollars (Chertoff's department estimated three million dollars a mile, with an upgrade for rough terrain), America's defiled image, the fence's ineffectiveness, or Calexico's quality of life.

It is a heartbreaker to see the physical evidence of America's attempt to fence itself off from the rest of the world—this variation on the Berlin Wall. We are turning into a national gated community. We're making the fifty states into our panic rooms—those so-called safe rooms now featured in some private homes, places where the occupants can retreat and cordon themselves off from the rest of the house if an intruder breaks down the front door. Trouble is, we're forcing ourselves to stay in our national panic rooms even when the intruder is a friendly one and comes looking for a job we need done, wants to buy something in one of our shops, study in one of our schools, or—God forbid—just come visit us.

Both the Mexican and the U.S. governments have struggled since they were established to secure their national borders. Many of the long-time original residents of North America who lived on the changing line between the two countries were nomadic. Arbitrary borders meant nothing to them. Long before the United States worried about illegal immigration from Mexico, Mexico labored to stop illegal immigration into its state of Texas from the United States.

Expansionist president James Polk instigated a Tonkin Gulf–like incident on the Mexican Army in Texas to start the Mexican-American War. In addition to the fight along the Texas border, Polk dispatched troops to steal Mexico's northwest, the land from New Mexico out to California. It was a war "unnecessarily and unconstitutionally begun by the President of the United States," according to a House resolution passed eighty-five to eighty-one just before the Treaty of Guadalupe Hidalgo was signed in 1848, ceding half of Mexico to the United States.

The gash on the south side of Calexico dividing it from Mexicali is a national disgrace. Sometimes we can obtain a clearer perspective on a mistake from someone outside of the family, someone who knows us—the United States—well. That's why I chose to talk about the barrier with Jorge Castañeda. Castañeda served as Mexico's foreign minister under President Vicente Fox and negotiated with the U.S. government in an attempt to improve conditions on the border and circumstances for Mexican migrants heading north. When we spoke he was Professor of Politics and Latin American Studies at New York University. It was he, as foreign minister, who coined the catchy phrase "the whole enchilada" for his wish list vis-à-vis U.S. policy to Mexico. But the attacks of September 11, 2001, interrupted the bilateral negotiations, and Mexico wasn't even left with chips and salsa once President Fox refused to sign up for George Bush's Iraq invasion.

Castañeda is arguably all but bicultural, comfortable on both sides of the border. When we talked he was teaching in New York, and he's taught at Princeton and Berkeley; he did undergraduate work at Princeton.

He writes for newspapers north and south of the Rio Grande (or Río Bravo, depending on your perspective). I wanted to know his emotional response when he looks at the wall that now bisects Calexico and Mexicali. After not even two days back in the borderlands and seeing the extreme wall for the first time, I knew mine.

"It evokes very negative reactions on my behalf," he told me without hesitation, "not only because of the suffering and danger and grief it imposes on Mexicans, but also because of the way it denies what I've always considered the United States to be."

And what is that?

"A country that's open-minded, a country that's liberal, a country that's tolerant. I get very upset about it mainly because of what it does to my countrymen, but also because of what it does to my idea—a foreign idea, granted, but an idea that has been built over the last fifty years—of the United States. I think it absolutely betrays everything I thought the United States was."

Add to betrayal, irony. The wall I was looking at likely was thrown up with the help of undocumented Mexican workers. One of the stark realities of early-twenty-first-century America is that there aren't enough workers legally living in the country to fuel the economy. With raw unemployment numbers running at about seven million and estimates of the number of foreigners in the country without proper documentation ranging from twelve to fifteen and on up to twenty million, the math dictates that we need the outsiders. Even if all seven million legal workers are out of a job because a foreigner without proper papers took it, that leaves five or eight or thirteen million jobs we need performed that are filled by the so-called illegals undaunted by the wall, despite the ebbs and flows of the economy.

I checked in with Jason Booth, a friendly and stoic chap who shouldered the challenge of working as the public mouthpiece for the Golden State Fence Company. Golden State Fence was fined hundreds of thousands of dollars for employing fence builders who carried inadequate identification with which to prove their legal residency in the United States. Two of its executives were sentenced to three years' worth of probation for violating federal law. Few employers are targeted by Immigration and Customs Enforcement; it's the workers who usually bear the brunt of our xenophobia.

Mr. Booth has a theory for his company's misfortune. "Quite possibly it's because Golden State is one of the largest fence companies in this part of the country," he said from their Southern California headquarters when I contacted him. "Golden State had been the subject of several raids over the years, and they thought it would be a company that would just be good in that respect. I mean, it was an easy target for them, I suppose." Translation: You simply cannot get enough fence builders unless you hire "illegals."

Golden State Fence won a contract with the government to build sections of the high-profile fence along the Mexican border. I wanted to know whether any of those undocumented workers on the payroll were building the Mexican barrier. Booth insisted, "No, there's absolutely no indication of that whatsoever." However, he was understandably cautious when I asked him if Golden State Fence could stay in business without "illegal" workers.

"You know that's not really a question I'm in a position to answer," PR professional Booth told me, and then he tried to clarify his answer. "I know that Golden State Fence, as you pointed out, always struggled to find workers particularly willing to do the kind of work they do, which is usually hard work. It's skilled work and nearly always outdoors and also in a part of the country where we get very extreme weather. In the construction industry I would say it is difficult, but nothing is impossible."

With the government charging that as many as two-thirds of Golden State Fence workers were working in violation of immigration laws, it's quite likely their border fence workers were "illegals" out on *la frontera* building the wall designed to keep out their brothers and cousins. Despite Booth's denials.

Before I said good-bye to Jason Booth, I noted his prominent and distinguished-sounding British accent.

"Are you in this country legally?"

He laughed, "Yes, absolutely."

"We let you into your former colony?"

"Ah, yes," he said. "And thank you very much."

"Hey, it's a pleasure," I told him. "But don't forget the Boston Tea Party and what we think of King George." We want him on his best behavior.

Frank Salazar is a Calexico politician, a former city councilman and aide to the Valley's longtime Democratic congressman Bob Filner. He's been to Washington, where he labored for the Clinton administration. He came home to the borderlands to work as a well-connected political consultant, convinced there is a future in Calexico as well as a past.

But when I sat down to talk with him at the Barbara Worth Resort, he immediately made it clear that he is impressed by that faded glory of Calexico's good old days.

"We had power. We lost it. You know, they show pictures on post-cards of the Salton Sea and Sinatra's playing at the lounges. Back in the twenties and the thirties in Calexico, you had John Wayne getting drunk in Mexicali and staying at the Hotel de Anza, and you're think-ing, are you kidding me? Really?"

John Wayne did indeed make a stop in Calexico. The moment is documented in the hundredth anniversary issue of the weekly *Calexico Chronicle*, with a photograph of Mr. Wayne posing in a skipper's cap with local schoolchildren in the lobby of the Capitol Theater. On the same page of that issue is an image of the downtown Calexico port of entry in 1941. Dramatically missing: the Wall. Instead, there's a sim-ple border hut for a checkpoint, under a festive sign reading, MEX-ICO. When I talked about John Wayne's visit with Salazar, the almost restored Hotel de Anza was an old-folks home and headquarters of the just-opened Calexico Cultural Arts Center.

"They had dances there, I had a prom there. But it's past its glory. It's now a senior citizen complex. I saw Molly Ringwald there when they filmed the movie called *Baja*. I think Tom Cruise stayed there as well when they made the movie *Losing It*. *Losing It* was all filmed in Calexico. My sixth-grade teacher was in it. I couldn't see it because it was an 'R' movie. It was about a bunch of guys going to Tijuana to get laid, but it was really not Tijuana, it was Calexico. They made several parts of *La Bamba* in Calexico as well. Yeah, Calexico's interesting."

I asked Salazar about the newspaper editorial assaulting the Pacheco brothers.

"Oh, the Pacheco brothers. Yeah, I know them all. Lewis Pacheco, Sal Pacheco, Sammy Pacheco, all the Pachecos. How frank do you want me to be in this?"

"Completely frank," I told him. "After all, your name is Frank."

He leaned back in his chair, smiled and guaranteed, "Sure, there's nepotism or the *compadrismo* system. Does compadrismo exist south of The Eight? Well, let's go north of The Eight. What do you call that? *Farmismo*? People think that their poo don't smell. It smells every-where. We're in the Imperial Valley.

"Every story about Calexico in the *Imperial Valley Press* is a nega-tive story," said Salazar. "It's a compadrismo story, it's a corruption story, it's a story dealing with drugs and border tunnels. Why don't you look north of I-8?"

Why the negativity about Calexico?

Salazar *was* frank. "I'd say because we're 85, 90 percent Latinos, and it's hard for anybody north of Interstate 8 to tap into the system in Calexico, because they feel like fish out of water. As you do today," he said about me, because I was talking to him at my hotel on the north side of The Eight. But I felt pretty comfortable, not like a fish out of water, wandering around Calexico. That's the conceit of a journalist—that's the job of a journalist: secure an adequate comfort level quickly.

"You guys are at the Barbara Worth Resort," Salazar pressed on about the contrasts. "Go to Calexico. Go to the Don Juan Hotel."

"What's the difference?" I asked.

"Oh, you'll see the difference," laughed Salazar. Look up the Don Juan at Yahoo Travel, and there's only one customer review reading: "It's just okay." Markos and I opted for the relative comfort and high-speed Internet of the Barbara Worth. But I asked Salazar to explain the north-of-The-Eight/south-of-The-Eight divide.

"Stay at the Don Juan," he said again, "because that'll be Calexico at its best. You'll see the rustle and the bustle of the morning and the nightlife. You ask for wi-fi, they don't know what the hell you're talking about! It's just different. This would not survive Calexico," he gestured around the Barbara Worth, "because it's supported by the establishment. Calexico has never been supported by the establishment. I tried as much as I could to reach out past Calexico, north of The Eight, past parochialism," he said about his time in city government. "We need to reach out to the El Centros and the Holtvilles and the Brawleys and go north. But sometimes we're just so stuck being in Calexico that we're like fish out of water, too."

I prodded him to explain the cultural differences he saw between his hometown and those cities to the north.

"I'd say the culture in Calexico is extremely social. We're very social. We're very Mexican-minded. We are Mexicans. When Calexico people go to the San Francisco or L.A., and they hear the word *Chicano,* we freak out. We're rooted in Mexico. We're Mexicans." He went through a litany of examples of how some Californians of Mexican descent feel otherwise and call themselves Chicanos or Mexican Americans, and how they try to convince him that should be his identity, an identity he rejects. "I'm a Mexican. It's a culture. We're Mexican. We speak

Another Valley air conditioner awaits the summer's triple-digit thermometer readings.

Spanish first. The Mexican currency is accepted in Calexico. You have fifty pesos, go to McDonald's or go to Jack-in-the-Box," he snapped his fingers, "they'll take it."

Indeed, my traveling companion Markos was the only English-speaker I encountered wandering the streets of downtown Calexico.

"Go to El Centro, give them fifty pesos, and ask if they'll accept it. Chance is they won't. It's a culture. Go to the Calexico Walmart, and they'll probably take the peso. Not in El Centro. You ever thought about that?"

I told him about Felicia, the barber I met from Holtville, who insisted, although she was born in Arizona and spent the bulk of her life in the Imperial Valley, that she's 99.9 percent Mexican.

"We've always been Mexicans. We're always Latinos and Mexicans, we hang out with us. When we go out and we see whites, Anglos, Caucasians, blacks, Asians, they look at us as Mexicans." I was getting a crash course in Imperial Valley race relations and borderlands culture from Salazar's point of view. "We hold on to our culture. We can see the border across the street. We have dual lives. Tomorrow I have to meet with a client in Mexicali. During the weekends, I want to visit my

Neon nights at the Border Motel offer an alternative to the Barbara Worth Resort.

dad, I go to Mexicali. I want to go get some good tacos, I go to Mexicali. I want to buy groceries, I sometimes go to Mexicali. It's just a dual life. We're like the Mexican Californians. You know, we're just chill. We're more relaxed. We don't have freeways."

The speech sounded so pat, so political, such a set piece.

"How much of what you just said is simply your public political act?" I asked Salazar. "You're explaining, 'Hey, I'm a Mexican from Calexico.' But you're no simple local boy; you've enjoyed a career in your nation's capital." He must code shift. One voice for his Calexico self, another for the corridors of national politics.

"People I work with in government in San Diego say to me, 'Why do you want to go back to Calexico?' I say, 'Because I love my Valley. It's me. I like it. You know? It's different. It's not the same hobnob like at the Capital Grille in D.C. You focus on your family, you work hard, you sweat hard. It's a hundred degrees today. I want to go home.' Catch my drift?"

His drift I caught.

"That's how we are in Calexico. We don't like outsiders."

I was not quite ready to accept that broad statement; I had already been made to feel quite welcome by the Calexicans I met casually on the street. Maybe that's because I presented no threat to the status quo. But I had begun to look at the California borderlands south of The Eight as some sort of a free zone, almost an outlaw region, a liminal space where two distinct cultures—gringo and Mexican—are interacting without mixing well. It's not quite as separated an act as water and oil, but they sure are not dissolving into an integrated new compound with the smooth and easy transition that rum and Coca-Cola make to become a Cuba Libre. There seems to be a mentality of, "Leave us be because we've got it covered here, and we'll give lip service to your rules and regulations, but we'll take care of our own act here."

Frank Salazar disagrees with that representation of his hometown.

"No, we do abide," he says, using—consciously? Who knows, it seems rude to ask—the line from the Coen brothers' *The Big Lebowski*. "We do abide by whatever we need to, but it's a certain way we go about it. Yes, we do operate differently. We have our own . . . what's the word I'm looking for? We have our own mode." Low and slow, like a lowrider, maybe. And even that mode annoys Salazar sometimes; Salazar, local boy made good in the capital city, comes home and can't quite slow down to the Calexico pace. "Sometimes when I call somebody and they don't call me back, I'll e-mail them and they don't e-mail me back, I fax them and they don't fax me back—I feel like I'm bugging the hell out of them. And chances are I *am* bugging them in the Valley. When I have people come from the outside, clients of mine, I say, 'Don't worry, that's how the Valley is. But at the end we'll get our job done and we'll be loyal.' That's one thing that the Valley has, Calexico has, is loyalty, more than anything. Like a *familia*. You break your back for me, I'll break my back for you. It's loyalty. It's something I don't see in the bigger cities."

I talked border and border fortification, and Salazar grumbled about the post-9/11 changes bifurcating the Mexicali–Calexico experience.

"It has kind of cramped our lifestyle. Cramped my style." He ticked off the factors. "Terrorism. Security. Bush administration legacy. We'd freely go in our cars, have a nice dinner, get some drinks, come back, go to bed. I miss Mexicali myself. I don't go as much as I used to. Yes, the lines are longer. Before you would come home at one o'clock in the morning, and by one thirty-five you'd be across. Now, it's like you make line at one, two forty-five you're done. You waited an hour and forty-five minutes in this long line, and you're hoping to God that your air conditioner and your radiator won't go out." I noted the local jargon: "make line."

It's not just an inconvenience for Salazar and his friends, an entourage he calls Mexican Yuppies. He cited real damage to his city's economy. It must be devastating to business in the Calexico backwater, losing customers from the metropolis to the south because of the long waits at the wall. Salazar did not appreciate my terminology. "You mean 'border,'" he interrupted when I referred to the wall. And he pleaded with me to use another term when I called Calexico a "backwater" to Mexicali.

"Calexico is suffering because of the border waits. A lot of the mom-and-pa's that we once had are closing. Businesses that were once thriving and booming in downtown are not making ends meet. Times are tough. You just don't see the hustle and bustle as much anymore. Calexico relies on Mexicali. If you were to go downtown right now and ask everybody there, 'Where you from?' I can say about 85 percent of the people are going to say Mexicali. There's a McDonald's in Mexicali. There's a McDonald's in Calexico. Where are Mexicali people going to go? The Calexico McDonald's."

Why?

"It's Calexico. It's the United States. There's a Walmart in Mexicali. There's a Walmart in Calexico. Where are they going to go? The Walmart in Calexico."

Crazy. There's no consequential price differential. The American side is perceived as better: better service, better return policies. And different. It's not Mexican. Mexican-made Coca-Cola is sold at premium prices in San Francisco taquerías; it tastes better, say aficionados, because in Mexico cane sugar, not high-fructose corn syrup, is used for a sweetener.

Frank Salazar wishes Calexico would harness its strength, that its role as a port of entry means it holds power, power that can be exerted to draw attention to its problems.

"Let's block the border," he gave as an example. "We could do that." His eyes sparkled at the mischievous notion. "We'd get attention." He offered other headline-grabbing ideas. "We could drive a tractor or cars into the New River to stop the flow." But inaction, not radical protest, is the norm. "We look the other way and say, 'Mañana.'

Political operative Frank Salazar holds court.

We just put our heads down and work day in and day out because we don't want to lose our jobs. People don't want to stick their necks out, and I understand."

Quite the image, homeboy Frank Salazar leading marauding Calexicans blocking the border and sending the polluted New River back to its Mexican origins.

I left Frank Salazar at the Barbara Worth and drove the few miles to Calexico to cruise up and down its streets. It was nothing like I expected to find. No quaint Main Street block heading north from the border to study as a representative sample, to get to know intimately. No row of intriguing all-American-looking red-brick commercial buildings packed with vibrant shops under cozy apartments. No crowded street scene, no sidewalks packed with neighbors gossiping in a Mayberry RFD–like scenario. No nineteenth-century Americana architecture: the border city wasn't founded until 1908.

Instead, I found the downtown opening of the physical abomination that identifies the border, the official crossing point and its huge inspection shed for those driving or walking north, flanked by the harsh barrier that rejects the innocuous label "fence" that so many proponents of the barrier use. But it is a wall, not a fence. And from my perspective of having lived in Berlin when that city was divided, it was impossible not to see it as a variation on the Berlin Wall theme every time I saw it: ugly, monstrous, insulting, and—ultimately—doomed to failure.

I watched as an SUV was being inspected thoroughly in "secondary," the lane where officials pull cars and trucks they suspect of harboring contraband or secreted immigrants. Then I strolled along the sidewalk toward the bus station, past a stinking sewer that I would recognize and try to remember to avoid because that street corner, directly across from the main Calexico port of entry, stank throughout my visit, a nauseating smell that quickened my steps. I was on First Street, literally the first street on the USA side. The second stories of the buildings stretched out over the sidewalks, a reminder of the need for protection from the perpetual desert sun. I turned up Paulin Avenue and walked the block to Second Street. Bleak. Those shops not vacant were adorned

A mom-and-pop holdout still manages to compete with the Walmart that's strategically positioned just a few blocks from Calexico's struggling old downtown.

with signs in Spanish. "Cilantro. Mazo Grande. 4 × 99¢." There was no sign of anything "downtown" where I could sit for a leisurely meal. I went back to the Mazda, cranked up the air conditioner, and reluctantly headed north on the main drag, Imperial Avenue, up toward the lights of the strip malls stretching into the farmland.

I beat it north on U.S. 111 from the border wall, passed under The Eight, and headed for Imperial Valley College and the scheduled noontime poetry reading. A few miles north of the border, I turned left on Aten Road and found a spot for the Mazda in the college parking lot. The campus newspaper is called *Left on Aten*, suggesting a Calexico orientation. Driving to IVC from El Centro would require a right turn on Aten. The campus sits like an oasis on the desert landscape, its squat utilitarian buildings well air-conditioned, its lawns irrigated to country-club verdant. In a courtyard behind the library, about a dozen participants were gathered for the poetry. A boom box wailed, a singer plaintively offering, "I really want to grow . . ." Student Angel Sandoval, in a black T-shirt festooned with the legend, "I'm not an alcoholic, I'm a writer," moseyed confidently over to the microphone and graciously announced, "First of all I'd like to thank Professor Alicia Ortega. Thank you very much for your time, for your clout, for your class, and for your students." Applause. The courtesy of such heartfelt appreciation sounded like a throwback to a bygone era. But he wasn't finished. "And also the staff of the library—very helpful putting this thing together." The format was open mic. "Hopefully, you have pieces you want to read, and we'll get this going, man. We've got an hour, so we've got to keep it moving, all right?" He turned down the music.

Angel read some lines based on the hip-hop work of Jay-Z, lines he adapted with his own autobiographical opening, "I come from Valle Imperial, where it is hot as hell," making it fit neatly with an approximation of the original "American Dreamin'" Jay-Z lyric, "You've got to survive the drought, so I wish you well." He finished the verses, took a swig from a water bottle, and smiled. "I'm a little dehydrated, I'm trying to survive the drought." It was noon. It was hot. I found a shady place for my chair, but the locals were acclimated; they sat in the sun without complaint.

Arena Márquez took the microphone. In accent-free California English she announced, "Hi, guys! Today I want to read a poem from Sor Juana Inés de la Cruz." We were far from the strip malls of

Highway 111 just a few miles south, far from the deteriorated Calexico downtown and the marauding border wall, as this junior college student launched into the seventeenth-century Mexican nun's feminist verse—in flawless Spanish. Ms. Marquez followed her reading with an appreciation of Sor de la Cruz in English. "I really admire Sor Juana Inés de la Cruz. She got a lot of criticism in this new country of Nueva España." Márquez was transcending the border, referring to the historical Imperial Valley as a land without the southern border at the wall, but rather as just one colony, the New Spain that stretched from Guatemala north. "Because she was a nun, she was able to write and was not persecuted like other people would be, for being a woman and for being someone from the Catholic Church who was speaking up against a lot of the norms back then."

A classmate followed Arena with more of Sor de la Cruz's work, translated into English and as contemporary-sounding as anything Jay-Z writes; in fact, its phrasing sounded almost hip-hop. "Stupid men/Quick to condemn/Women wrongly for their flaws/Never seeing you're the cause/Of all that you blame in them."

Wearing a suit and tie, and looking cool as the temperature approached one hundred degrees, Mark Perez announced that he was on his lunch break but could not pass up the opportunity to share a cathartic personal poem. "I agree with Angel," he announced. "Writing is power, writing is freedom." Then he launched into an ode to his divorce. "Forgive me for not paying attention to your very own needs/Forgive me for stepping all over you in your time of need/Forgive me for pushing you farther and farther away from me/Forgive me for wishing you dead." He continued in similar fashion for a stunning several stanzas. Before he returned to his office, he announced the inauguration of a poetry club with monthly meetings scheduled for the Calexico public library. "A librarian will be in charge of the meetings," he reported to the audience, "and I really encourage you guys to go. If we get together, we can make changes in this community with our writings and by inspiring each other." More applause.

From Angel next came the news that Calexico had just opened a cultural center. "It's a great idea, the cultural center. It has so much potential. We should really take advantage of it. It's a very good thing that Calexico is doing, taking the leadership role in cultural awareness and the arts. It's about time. Poetry is revolution, and we need more revolution in Imperial Valley. Who's next? Come on!"

I was getting some severely mixed signals. While the morning paper was writing Calexico off as a hopeless and corrupt backwater, the local next generation was seeing it as a potential Left Bank in the twenties. "Only in Calexico" was starting to take on a greater meaning.

"Who's next? Come on!" implored Angel, and a surprise guest came forward: the new superintendent and president of the college, Dr. Ed Gould. His cheerful smile was wide, and he looked relaxed in an open-collared sports shirt. His neat hair looked freshly barbered as he strode to the microphone.

"Poetry is something that not only stimulates," Dr. Gould said, "but really is the product of an era. I'm going to read a couple of poems by Rod McKuen. Now, you probably don't know Rod McKuen," he told his students, "but he wrote for those of us who were part of the Vietnam era at a particularly difficult time in our lives, as we were deciding what we were going to be in relation to this country of ours. It was a very, very difficult time." Gould was relaxed at the microphone as he transcended generational distances and connected Vietnam and Iraq, civil rights with immigrant rights, then and now. He was teaching history and current affairs with a warm and comforting voice of authority.

"We would sit around the residence hall, and we would look for meaning. As the racial tension grew in the country, and because of the war issues between our generations, the separations between us and our parents became a reality in the late sixties. We were looking for meaning in life." His audience was rapt. "What Rod McKuen brought to most of us was an escape from that day-to-day into love songs." Gould made McKuen further accessible by placing him as a neighbor. "He grew up in Oakland, spent a lot of time in San Francisco." And then he read "A Cat Named Sloopy" and "Gifts from the Sea," while desert birds sang for his background music in the open library patio. Applause for the superintendent and president, and the perfect opening faculty act for what was coming next.

But first, dear reader, a footnote. Rod McKuen? Rod McKuen as a twenty-first-century muse to make sense of life in Calexico? Rod McKuen, who has sold millions of recordings—his work still sells—and whose oeuvre is disparaged by the elitist likes of the British award-winning (the T. S. Eliot and Whitbread prizes, for example) poet David Harsent, who is quoted as calling McKuen a poet "with a formula likely to appeal to the groupies and grannies alike." McKuen is a fellow Californian. I figured it appropriate to check in with him and get his reading regarding this example of a place where his writing remains in vogue and was introduced to a new generation of readers.

One of the best-selling poets of all time lives in Oakland, but I caught up with him when he was on the road in Southern California, intrigued to check in with him about his current celebrity at Imperial Valley College. I told him of the noontime poetry reading, how it was something quite special, with original work being recited by students and faculty. And I told him of how Dr. Gould came up to the microphone and invoked McKuen's name and work. Does that resonate with you? I asked him. Were you writing for people who were feeling disenfranchised like the young Dr. Gould?

"You know, it does resonate now," McKuen responded without hesitating. "I'll tell you why. Because frankly, I wrote about what I believed in and what I felt and what was happening to me. I don't write to an audience so much as I write to try to explain things in my own life. It was very difficult for me during the war," he said, because he was publicly opposed to the war. He recalled decrying the U.S. action, deploring a government sending its children off to die, and mused, "By the way, does that sound familiar?"

Does it ever.

"At the same time I made several trips over there to entertain the troops, because I had nothing against the kids. I certainly don't like war, and I was perplexed that it was going on for so long. Everybody knew it was something we couldn't win and that we were pretending that it was possible to win."

His memories of the Vietnam quagmire didn't just sound like a retelling of the Iraq War; they sounded like a summary of U.S. border policy: everybody knew it was something we couldn't win and that we were pretending that it was possible to win.

I recounted to McKuen how Dr. Gould connected Vietnam to Iraq, and the civil rights movement to the current movement for immigrant rights, how he was teaching history and current affairs with a warm, comforting voice of authority, a terrific example of what should be happening in a college environment. And I told the poet that the professor reminisced to his students, "What Rod McKuen brought to most of us was an escape from that day-to-day into love songs."

"Gee, what a nice thing to say."

Is that what he was consciously doing at the time?

"I'm sure it was. I think it was Johnny Mercer who said of my early songs, 'Rod, you write all these songs about looking back and about lost love, what's going to happen when you get older?' Well, I'm still writing the same songs."

Love is omnipresent, and that never changes—Iraq or Vietnam, immigration or civil rights.

"No, it doesn't. I mean you, here we are. You're a writer, I'm sure it's true in your work. You talk about what's going on around you and what affects you. Probably the reason you're successful, and probably the reason that most of us with any sense like radio better than television, is because we can make up our own minds. The same is true with a poem; it can be read so many different ways. When they present something to you on television as a fact, and you see the picture, it destroys the illusions you can make in your own head. I'm sure that you as a broadcaster must also speak from your perspective as to what's going on in your life and what's going on around you that affects your life."

The connection he made between radio and poetry was intriguing, because the poet is creating images, and radio is unique in media, and certainly in news media, for stimulating the imagination by default because there are no pictures. There's not even any typography to put any kind of context into what's coming out of the speaker other than what the listener adds.

"What the listener brings to a poem, or a thought or a scene described in radio, is every bit as important as what the author or what the commentator can bring into it," said McKuen.

Right he was, as was made clear at the Imperial Valley College noon readings of his work. Dr. Gould provided an interpretation for the students, one they put into a borderlands context, just as I took the exuberant lines of the poem "Calexico" with the prejudices of a big-city type looking at the rural border, when it was read that noontime.

I asked McKuen for his reaction to Dr. Gould's choices, "A Cat Named Sloopy" and "Gifts from the Sea," as examples of poetry that allowed him to escape from the difficulties of the sixties.

"It's difficult for me to relate to them. 'A Cat Named Sloopy' is probably one of the most-read and requested of my poems, and yet I like to think I've gone way beyond that. My problem, I think, is that, frankly, if I could, I'd rewrite everything I've ever written."

Isn't that the case with most writers?

"I don't know, but it sure is with me. I have a website and even when I reprint poems on the website I find myself rewriting them."

McKuen wrote "A Cat Named Sloopy" in the mid-sixties; it's understandable that almost a half century later he might want to revise it. "I write about everything," he told me, but there's no work in his massive collection that directly speaks to the crises on the border.

"I've never addressed immigration because I don't frankly know how to address it." Not that he is without opinion. "I think our borders should be open and free, because America's always been an open society, and that's how all of us got here. I don't like walls. I don't like fences." He considered those types of border crossers that he may wish to see excluded. "I don't think it's as simple as banning people from coming into the country because of drug problems." He suggested he's not prepared to write off lawbreakers. "I think that everybody has a useful contribution to make." But he, as are so many, is stumped when asked for solutions. "I've never been able to get a handle on what should be going on at the border."

McKuen has made visits to Dr. Gould's borderlands neighborhood.

"I have to say it's scandalous. It's a waste of money, because the money could be put to better use, just as the drug laws are a waste of time and money when, instead of filling our prisons with people, we should be getting people over drugs."

I asked for a poem that reflected his thoughts on the border—or, I queried, is he kept busy writing the escapist work that appealed to Dr. Gould in an effort to provide a little separation from the problems of the world?

"I think I do a bit of both. I've yet to write a 9/11 poem that I really like. I've worked and worked and worked on that, and I just haven't been able to harness it. During the Vietnam War we were in a less complicated world. It is really, really more complicated today."

Before we said good-bye, I suggested Rod McKuen offer an impression, what may be a first line of a poem for Dr. Gould and his students, a poem that addresses the borderlands.

"I'm not sure if I could do that, but I can certainly tell you a line that I live by."

Fair enough.

"I close every concert with this: I figure it doesn't matter who you love or how you love, but that you love; because if you're not loving somebody or something, you're not alive."

Not bad.

"If we approach each other with that attitude," he said, "I don't know how we can go wrong." And with that he asked for Dr. Gould's address, so he could drop him a note.

"Vamos a tener una voz en español," said poetry instructor Alicia Ortega, as the Imperial Valley College poetry reading continued, "y creo qué van a entender todos. For any of you who do not understand Spanish, you're going to understand the feeling," she said about the next act on the program. "It is to celebrate Calexico's hundredth anniversary." Only in Calexico! I had arrived to celebrate the poor city's centennial.

Spanish instructor María Luís Grivanos swept to the front of the assembly. Her makeup was theatrical, with her dramatically arched dark-black eyebrows drawn to match her equally dark-black pixie-like hairdo. The words came out of a smiling mouth rimmed with red-wine-colored lips, and her eyes were wide with the excitement of performance. She held her position in silence for a moment, then thrust her arms to the heavens and exclaimed, with no need for the microphone, "¡Calexico! Dos culturas, dos mundos, un siglo." I was transfixed as she pronounced in Spanish:

Calexico! Two cultures, two worlds, one century.

Land of energy, courage, and harvest.
People struggling against nature's adversities in the desert,
Who build tracks in the sand,
And form this land with the sweat and souls of men and women.
Men and women with cracks in their hands,
From laborious work under the ardent sun,
Who cultivate life,
Life among the sand furrows of hope and prosperity.

Two cultures, two worlds, one century.
People thankful for this land,
With secure and happy childhoods,
Who sow dreams and illusions,
Who harvest opportunities and triumphs,
Seeking a better life.
Melting pot of dusks, dawns, and life.

Hot oracle of harsh sun on the path of this incomparable valley,
Brilliantly reflecting the colorful future.

Calexico! Land that fosters successful natives, immigrants, or
friends.

Calexico! Two cultures, two worlds, one century.

It was epic. An ode to the Calexico I was looking for by an actress
placed on the stage by Central Casting. "Calexico!" Señora Grivanos
had shouted out to grab our attention, and from that first shout, her
overacted emotive performance, her pleading paean—here a plaintive
whisper and there a yelled demand, sometimes a staccato rush of words
and other times a dirgelike assault of symbols—enthralled me. Markos
agreed, saying, "I'm sure the name Calexico has never been pronounced
with greater passion or power."

The soaring voice and animated gestures of Spanish teacher Maria Luis Grivanos captivate audiences whenever she shares the epic paean she's written to
her adopted hometown, Calexico.

"Gracías," she said quietly when she finished reading. She smiled at the applause and exited stage left. I grabbed her. She was flush with the afterglow of performance, bristling still with adrenaline, and reticent about speaking in English.

I sat in the shade with María Luís Grivanos, entranced with her reading. She told me she wrote the poem because she wants others to know how she feels about Calexico. Her creative process, she said, included interviewing friends, other citizens, and migrants. "I question them, how you feel about your town?"

Calexico has been her address for over a quarter of a century, since she crossed the border from her family home in Mexicali. "When I came in here I found a lot of opportunities for jobs, for study, for a life here with my family." Her two children were born and raised in Calexico.

"Calexico is a beautiful place to live, and it's growing," she said, "but it's only a baby. Calexico is a baby city." Therein lies at least part of its charm and appeal.

I found one of the ultimate examples of Imperial Valley boosters when I met Elvia Machado, the secretary to the English Department at Imperial Valley College. Imperial Valley. One of those places that we arrogant and chauvinistic coast dwellers refer to as "flyover" lands. The kind of place we tend to drive through fast on a journey to somewhere else while we ask each other, "What do they do here?"

Unlike so many of her compatriots who left the Valley for the big city, or left the Valley and ultimately returned as a prodigal son or daughter, Elvia Machado has—essentially—never left home. She's lived in the Valley all her life—for thirty-four years—and she's barely traveled. Unless you count a two-hour drive west to the beach. "I have been to San Diego," she admitted, but not often.

"And not any farther south than Mexicali?" I asked.

"No. Absolutely not."

It's not, she insisted, that she doesn't want to travel; it's more that she wants to stay home. "I just don't ever leave, I guess. I don't have a reason to, is what I feel in my mind. I have all of my family here, and I just love the place, even though it can get really, really, really hot, and most people are uncomfortable with that."

One hundred seventeen degrees in August. The beach—one would think—over there just two hours west in San Diego at seventy-one degrees would be appealing and would draw her out of her nest. But nope.

"I just don't like the water, the whole shark thing, and, you know," she's laughing now, at herself and at the absurd reality of how happy she is to stay at home, "the unsafe riptides and all of that just kind of doesn't attract me. It's beautiful to watch, it's not something that draws me there."

With all due respect to her Imperial Valley, there is a certain harshness to the place: topography flat and austere—even bleak—climate often unbearably hot, architecture rarely inspiring. The air quality is the worst of any county in California. And one could make an argument that traditional cultural opportunities are not in abundance in the Imperial Valley. Does that ever factor into Elvia's decision-making process and make her think, "Maybe I should get out of this place for a while?"

Dream on, city slickers. "Not at all!" she insisted. "I know that the air quality is not as good as it should be, and I, for one, am fortunate enough to not have the respiratory problems that others have. I thank the man upstairs for that. But I'm okay with everything the desert has to offer. It's just suitable for me. So."

Thirty-four years of hanging out in the Imperial Valley. When she reads the newspapers or checks out what is going on in the rest of the world, she must at times reflect, "Hey, the Eiffel Tower, that would be fun!" or "I'd like to go to the Met in New York and see some of those paintings!" or "A ride up to San Francisco to the opera or a Giants opener would be cool!"

"None of that?" I asked her.

"Well," she allowed, "every so often I'll see things on TV and it attracts me, but I'm not one for busy, for all of the hustle and bustle. Even when I go to San Diego, which is the nearest busy town, it's just anxiety for me. It overwhelms me, all the traffic, and it's just so fast-paced. Nobody ever has time anymore to do anything. It seems like everyone's in such a rush. Going there makes me feel there's more to life than just hustle and bustle and the fast-paced life. Here," she said about home sweet Imperial Valley, "it's a little slower. It's more family-oriented, I say. And that's just my interests."

I asked her for an example of a Friday or Saturday night in her life.

"Most people would probably think that my life is not as fun as it could be, but a night out is the drive-in movie theater. There's not too many of those around anymore, and there is one here! We go and watch movies. Go out to eat. Back in the day it used to be cruising, where you would just take a cruise out and just enjoy the atmosphere. That's what I enjoy."

Cruising despite gasoline prices?

"The gas is expensive but, as with everything, you tend to work around these things, and we surely are. Cruising does take up a lot of gas, but you know what? It's the quality time spent with the family that is much more valuable to me than money."

Plenty of us in the big city should take note.

How does a vivacious woman with a PhD from the University of California at Berkeley end up in the Imperial Valley, chairing the Imperial Valley College Humanities Department, teaching debate to intense and motivated students from Mexicali and Calexico? Let's let Dr. Melani Guinn explain for herself. Oh, yes. One other point: she's married to a former Border patrolman. And how did that happen?

"It's funny, when I met him in New York he was in the dot-com industry. He was a harmonica-playing dot-commer, and that was right around the time that they all started crashing, when the bottom fell out of the dot-com market. He was thirty and some friends told him, 'You know, you really ought to pursue your dreams, like really, what do you want to do?' And he said, 'Wow, I've always wanted to be in law enforcement,' and little did I know, you know?" She laughed. "Dot-commer, harmonica-playing, long hair—no clue. I never saw myself as a cop's wife, not in my demographic, you know?"

We were talking in her tiny office at the college, a windowless cubicle, chilled like an icebox. She offered coffee. "It's organic, I go to Yuma to get it."

She talks New York fast, strong coffee fast. Her husband wanted to be an FBI agent, but he applied to the usual suspects, too: municipal police departments and the Border Patrol. The Migra called, off he went to the academy, and after graduation the two packed for the Imperial Valley. While Dr. Guinn was deciding what to do with her new life, she figured she would take a few community college classes. No deal, Imperial Valley College told her, unless she paid hefty out-of-state fees. During her time in New York she lost her California residency. "And I, just out of frustration, said, 'What about teaching?' I didn't even want to teach, but I was just kind of mad." One class led to another, and before she knew it, husband Chris had left the Border Patrol because of health concerns, and Melani was chair of the Humanities Department.

It was Chris and the Border Patrol that brought the couple to the Imperial Valley, but Melani's job kept them there once he was mustered out of the force and they were free of his commitment. "I didn't want to leave. I love my job here. I love my students. I like a lot of things about the Valley. I like the wide, open space. I really like the desert." I expressed skepticism: this from a woman who studied in Berkeley's perfect cosmopolitan climate?

"I mean, it's hot," she acknowledged. "This is nothing," she said about the temperatures that day, temperatures we watched approach 100. "This is our temperate time. I mean, this is when you don't have to seal your windshield with one of those crazy accordion things. It gets to be 120 and, like, 65 percent humidity here for a couple months in the summer. It's really intense." Then she made a counterintuitive statement. "But that means that crazy people don't come here, because it's an extreme place."

I asked for an explanation, and she came back at me with a ready answer, and an unexpected comparison.

"You know how when you have a place that's very pleasant, like San Diego? It is year-round pleasant. You draw a certain type of person who's very pampered, used to kind of having things easy. But when you live in extreme places, you draw a really hardy kind of soul. And Imperial Valley's like that. I mean, nobody stays here who is a wuss. New York was like that. That's why I like both of them."

The coffee was percolating, made with filtered water. "My first real cup of coffee since we left San Francisco," Markos said later. "Melani was able to squeeze a bit of big-city comfort into that ten-by-ten air-conditioned office. It could just as easily have been an office off of Washington Square in Greenwich Village."

When the air pollution gets severe in the Valley, Melani and Chris drag their Airstream up into the mountains and camp above the pollution.

"It's hard to be green here," she told me, "because we have to order a certain amount of stuff on Amazon. And shipping isn't the greenest thing. We joined a co-op in San Diego, and we take the Prius—we have a hybrid, we had to get a hybrid—because you have to drive a lot here." She was smiling; she knows she's making their lives sound like a caricature. I teased her about the Prius, suggesting it's just in the driveway to rationalize the Airstream with carbon credit.

"We had to buy a truck for the Airstream," she acknowledged, "because they don't have hybrids yet that can pull them. We'll get one when they have them. But we only use the truck to pull the Airstream.

You have to find a balance, and we use the hybrid—the Prius," she is specific, "to go to San Diego to the co-op, once a month. We stock up on all the good stuff that we're getting at least semilocally. It's two hours away," she admits about San Diego, "but we're thinking about growing a garden in our backyard, a little organic garden. And doing xeriscaping in the front, even though, as you notice, very few people do here, which is just insane."

I told her we were living at the Barbara Worth Resort, watching precious Colorado River water flow in an attempt keep the golf course green—green. Not very green of the Barbara Worth.

"It's just insane!" she knew my home away from home well. "We got married at the Barbara Worth, because it's pretty much the only place. We had friends from New York come, and they're like, 'Oh, my God, why are they watering?' Three times a day in the middle of a very hot time of year."

I was talking humanities with the humanities professor, about adapting to a culture foreign to a San Francisco–New York sophisticate. Watching the politically incorrect watering of the golf course "was an adjustment. The food was definitely a big adjustment."

I told her Markos and I had eaten dinner the night before after eight in the evening, and we asked her to guess where we had dined.

"After eight o'clock? Let me think. Let me think. Applebee's?"

"Close. Guess again."

"Was it at the mall?"

I told her all the restaurants at the strip malls in Calexico were closed.

"The mall was closed," she said and barely paused before she announced: "Denny's!"

We laughed and I asked her if she crossed to Mexicali regularly for a dose of big-city culture.

"To Mexicali?" she sounded incredulous. "No, we don't."

I acknowledged that my question was arrogant, suggesting that there is something wrong with Imperial Valley culture. Your culture is wherever you are, it's your job, it's your neighbors, it's your books in your office. Who was I to be indicting Applebee's and Denny's?

"Yeah, yeah," she sounded as if she agreed but then said, "it's a valid question," and told me a story. "We had an instructor here at the college who we hired who mistakenly thought that he was—I don't know how he got this wrong—but he thought he was applying to a school in Los Angeles. He read the fine print wrong. He moved here and took a tenure-track job. He was miserable. He's from the Bay Area and a bit of a prima donna. But I do think it's something that you have to deal with when you're drawing other instructors here; some people are going to feel really not at home here."

I suggested, chauvinist from San Francisco that I am, that we can be as pretentious a bunch in San Francisco as can New Yorkers. Folks in the flyover American cities exert a quiet and comfortable sense of prag- matism: doing their jobs, enjoying themselves, and not patting them- selves on the back all the time telling themselves just how cool and hip and hep they are.

Dr. Guinn jumped to agree. "That is what I like about it, I have to say. I lived in the Bay Area, New York and L.A.—there's no pretentious- ness here. If people are, it's a joke. The farmers are rich, but they're not of another class. They're still middle-class, even though they're filthy rich. Culturally they're middle-class, and the migrant workers are mov- ing their kids into the middle class. No, it's not pretentious here and I really like that."

That cultural leveling, she theorizes, is an aspect of what makes the borderlands unique.

"We don't belong to Mexico, we don't belong to California." Dr. Guinn was retelling a Bud Light map lesson I soon would learn. "My dad visits from Texas, and he always says, 'I hate California.' And I say, 'Dad, I live in California.' And he says, 'This is not California.'" She wants her father's point to sink in and repeats it. "This is not considered California to Californians or Texans. It's just its own strange free zone."

Her father's term is an intriguing identifier for what I was recogniz- ing. These Borderlands are north of the Mexican border, but he's cor- rect: they don't quite feel like the rest of California. What goes on in this free zone? What is different about it from either California or Mexico?

Melani Guinn pondered the point. "We're kind of isolated," she said. "We have more in common with Brownsville, Texas, than with the rest of California. There's another dimension. We're very rural. We have a lot of space around us. Our students live a kind of protected life, which is both freeing and not freeing. They can't wait to get out of here and go to San Diego." But plenty of them come back, I've been learning.

Where others see desolation, Melani sees opportunity. She recounts for me a conversation she had with the teacher who left town in horror. "He complained, 'We have no good bookstores. We have no good places to get records.' I told him, 'You can do anything you want here.

You can open a record store!' I don't know if you have been down the main street. I said, 'You could probably rent something there for very little and start your own used bookstore.' This place has all sorts of opportunity. You know, if I were an entrepreneur type, which I'm not, I'd open a coffee place. You should see how bad the coffee is. It's like brown water. It's terrible. That's what I mean by freedom."

Not that all was idyllic from her perspective. When the college was planning a new building, after Dr. Guinn came to work she learned that it was not going to be equipped with solar panels for power generation, despite the fact that the sun shines almost every day of the year in the Imperial Valley. She told her colleagues that she wanted to contact the local newspaper to draw attention to what she saw as a mistake. The local power provider is the all-powerful Imperial Irrigation District. The IID controls the lifeblood of the Valley. Literally. Without the Colorado River water that the IID brings to the Valley, the desert would reclaim Calexico and everything around it. Farms would dry up. There would be no reasonable excuse to live in the Valley, but more important, there would be no water to make life in the Valley possible. The IID, Melani was told, offered relatively cheap electricity and no incentives for solar installations. Ridiculous, was her San Francisco–New York response. When she called for attention from the newspaper, peers at the college suggested quietly contacting the IID instead.

"It was very strange. I started feeling like I was in the fifties. That's another thing that's a little weird here. There's a little bit of the fifties going on, in a good way and a bad way. We've got that good-old-boy stuff, and students are extremely polite."

I had noticed a general sense of polite behavior at the poetry reading. And students in ties in hundred-degree weather.

"Yeah, they're very polite, very respectful, and there is this kind of distance you used to have with your teachers." Her assessment of her new home kept going back and forth: charming, full of opportunity, and yet disarmingly antiquated, especially in an urban California context.

"It's very strange. I mean there are some weird things, believe me. I didn't take my husband's name. I got married after we moved here, and I didn't take his name. I had no intention of ever taking his name. I'm just not that kind of person. I got back after taking a couple days off to get married, and my students said, 'Oh, Dr. Guinn, what shall we call you now?' And I said, 'Dr. Guinn.' And they said, 'What?' It didn't compute. I said, 'I didn't take my husband's name.' And this

Calexico RFD.

guy raised his hand, and he said, 'Isn't that against the law?' My brain just couldn't compute that they thought it was against the law."

Vikki Carr is the executive assistant to the president of Imperial Valley College, an Imperial Valley local who did what is expected so often of people from small towns. She went off to the big city. In fact she escaped the Valley a few times—and she kept coming back.

I met with her after the poetry reading. Dr. Guinn suggested Vikki Carr as just the archetype to help explain the lure of the Valley, a place I was beginning to appreciate, but nonetheless, for outsiders still a backwater. She was prepared for my prejudice with ready answers.

"Let me tell you the reasons why I keep coming back to the Valley. The most recent one, of course, is the housing opportunity in the Valley. Living in most of urban California is expensive by national standards, and Imperial Valley offers some of the lowest housing prices in the state. As a first-time homeowner, this is a perfect place, where you can come and actually start a family and be able to afford your house."

That's intriguing for those of us sobered by the high cost of homes in places like San Francisco, where, even after the market slipped, a half a million dollars barely provided a fixer-upper for shelter. Vikki told me about the five-bedroom, three-bath palace she picked up for $279,000 and compared it to the same type of house she looked at when she was living in San Diego, a house that she couldn't consider buying because of its $700,000 price tag.

But it wasn't just the relatively cheap housing.

"My parents. My parents are lifers, that's what I want to call them, here in the Valley. They emigrated from Mexico to the Valley forty years ago, and my dad is set on Holtville, which is one of the little cities here. They've been farmers all their lives, so they're getting into some health issues. They really need our help. That was the other draw back to the Valley: my parents."

It was a story I was beginning to hear repeated. The rural lifestyle, the affordability, but—most important—the continuity of family keeps people in the Imperial Valley.

"Not just with your blood relatives," Vikki pointed out, "but with the community in general."

Markos's high-school buddy George, the fellow we met for a beer just after we arrived in the Valley, is one of those wealthy growers Dr. Guinn labeled middle-class. He and his wife Maria lived just a few miles south of our resort home, down Barbara Worth Road and up over The Eight. We sped the Mazda past the fields and parked for a few minutes on the top of the overpass, watching the east–west transcontinental traffic hurtle past, so much of it unaware of the subtleties of life in the Valley, the Valley just an obstacle between Yuma and San Diego.

Their home is luxurious but not ostentatious, set by the side of Barbara Worth Road and surrounded by their bountiful fields. They grow year-round, except for the hottest days of summer, corn and cantaloupes, among other crops, crops destined for high-end markets such as Whole Foods. When you pay 79 cents for an ear of corn at your local Whole Paycheck, know that George and Maria receive only about twenty-five cents for it; the rest goes to middlemen and transport and profits along the route to the checkout counter. Some of their acreage is organic. Labor comes via a labor contractor, although George is beginning to bypass the contractors and hire directly; stoop workers earn over seven dollars an hour. He's conscious of the harsh conditions, mitigating them at times with techniques such as cutting the tops off the corn stalks prior to harvest in order to minimize the allergy-triggering effects of pollen on the workers.

His battle is not just with the elements. Irrigation pipes are stolen regularly; it's impossible for him to police his widespread fields. Even his tractors—each with a sticker price upward of a hundred grand (air-conditioned cabs are a must or he cannot find workers to drive them in the Valley sun)—get swiped. Hustlers try to get them across the border to Mexico before he notices that they are missing. The Border Patrol chased two of his tractors when thieves took a sharp right turn off The Eight and struck out cross-country, hoping for a quick sale and a fat paycheck south of the border. Look on the south side of The Eight as it hugs the border eastbound toward Yuma. Metal barriers are in place in an effort to stop cross-country sprints north, cars and trucks filled with migrants or drugs, and trips south, smugglers running from the Migra, or thieves, such as the ones who hit George and Maria's place, piloting high-dollar-value vehicles to a new home in less-regulated Mexico.

Maria is a homegirl: her father came to the Valley as an immigrant from Greece.

"When he came to the United States," she started his story as we dug into a fine meal she made for us—baked salmon (the Pacific fishery is just two freeway hours from the Valley). The story was typical. He saw a help-wanted ad for farm workers in Greeley, Colorado. He took the train to Greeley, where he worked for a family on their farm, on the railroad, and in the mines. Maria told us, "He worked in the mines for a day and came out of the mine and said, 'I'm not doing that.'" He saw another ad, this one looking for a sheepherder in California. "He didn't know anything about sheep, but he convinced the sheep ranchers that he did." She laughed. Eventually he made his way to the Imperial Valley and went to work for a farmer from the same Greek island her father called home, John Zenos. "And John Zenos was the one who introduced carrots to the Imperial Valley."

That's not what they say in Holtville, where the name Maggio means carrots.

"If you speak about carrots in Holtville," Maria agreed, "Joe Maggio has the name. But Joe Maggio was after John Zenos. John Zenos was first. John retired and then Joe started farming. He farmed carrots on the grandest scale and became known as the Carrot King. But before

Maggio it was John Zenos, and he was the one that introduced carrots. I have that firsthand from his wife."

"If you can't believe the guy's wife, who can you believe?" George asked between mouthfuls of fish. Maria said it did not take long for her father to strike out on his own.

"Being Greek, my dad felt he was making money for John, but he wasn't getting, like, his fair cut. He got mad and he decided, 'If I can make money for you, I can make money on my own.' That's when he broke away and started farming on his own." Her father developed his own specialty: lettuce. But soon he saw the value in watermelons. "His biggest thing was being a watermelon grower; he was well known for his watermelons."

Maria numbers the Greek community at the time her father arrived in the Valley as several hundred. Why did they come to Holtville and Calexico? Same reason Mexicans come today. "What brought them here was just knowing other people, and they all came. Like my dad."

Swiss immigrants came to build and work dairies. Japanese and Filipinos came to grow vegetables (until the Japanese were rounded up in World War II and sent to internment camps). Up the road at the Pioneers Museum, the main hall is one alcove after another celebrating the long list of ethnic groups attracted to the Valley (the trombone played by Walter Enz in the Holtville high school band and the Swiss band back in 1940 is one display): Koreans, Portuguese, Indians (the ones from India), Chinese, Italians (the egg scale used on Mr. Maddalena's chicken ranch is on display, with a note that the ranch housed 10,000 chickens), French, Lebanese, and African Americans. There is a photograph on the wall in the Japanese alcove showing a merchant pointing at a sign posted over his cash register (after World War II) that reads, "We don't want any Japs back here, ever!"

There's nothing new about rejecting the Other in the Valley. A poster in the local museum dated December 4, 1944, announces, "Sure we remember the sneak attack of the Japs on Pearl Harbor, that infamous treachery we will never forget. Your son, father, brother or sweetheart are today in the Pacific teaching those fanatics an unforgettable lesson. They'll remember Pearl Harbor, too." It was a call to a meeting. "Do we of the Imperial Valley want the return of the Japs?" it asked. "Attend the public meeting protesting the return of the Japs. Hear Dr. John R. Lechner, noted speaker, an authority on Jap atrocities in California."

As we ate, Maria summed up the migration succinctly: "They came because they didn't have money, and they were able to make money. That's my theory. Because if you had money, you'd think, why would they want to come here?" Harsh but true words for her homeland's harsh but productive climate. "And once they made their money, they went to San Diego and lived like kings. I'm talking about the Greeks. Others stayed. The Greeks made their money and lived very well in San Diego. In fact, John Zenos bought the Chrysler Mansion in La Jolla.'" That's a lot of carrots sold. According to Maria's mother, the Carrot King swallowed a false tooth and choked to death.

"I think his wife, Annie, sold it," said Maria, "and got a smaller place in La Jolla."

"Sold the tooth," George suggested. His droll humor was a welcome addition to the stories.

"Sold the mansion," said Maria firmly.

"Oh, I see," George acknowledged, smiling.

We talked about the wall just a few miles south of their place down Barbara Worth Road, where it met the road that parallels the border. Do the longer waiting lines keep her from Mexicali? Indeed, she told us it had been years since she visited the metropolis just south of their farmland.

"Literally years since you've been over there?"

"Yes. I want to go over there and eat, because they have some fabulous restaurants. There was this one, Lucerna, that had outstanding seafood. I want to go back there. Everyone was wanting the wall, not because they don't like the Mexicans, but because the terrorists are sneaking their way through. That's who we do not like. Or want."

The border was just eight miles south of our dinner table.

"When you're Mexican," George said about workers he employs and who cross daily and legally, "whether it takes fifteen minutes or whether it takes two hours and fifteen minutes, you're going to cross the border. It's just another inconvenience.

"It's not quite like the Salem witch hunts," he said, "but people are so traumatized by the media . . ."

"Lou Dobbs?" I interrupted. The demagogic ex–CNN anchorman is well known in the Valley for his tirades about the porous border.

"Exactly. Exactly. It's a shame. It really is. If I'm going to wait in line two hours, I'll just go to San Diego. It's two hours away. And I'm not having the frustration of waiting in line, or sitting in traffic."

It's not just the U.S. policies that keep Maria and George out of Mexico. They used to own a vacation place in San Felipe, on the Sea of Cortez.

"I loved San Felipe," Maria said. But no longer. "The last time we were down there, Jimmy was a baby in a car seat in the back, and we were stopped by *federales*. They had their machine guns. They wanted to see in the glove compartment. Jimmy was sound asleep, never woke up, and they asked me if he was sleeping. I said, 'Well of course.' But maybe they thought something had happened to him. That kind of spooked me; I wasn't real anxious to go back. And then you hear all the fighting amongst the drug lords in Tijuana. That kind of scares me. If an accident happens, what kind of red tape am I going to be in? Am I going to be able to get back home? If it weren't for that, I'd love to go there. I loved Mexico and I loved San Felipe. I like San Felipe better than Mission Beach."

Drugs, rogue cops, post-9/11 paranoia. They conspire to radically segregate two places that throughout pre-9/11 history existed as cooperating, commingling communities.

Maria and George's homestead sits about midway between Holtville and Calexico. They've watched white flight from Calexico north.

"It's no different than the inner city," was George's interpretation of the changes to Calexico's demographics. "It's no different than the Mission District." He used his hometown, our San Francisco, as an example. The Mission District is now a majority Latino neighborhood. "First the Irish came and then as the Irish became more accepted, they moved to more compelling neighborhoods. Then the next group of immigrants came, and when they became more accepted, they moved. It's just the evolution of becoming Americanized, I guess."

So where do upwardly mobile Calexicans move?

"They move to El Centro."

What is the draw of El Centro versus Calexico? El Centro just looked to me like a bigger version of Calexico.

"I believe it was more of a racist kind of thing, to be perfectly honest with you," said George. "I think as the Hispanic population began to have the ability to afford to live in Calexico, and as more and more Hispanics began moving in, the city was getting older, there wasn't really any internal growth. It's not like San Diego, which drew other Anglo people to the area. This area was stagnant for a zillion years until just recently. The only influx of outside population was the Mexican people coming from Mexico who had two nickels finally to rub together and said, 'Hey, you know what? I want to make a better life for myself and move to the United States side.'"

Meanwhile, other parts of the Valley were growing, filling with affordable housing developments, even attracting commuters from San Diego. Twice the house at half the price, plus a two-hour commute. Not an uncommon California equation, despite four-dollar-a-gallon gasoline. The increasing population will result in more business opportunities in the Valley, compensating perhaps for the loss of business to Mexicans not prepared to continue waiting in long lines to come shop on the U.S. side.

We started to talk presidential politics. And then stopped. Delightful hosts, Maria and George turned out to be delightful Republicans. We instead discussed dessert.

≈ ≈ ≈

Wednesday

Crossing the Border(s)

I punched "scan" on the Mazda's radio, and it skipped right over to KXO, "1230 on your AM dial." I cranked up the volume. It's an oldies station, and one after another, they were some of my favorite pop tunes. What a great mix of musical memories. Markos and I felt as if we were in our own buddy road-trip movie, speeding across the Imperial Valley in Uncle Hertz's automobile, singing those great old American songs, en route to El Centro. The music stopped. Time for a traffic report. A traffic report on the local radio? We'd seen no traffic. It flies along The Eight, and it's hard to slow down coming into Calexico; why bother, except for the speed limit sign?

"An hour-and-thirty-three-minute wait at Calexico," said the announcer. The traffic report was for the wait at the border coming north across into the United States. A repeat, in case you don't believe it: "You're gonna be in that line over an hour and a half." And how about Calexico East, the new port of entry east of Barbara Worth Road, far from downtown Calexico? "Not a whole lot better. Eight lanes open. It's a fifty-to-sixty-minute wait over there."

And then back to the rock 'n' roll.

We cruised the main El Centro drag and saw a version of Calexico, only more of it. Paint peeling off worn facades, plenty of storefronts available for rent (to open that record-store-cum-coffee-shop Dr. Guinn proposed?). The bail bonds operation run by Gustavo Abril and Tony Diaz ("We take pink slips for collateral. Fianza para encarcelados. Call collect. Se habla español."). Hand-drawn signs announcing business attempts: "Old Time 60's Deli." Brave attempts at combating the chain stores at the new mall just south of The Eight, like COL-R FABRIC, each letter a different color and no explanation for the hyphen instead of the "O." Amelia's Hair Designer & Barber. Divine Thought Pensamientos Divinos: spirit guides, jewelry boxes, books, Bibles—the English

The air conditioning at Carroll Buckley's radio station, KXO, keeps his office cool enough on scorching Imperial Valley days for him to tie his necktie tight.

separated from the Spanish with a yin-yang sign. The Main Street Mall, a struggling effort housed in what looks like a department store building from the fifties. A nightclub: "Musica en vivo todos los fines de semana." Downtown El Centro is passed by, struggling to survive. And home to the offices and studios of KXO, the radio voice of the Valley with its local news reports.

I sat down with one of the owners, Carroll Buckley. A transplanted Pennsylvanian, he's another Imperial Valley booster and lover. It was the moustache that caught my eyes first. It was impossible not to focus on the white 'stache with its Gay Nineties flourish: the ends came to a point and were turned up. It looked like one of those clip-on Halloween moustaches, except that it was white and they were always black. It looked cute and made Buckley look Santa Claus–like accessible. It was close to a hundred degrees outside, yet cool with air-conditioning inside, rationalizing his tight shirt collar, fixed with a tie knotted in a smart and tight Windsor. His long sleeves were not rolled up, but buttoned down

Faded glory on El Centro's main drag.

tight. His blue eyes wide, he was ready to talk Valley—with intensity. I started with the traffic report, and the long waits at the border. He took his cue and rhapsodized about what lies south of the border.

"It's a beautiful city and unlike many Mexican cities. It's the state capital of Baja California. There is a large middle class in Mexicali, unlike a lot of other Mexican cities. The people in Mexicali are great people, educated and very urbane, even though Mexico City looks on them as the hillbillies of Mexico." Then Buckley made clear just how important those one and a half million Mexicans in Mexicali are to Calexico and the rest of the Imperial Valley. "Our economy here depends on them." A simple, straightforward fact. "Not just for labor, but for retail and service."

Of course radio, unlike so many other businesses, mocks the border. No matter how severe the physical barrier on the borderline, no matter how high the fence, nothing separates KXO from penetrating that imaginary line and blasting oldies and commercials to its Mexicali audience. Even the wait time at the border can be an audience builder: hours of tedium punctuated by informative traffic reports and finger-snapping, foot-stomping, sing-along oldies.

"Exactly," Buckley said about my assessment. "Radio doesn't stop at that fence. And Mexicali loves our station. They love AM 1230 and the oldies. The tunes are nongenerational, nonethnic. Anywhere you go in the world, you're going to hear Motown and the sixties and the seventies. Everywhere. Go to a wedding reception. Play rap, two people are moving. Put on the polka music that I grew up with, and you've got nobody moving, unless of course they think it's the . . ." He paused and thought for a moment. "What's the one, Mexican genre . . ."

"Ranchero," I offered.

"Yeah. The oompa, oompa. But you put on oldies, and everybody moves. We're doing a local news product. We don't read the newspaper on the air. We generate our own product. And son of a gun," the moustache smiled, "if that's not what people want!"

Carroll Buckley told me that he and his business partner Gene Brewster manage to make a living serving the community, instead of operating as an outlet for nationally syndicated programs as do so many local stations around America. "We are a community station. Of thirteen stations licensed to this market, there is one other that is live. And they do well. Everything else is syndicated satellite."

We talked about divided Berlin and compared it to the Calexico–Mexicali forced split. What were integrated twin cities are being forced further and further apart by the arduous realities of the contemporary border.

Buckley took issue with my premise. "That fence is not dividing the communities. The relationships that have been built up since literally the turn of the twentieth century are here. Whether there's a wall or a fence there hasn't put up a divide." He was living in the past. During my time in Calexico I would hear again and again of how the border was, in fact, separating those intermingling borderlands he still imagined. Buckley launched into a short, familiar speech about the importance of the Mexican workforce in the United States.

"Politicians in Mexico see the United States as the great safety valve that is keeping their country more stable because so many people are going north and sending money back. What would Mexico be if people were not in this country working? And Lord knows they're doing work that I have done and would not do today. I picked pickles when I was a kid. They grow them around Kalamazoo, Michigan. It's work that I wouldn't do now. God bless these people for doing the work."

He dismissed the long border waits, too.

"It's not a whole lot longer than it was before. You have to keep in mind the volumes of people that are moving through. This is the second-highest-volume land port in the country, next to San Ysidro. How do you move that many people through one gate? These are people that work over here. Or these are people that live in Mexico, work in Mexico, and have disposable income that they prefer to spend over here."

There are crowds of Mexicans in the borderlands with valid paperwork to come over to the United States for their workday and return home to Mexico for the night. And Mexicans living in the borderlands can qualify for visas to allow them to come north to shop and visit for a short period of time. Shopping on the U.S. side of the line appeals to many Mexican consumers.

"For years in downtown Calexico, on First Street in Calexico, there were grocery stores everywhere. And they came over for chicken, eggs, milk, and bread. The staples. And to a degree they still do."

Not much. I saw those stores struggling, and I saw the empty storefronts. Chicken, milk, bread, and eggs are all available on the south side of the line.

"Yes, they are," he of course agreed. "It's perceived as superior quality here." He considered the lure of the foreign. "I prefer the Mexican beer. And I'm not talking about Corona. I'm talking about real beer."

"Modelo Negro," I suggested.

"You got it!"

So Modelo-drinking Carroll Buckley came from polka-rich Pennsylvania via pickle country in Michigan to the Imperial Valley. I wanted to know what lured him to this edge of the States.

"A job." Certainly not the weather. "When I got out of the service in '71 I got a job here as news director at Channel 9." Next came an old radio joke. "I quickly realized that I had a face for radio and got back into my real love. TV, it was a job. Radio has always been my real love. It didn't hurt that I married a young lady from here who I met at San Diego State."

It was that common theme again: family ties.

"It was not our intent to stay here." But stay they did and it worked out well. "Oh yeah. I've raised two kids here, and I would far prefer to have raised them here than most big cities."

I told Buckley that I was grappling with why so many of the people I had met came back to the Valley or stayed put and never left, despite the ghastly climate, the dirty air, and the sorry statistics regarding wages and education. Imperial County ranks lowest in all categories for California counties. He answered without hesitation.

"The people." He quickly added a critical qualifier. "And it is still small-town. I had a conversation with a gentleman about two weeks ago, talking about growing up in El Centro. I laughed and told him that growing up in Michigan, if you stepped out of line, the neighbor kid's mother would whack you upside of the head and tell you, 'Don't do that.' I had to be home when the streetlights came on. The neighborhood watching out for the neighborhood. You get a lot of that here."

Ah, I announced, again with the arrogance of an interloper, that's why the oldies are so appealing. KXO is playing songs from the era that in some ways the Valley still embraces and . . .

He interrupted with a harsh, "No."

No?

"No. The Valley is far and away advanced socially and economically from where it was then. The power shift has been huge. I was born in Pennsylvania, eastern Pennsylvania, and grew up in a very ethnically mixed neighborhood. I knew the difference between a Serb and Croat. There's a lot of that here, the blend of the cultures is marvelous. Where did you have breakfast?"

The Barbara Worth Resort.

"Well then, you missed out on the real flavor of the Valley."

I told him I already figured that out, that the Barbara Worth Resort was a Valley oddity (and therein lies its charm), and I asked him where he recommends for breakfast. I asked him to set the scene for what he calls that real Valley flavor.

"You will be sitting in the Owl Café downtown or Junior's Diner over on Adams Avenue, and you will see two people sitting, one eating ham and eggs, the other eating *chorizo y huevos*. One speaking in English, and the other in Spanish, the two of them conversing. Not uncommon in the least. So many of the people in this Valley are second, third, and fourth generation. This is not a transient population the way the L.A. area is. The people that are here are legal. They've been here. They may have a kid named Sean Garcia and Peter—not Pedro—but Peter Gonzalez. The cultures have been intertwined and it's great, because you celebrate Cinco de Mayo, which is not a big deal in Mexico, but it's a big party deal here." Fourth of July is an even bigger party in the Imperial Valley calendar. The Imperial Valley College campus is crowded with over fifty thousand revelers celebrating the American Revolution, about three-fourths of them Hispanic, and Buckley loves it. "It's a really unique culture, and it's the people that drive it. It's certainly not intimidating. You know, as a middle-class, middle-aged white guy, it's certainly not threatening the way in some communities it would be."

He finished his booster speech, and it was a convincing one. Booster Buckley admitted his improbable paradise would be impossible without the Colorado River water, but he acted unworried about that lifeblood ever drying up for the Valley. The major reason: the world needs what the Valley grows.

"Ask somebody in L.A. where does milk come from? Safeway is their answer. We've got two extremely large dairies here because they've chased them out of the L.A. Basin. They were in Chino. And there are several others still in Chino that are looking to come down here. We've got wide-open spaces. We've got water. We've got labor. And we'll accept agriculture. What have they done to them in Chino? What do the people who chased this industry out of Chino do for milk? They go to Safeway because that's the source of all milk. I heard somebody say, 'You guys grow alfalfa. Nobody eats alfalfa!' You drink milk? You like ice cream? How about cheese? The alfalfa feeds the milk cows."

I queried Carroll Buckley about his downtown studios. Why did he and his partner choose to stay in the fading, deteriorating, sad downtown of El Centro? Again, Buckley defies my expectations.

"I don't think we ever made any conscious decision. This is where we are, and for a radio station, who cares where the studios are?"

I prodded him, leading the witness, asking him if he was doing his part trying to bring downtown back to its vibrant old reality from the days before the swank Barbara Worth Hotel burned to the ground. He allowed that was part of his reasoning and showed off a photograph dated 1928, a picture of the station's old studios just three blocks down the street.

"Historically we have been downtown. Our view is we're not an El Centro station, we're an Imperial Valley station. Our news is not El Centro news, it's Valley news. That's another marvelous thing that's beginning to happen. The Valley has learned in the last two or three or four years to work together, to realize together we're huge and strong. Separately, El Centro is 45,000. Calexico is 30,000. Brawley is 20,000.

KXO plays those hits "off the charts, but still in our hearts" and cranks out local Valley news.

Individually there's not a whole lot of weight there. Put them together, and it becomes Yuma. What Yuma really has over the Imperial Valley is they've got one city; we got seven." It sounds so parochial to consider a rivalry with Yuma. But nothing is more important than what's going on in your hometown, no matter where that hometown is.

I was about to say good-bye to Carroll Buckley when he offered a compliment. "I appreciate your approach," he said about our interview. "Oftentimes people come in from somewhere else and suggest, well, you live in the Valley, you must be an idiot. Most of the people that are in the Valley are here by choice or stay here by choice, and they're not idiots. Well educated. Well spoken. Not nearly as uptight as our brethren on the coast. And they're supposed to be laid-back."

I offered a theory of pretentiousness. Lots of it on the coasts, and a delightful lack of it in flyover America.

"Exactly. People here will see through the pretension in a heartbeat. And I like that. I'm still married to the same woman. My blood pressure is under control. No ulcers. Raised two kids with no major issues. I've been happy here. I like this place. You know, I like to get out of this place, too, but I'm here by choice. There are flaws, there are pimples, there are warts. I could give you a whole laundry list of things that I would love to see changed, but they are changing. Sometimes it takes generations. But there's just a flavor down here." That seems enough of an explanation for him. A flavor. And for Carroll Buckley the radio business is, if not booming, doing okay. His line, "There's just a flavor here," is a variation on George's theme of "You can make it here." No superlatives, but things are okay. He praises the new shopping mall, a coconspirator with the border wall in eviscerating the vitality of the Valley's downtowns, sparkling in its cookie-cutter splendor just south of The Eight at Highway 111. All that new retail is good for the commercial radio business.

"I've yet to see the new mall," I told him. I had made a vow to stay off The Eight and not visit the mall. Getting to know Calexico sans generic shopping center and freeway was a secondary goal for me in the Valley. Macy's and interstates we have in San Francisco.

I opened up the baking Mazda, turned the air conditioner up to a Spinal Tap 11, and hit the road, heading for the sparkling new Border Patrol headquarters. Millions of dollars of gleaming Homeland Security money brought home to the Valley. I was scheduled for a sit-down with Border patrolman Enrique Lozano. I cranked up the radio. KXO, of course. And there was Carroll Buckley, reading the news.

First I heard an announcer identify the station: "AM 1230 KXO. All right, time to check in with local news, brought to you by Martinizing Dry Cleaning. Make it easy on yourself; use their drive-up window." A jingle, and then the news.

> This is KXO local news. I'm Carroll Buckley reporting. The Seventeenth Annual Mariachi Festival sin Fronteras will take place May twelfth through seventeenth in Calexico. The theme is Jalisco en Calexico, celebrating the Calexico Centennial. The concert itself is May seventeenth at Crummett Park. Gates open at five, the concert begins at seven p.m. For information or tickets, you can contact the Calexico Chamber of Commerce.
>
> The Spring 2008 production of the Imperial Valley College Theater Arts program will be *As You Like It* by Don Negro. It is the

record of one company's attempt to perform the play by William Shakespeare. It's a bare-stage comedy. It represents a ragtag group of amateur actors led by an actor trying to impersonate all of Shakespeare's characters. The production is directed by Dr. James Patterson, Associate Professor of Speech and Theater Arts at IVC. Performances are scheduled for Thursday and Friday, May eighth and ninth at eight p.m. at Rodney Auditorium on the campus of San Diego State University in Calexico.

For this Cinco de Mayo, the Calexico Police Department will conduct a sobriety checkpoint to educate the public on the dangers of impaired driving and to remove impaired drivers from Calexico's roadways. Motorists approaching the checkpoint will see signs advising them that a sobriety checkpoint is ahead, and motorists will be detained just momentarily while a Calexico police officer explains the purpose of the checkpoint. Checkpoints are scheduled for Monday, Cinco de Mayo.

And the Red Cross Imperial Valley Chapter will celebrate World Red Cross Day with Rhapsody in Red. We're asking you to consider becoming a sponsor or simply attend the Rhapsody in Red World Red Cross Day reception at the Pioneers Museum on May eighth. Call 352-4541 for more information. There will be live music, great food, and good friends.

That'll do it for this look at local news on KXO. For information on these and other local news stories, you can visit our website, KXOradio.com. I'm Carroll Buckley, reporting for KXO local news.

Buckley shut off his microphone, and the announcer returned to the airwaves: "Local news brought to you by Martinizing Dry Cleaning. Where customer service is our number one priority." Our oldies disc jockey was back with us with this bizarre self-introduction: "You got Traci Lyon Ramírez. She ain't nothing but a low-class white trash. She probably didn't even finish high school. 1230 KXO!" A screaming glissando of a jingle with a noisy stinger at the end of it. Cue to the music, and Markos and I rock out down Highway 111 singing along with Donovan, "Sunshine came softly through my window today," as Markos snapped pictures of the Valley landscape we saw through the tinted windshield. It was another of those songs with lyrics hardwired into our California consciousnesses. Sunshine baked hard on my Mazda that day.

Interstate 8—The Eight—provides an east–west physical marker for Imperial County's north–south divide.

We stopped off at the Pioneers Museum, where the hundred years of Valley history is outlined with memorabilia, to preserve, as the museum's mission statement proclaims, "the ideals and deeds that make this desert bloom." I caught up with the curator, Norm Wuytens, and talked with him about what is on display, especially the Barbara Worth and Harold Bell Wright relics.

The original handwritten manuscript of the novel—written in pencil—is in a glass case. China from the Barbara Worth Hotel in El Centro can be admired, china salvaged after the building burned. Wright and his heroine seem such icons of the Valley, I suggested to Wuytens that reading the novel ought to be a local high school requirement.

"Yes," he agreed. "Absolutely!" Then he thought for a moment and considered, "You know there are some things here in Imperial Valley that are the best-kept secrets in the world, and the news doesn't seem to get out, but I would think that it would be good reading material for students while they're in school."

The Pioneers Museum is a repository of Barbara Worth memorabilia.

Not a secret is the weather.

"Our summers down here are so miserable that at vacation time nobody wants to vacation here, and in the wintertime everybody's busy and their kids are in school, so this is not a place to visit on vacation."

It remains a secret. I asked Wuytens how hot is hot.

"Ah," he sighed, "118, 120. But 115 is not abnormal at all. We have a lot of days in July and August that are 112 to 115."

"Curator Wuytens," I addressed him formally with his title, "I want to tell you something, friend-to-friend, colleague-to-colleague, peer-to-peer: 115 *is* abnormal."

"Yes," he admitted, "but it doesn't sound near as bad in Celsius."

"Maybe that's the new marketing campaign for the Imperial Valley," I suggested, "It doesn't sound near as bad in Celsius."

Barbara Worth: the heroine of Wright's novel, the adopted daughter of the banker modeled after Holt of Holtville, the banker who really did find the financing to bring the Colorado River water to irrigate the Imperial Valley. The bilingual heroine who does a good job of bridging the Anglo and the Mexican communities. "She's angelic in many ways, wouldn't you say?" I asked Wuytens.

"Yes, and that's what everybody thought when they read the book, too. Most of the characters in the book, although renamed, were actual characters. Mr. Wright, when he was writing his book, did a lot of research around the Valley. Even though it's a fictional novel, it is based on things that were really happening."

"This you may find curious, or maybe it's a story you've heard before," I said to Wuytens. "I was talking with a waitress, my regular waitress at the Barbara Worth Resort, Bonnie Peterson, and I was talking with her about this fictional character, Barbara Worth, and she said, 'No, I don't believe she's a fictional character, I think she was real.'"

"Isn't that interesting? Yes, because she is such a prominent name here that you want her to be a real person," said Wuytens.

"Was she a real person?" I asked the Valley history expert.

"No." He knew I was disappointed. "No, sorry to say, only in the minds of the ones that loved her."

"And the ones that continue to love her, such as our waitress."

"Right. Absolutely."

I found Border Patrol agent Enrique Lozano at the sparkling new Border Patrol headquarters in El Centro. The crew was still moving in, helped by a contingent of California National Guard troopers, dispatched for emergency border duty by Governor Arnold Schwarzenegger. The paint still smelled fresh. Here was a prime example of the government jobs fueling the Valley economy: Homeland Security, prisons, and education. Pick one of those industries, and you can live pretty well in Calexico, especially if you can stand the heat. Imagine a husband and wife each making $70,000. A couple hundred thousand for a house looks pretty affordable with those wages combined, especially when housing is at least twice the price two hours west in San Diego.

Agent Lozano hails from San Diego. How does a guy come from the coast and manage to survive in the desert? How does he go from seventy-one degrees 365 days a year, fresh fish, and pristine beaches to 117 degrees and sandstorms? Lozano said he's accustomed to changes of venue. He spent years in the Navy and told me he sees his Border Patrol work as a continuing opportunity to serve his country. "It still doesn't matter where I am. I'm still committed to defend this country, and this is why I'm here." "Here" is almost seven years in the Valley,

Border Patrolman Lozano—proud to serve his country—faces unending challenges at the busy Calexico border crossing.

a place he said he decided to grow his roots. "This is, to me, a perfect place for children to grow up. It's a small community and everybody kind of knows each other to a certain degree. We're Border Patrol agents, but we're part of the community." And then a line I hear over and over, "I think it's a great community."

Searing temperatures. And a harsh political climate. The borderlands small towns are not the same as Midwest idylls or New England crossroads or mining camps in the Rockies. He's facing serious law enforcement issues daily: death-defying illegal border crossers, death-dealing drug traffickers, a watch for terrorists. No big deal, he shrugs. All in a day's work.

"As Border Patrol agents, we adapt. It's our daily routine. We go out, and yeah, I know it's probably a hundred degrees plus; however, we've still got our mission. That's what we go out there and do. The climate, yes, it matters, but fortunately we adapt."

Walk on the shady side of the street.

Border Patrol agents and their cruisers are a constant sight in the Valley. The Border Patrol is the largest law enforcement agency at work in Calexico and its neighbors (and the largest uniformed police force in the United States, and still growing fast). Often its agents are the first on the scene of a Valley accident or crime, calling local agencies to mop up the results. Markos's friend George told me he's convinced that since its force was bolstered, there's been a trickle-down effect: a reduction of all crime, not just immigration and smuggling violations. Fewer of his irrigation pipes were being purloined. The uniforms and the cruisers dissuade criminal behavior. A downside of all these agents—and their numbers continue to increase—is a sense that the borderlands are militarized: the wall, the squad cars and trucks, the uniformed agents omnipresent, with their National Guard support. It is a characterization Agent Lozano rejected.

"It's not militarized by any means," he said without hesitation, explaining that the mission of the force has been the same since its inception in 1924: apprehending contraband between the ports of entry, with the added concern since 9/11 of terrorists and terrorist weapons. Nonetheless, as the number of agents increased at an extraordinary rate, it was easy for the border to be perceived as militarized. Agents and their laborers worked just that two-hour drive west, even as I visited the brand new Border Patrol facility, to string miles of razor wire between Tijuana and San Diego. With my memories of the Berlin Wall, the secondary fencing on the Mexican border, the razor wire, the stadium-type lighting used to make the no-man's-land light up like noon at midnight, the towers topped with cameras, all these elements made it easy for me to perceive the border as militarized.

We were sitting in a conference room at the new headquarters, joined by Lozano's colleague, Border Patrol agent Miguel Hernandez, a recruiter. I asked him for his elevator pitch. How does he seduce recruits? A litany of explanation followed.

Theirs is a tough job, the recruiter responded, citing relocation to a harsh climate, intensive training, and the Spanish-language requirement as examples of the difficult criteria facing applicants, and he knows it's not a job for everyone. His ideal candidate, he says, is a military veteran, someone who understands hierarchy and force discipline—someone willing to serve country. At the same time he seeks college graduates and minorities. "We're trying to expand our efforts throughout the United States, and we explain to people that if they are not able to apply right now because they're lacking one of the requirements, how to prepare for the next round." In the confines of the new Border Patrol headquarters conference room, the speech sounds idealistic. In reality, while we talked, the Border Patrol was desperately trying to fill its quota for new officers, scouring the States for candidates, rushing them through training, and—consequently—ending up with unwanted problems: officers—albeit a fraction of the force—charged with abusing migrants and taking bribes from smugglers. "We are offering a generous package of pay plans. Depending on experience they can start between thirty-six and forty-one thousand dollars a year. We let them know that. We give them the preparation manual: how to study, how to prepare for the oral interviews. We give them informational booklets on how to prepare physically and mentally to take the challenge. It's a well-established agency, the Department of Homeland Security. Serve your country, fight terrorism. I think there's no better place currently to serve your country. We put those things in perspective. And of course the pay," he returned to the value of the paycheck in a difficult economy. "Border Patrol has one of the most beneficial promotional processes that I can think of." This is the point where the salary-to-housing cost ratio can look mighty attractive. "In as little as two and a half years you could be making about seventy thousand, seventy-five thousand dollars a year. We want to make sure that people get the word, and if they want to seek a career with the Border Patrol, we want them to be here for a long time."

Job security seems a certainty given the increasing crises in the borderlands. If a recruit can make it through the entry process, then he or she can pretty much count on never having to look for a job again.

"Exactly."

It's a growth industry.

"Yes."

Keeping people out of the United States of America.

"Exactly." And back to the pragmatic. "The retirement plan we offer includes benefits similar to the 401(k). Of course, the medical benefits as well. The promotional opportunities are incredible. Just incredible."

Another fringe reality is danger. Hernandez readily conceded that his is a dangerous job.

"That goes for law enforcement in general. Every time you wear a uniform there's always a risk involved, because you're representing law enforcement. A lot of people who don't like law enforcement, they're breaking the law on a daily basis."

Risks specific to the Border Patrol include what they refer to as "rockings," rocks are hurled at agents from the Mexican side of the border. On occasion agents have responded with deadly force, instigating fleeting tension between the United States and Mexican governments. Squad-car accidents are a continuing hazard; high-speed chases are all but routine. The network of Valley canals presents a perpetual drowning risk, for migrant, smuggler, and agent alike.

There is always another side to stories. In my book *Wetback Nation*, I published a brief excerpt from a log of alleged Border Patrol transgressions kept by the immigrant activist group Border Action Network:

> Off-duty Border Patrol agent William Varas faces charges that he lied to authorities when he claimed that he fired his gun at immigrants only after they had first shot at him. Agent Matthew Hemmer was arrested on state charges of kidnapping, sexual assault and sexual abuse. A criminal complaint said Hemmer took an undocumented woman, then 21, to a remote location and sexually assaulted her before allowing her to return to Mexico. Agent Dennis Johnson, a former supervisor, was sentenced to seven years in prison for sexual assault and five years (concurrent) for kidnapping. Johnson sexually assaulted a 23-year old El Salvadoran woman who was in custody, naked and handcuffed. Agent Charles Brown, a 23-year veteran, was arrested for allegedly selling classified information to a drug cartel. Brown worked in the agency's intelligence unit.

The San Francisco Bay Area Independent Media Center posted a sobering video shot November 11, 2007, of a march at the Calexico barrier protesting the wall. It shows no aggressive behavior by the protesters as riot-gear-clad Border Patrol agents yell, "Get back, get back!" and pepper spray is shot into the crowd. Agents are shown attacking at least one protester with batons, knocking what appeared to be a peaceful demonstrator to the ground. Excessive and deadly force exerted by the Border Patrol against civilians is well documented, as is nonviolent criminal behavior: agents taking bribes to allow contraband to cross unimpeded into the United States.

As we talked, Agent Hernandez insisted that compassion is an important Border Patrol trait. "You have to show officer's presence, how to command people to listen to you. You don't necessarily have to be aggressive or insulting to get people to comply. You need to communicate.

You need to have cultural sensitivity, you have to be sensitive to those who are coming across." He offered an odd example and told me that just because a migrant might introduce himself with an Arabic name does not mean he is a criminal or dangerous. His parents, Hernandez offered, may have watched a movie, heard a name they liked, and picked it for their child. "Cultural sensitivity is a must."

What about their personal heritage, I asked the agents, pointing to their nameplates: Hernandez and Lozano? They must encounter suspects who appeal to Lozano and Hernandez for special consideration because of their perceived national and cultural shared pasts. Does that take a psychological toll on them personally?

"Yeah." Enrique Lozano acknowledged that some of the migrants he encounters do seek special consideration, appealing on the basis of Spanish surnames. "However, I am a Border Patrol agent, and I'm defending my country, and if you're coming here illegally, you're going to get processed according to the law. It's that simple."

Humanitarian work is part of the Border Patrol routine. Agents regularly save migrants stranded in the desert, parched and starving. Lozano came up with an example. "A couple of weeks ago there was a person that jumped in the All-American Canal. A Border Patrol agent, regardless of his safety, jumped into the water and tried to save this person. Unfortunately, he couldn't. But that shows you that there's sensitivity. We're humans and in this case, he jumped into All-American Canal."

Humans, indeed. Agent Lozano knows sacrifice. When we met, his wife was serving a Navy tour of duty in Iraq.

"We talk on the phone whenever she can, and e-mail is a great thing."

"Are you worried?"

"Yeah, of course."

"It must make your sense of mission here more intense, because you're thinking about protecting the country and by extension protecting her."

"Definitely."

I invited Agent Lozano to join Markos and me for dinner across the line in Mexicali. "After dinner, traveling with you," I joked, "we won't need to wait a couple of hours to return. We can jump to the front of the line."

"Actually, I have to get in line like everybody else. I don't have special privilege."

"You don't?" I was mystified.

"Nope."

I still was not convinced. "You don't get to jump the line when you come back from going over there for dinner?"

"No, I'm just a regular citizen. When I'm out of this office, I'm just a regular citizen."

"But what if you wear your uniform?"

"I can't wear a uniform in Mexico."

Of course.

I left the Border Patrol headquarters in El Centro hungry. But before we shook hands good-bye, I marked Enrique Lozano as a guy who knew where to find the best Mexican restaurant, with *auténtica* food. Letty's, he suggested without hesitation. "It's a very cozy place, pretty good food." I followed his directions down Fourth Street to the south side of the old and struggling downtown. As soon as I entered Letty's—located, just as its name suggests, in a converted modest house that looks left over from the late forties or early fifties—I was convinced Lozano had not let me down. The place was lunchtime-jammed, and jammed with just the type of people to suggest we'd soon be enjoying a heaping plate of comfort food: families and cops.

The waiter (Was it Letty? Probably, but I didn't ask.) took my order in Spanish. And while I waited for the *comida*, I looked around. All the specials were posted in Spanish. *Plato de Chile Chipotle: Pollo $7.99. Pescado o Camaron $11.59.* The fish chile chipotle was absolutely delicious.

Up on the far wall facing me was a sparkling image: a mirrored beer advertisement tempting us with Bud Light and a dazzling señorita. She looked at me with a seductive smile from under her cowboy hat. The buttons on her skimpy blouse struggled to contain her, and one thumb was hooked in the waistband of her jeans. But competing for attention with Ms. Bud Light was the background of the ad. It was a map of the borderlands showing the major cities from the Pacific to the Gulf. I looked at Calexico. There it was astride the border, along with Mexicali. What the ad screamed—as loud as it screamed beer and sex—was realpolitik. There was only one dot on the map representing both cities. In Bud Light World, Calexico and Mexicali were one. No border formalities. No separating artificial line. No Berlin Wall–type fortifications keeping beer drinkers apart. And the legend on the sign reinforced the potent graphic display of the map. *Aquí y Allá. Las raices se comparten.*

The lunchtime crowd fills Letty's, with no need to translate the sidewalk menu.

Today's special at Letty's.

Bud Light was making it official. There was no border separating
Mexico and the United States. At least that was my interpretation. After
I finished eating I started to track down the party responsible for this
corporate intrusion into international political policy. I finally hooked
up with Juan Torres, working hard in his St. Louis office to compensate
for the mess Washington and Mexico City made of the borderlands (and
selling some Bud at the same time). Torres holds the intriguing title of
director of Latino marketing at Anheuser-Busch. He knows how to sell
beer, and how to sell beer to Mexicans. American beer. That, I figured,
was quite the challenge, facing down the likes of Bohemia and Modelo
and Pacifico.

Juan Torres knew exactly what I was talking about as soon as I
mentioned the map. At first he referred to it by its trade name, a back
bar mirror, and then told me "it's in the category of point-of-sale, which
is material that we take to retailers and restaurants and stores to promote our brand." But I wanted to know the subtext. I asked him what
Anheuser-Busch was up to with this overt sociopolitical message—one

Unlike Hertz, Bud Light wants to erase the corporate border, and the company knows just the woman to best carry that message.

point on the map for the border cities. Obviously, they were selling *cerveza,* but what more was at work here?

"It's very observant that you notice the one point versus the other," he complimented me (he is a salesman and public relations expert, after all). But then he deconstructed the message for me. "Really, what it comes down to is it ties back to the entire tag line." He switched to ad-speak. "If you read it, on the creative it says, 'Aquí y allá las raices se comparten.' Translated into English loosely, let's say it says, 'On this side and on that side, or here and there, we share a heritage.' " He thought for a moment and refined his translation. "Or I guess more literally it would be, 'We share roots.' And really that's what it speaks to, the entire border culture—not just California, but also Texas, Arizona, and New Mexico. What we're trying to say very subtly is that there is a shared culture whether you're officially on the Mexican side or on the U.S. side. That the entire region is a culture unto itself and there's a way of life there that speaks to that culture." Spectacular. The

Anheuser-Bush marketing department is the vanguard of international relations. "Having one dot versus two is to really point out that those cities on each side of the border are, in fact, sister cities. The same family could have some members on one side and members on the other, or friends on one side and friends on the other. Families go shopping and do business on one side or the other. There's this shared experience that happens there. That's really what it speaks to; it's not that there are two different places, but it's a unique part of this country that is just a culture unto itself."

Bud Light embraces what Washington and Mexico City try to ignore. Bud Light understands and thrives with what immigrant-basher Lou Dobbs cowered from during his CNN broadcasts. In addition to selling beer, I suggested to Torres, the company is making an inclusionary statement.

"Inclusionary is a very nice way of putting it. Every day I try to address cultural nuances across this country. Whether it be in New York or in Miami or in Chicago, what I'm trying to do ultimately is speak to consumers in each of those areas in a way that they find relevant. And in a way that demonstrates that our company not only appreciates the consumer, but understands the consumer. We know that the culture is not a monolith, obviously, that there is a diversity of Spanish-speakers or Latinos in the United States. What we want to do is respect this culture. I think one of the best ways to do that is to demonstrate that we understand that each of these cultures is unique."

The sophisticated and diplomatic understanding Torres expressed for the transcultural and transnational realities of the marketplace was striking to hear. Not because I was surprised that Anheuser-Busch would make such a concerted effort to understand the marketplace, but because it was in such stark contrast to what spewed from so many politicians and pundits.

"There are about twelve million people who live along this border," Torres said, "whether it's on the U.S. side or on the Mexican side. We just wanted to say we understand that this populace is unique, that the shared heritage is unique, the shared history is unique. And so really it's not so much a statement as much as it is an acknowledgment of the uniqueness and how special that culture is."

All well and good, but from the standpoint of beer sales, I wanted to know how Anheuser-Busch can expect to sell Bud Light in the borderlands when Mexican beer is notorious worldwide for its taste and potency. The answer may well lie in its appeal as a gringo brand. The Aquí y Allá ad campaign is what Anheuser-Busch calls a "dual marketing effort"; it's mirrored—so to speak—on both sides of the border.

"Bud Light is a growing imported brand in Mexico, and it actually has a significant share of the market in northern Mexico," Juan Torres told me. "On the U.S. side, if you look at South Texas, if you look at Arizona, if you look at California, Bud Light is," he was careful with the wording, "in some cases the number one brand in that marketplace. The Hispanic consumer is a loyal consumer of the Bud Light brand on the U.S. side, for sure, and growing very much so on the Mexican side." And again, as the diplomat, he pushed Bohemia and Modelo and Pacifico back across the bar at me. "As much as we respect and appreciate the Mexican beers that are available to Mexican consumers, our brands happen to do quite well with that consumer. There is cachet to a U.S. beer in Mexico. What we're trying to do is just continue to be relevant and to be respectful of the consumer and of their culture."

Or, as the tag line for the Bud Light advertising campaign reads, "Todo por una." All for one.

The chatter was in both Spanish and English as Dr. Guinn's students prepared for a debate exercise in their Imperial Valley College classroom.

"All right! Is everybody ready?"

Dr. Guinn convened the class; she teaches debate at Imperial Valley College. The murmur of the classroom slowly hushed. Debaters had been given fifteen minutes to prepare for the exercise after being told the topic for the day, one Melani picked just for me: "Should the Mexican–American border be sealed tight?"

"There's a lot of excitement, and this is great," said the teacher. "But let's focus on the debate now."

The stopwatch clicked on and a shy-looking and soft-spoken Roxanne, her sunglasses resting on the top of her head, took the podium ("Go, Roxanne," encouraged one of her team members) to speak against illegal immigration. "It's a fact," she announced, "that an estimated eleven million illegal immigrants in the United States are not taxpayers yet receive social benefits paid for by U.S. citizens." Of course, this may not be her personal opinion; she was assigned to argue the point. "Immigrants take advantage of welfare, financial aid, hospitals. Illegal immigrants are taking our work and taking advantage of our education system." The young woman was channeling Lou Dobbs and the all but nightly televised assaults on migrants he was famous for when he served as a CNN news anchor. "For example, here at IVC, we have people that cross the border to study here. I've heard that there are some people who take advantage of that just to get a financial aid check." She offered a solution. "We want more agents"—her audience knew she meant Border Patrol agents—"and a crackdown on employers." But she had more Dobbsian worries, as she warmed up to the dangers. "A lot of immigrants," she continued, the qualifier "illegal" dropped (a mistake from nervousness or an intentional statement?), "a lot of them already in the country present a threat to national security." And then a nod to the local economy: "If we get more agents, then we will get more work." She hesitated as the clock ran, looking down at her notes before concluding with a reiteration of the need to fine employers who hire illegal migrants. Applause from her team and the audience of classmates. Dr. Guinn smiled.

"We shouldn't close the borders to immigration." A classmate was quickly in place at the lectern with a counterargument. A tall young woman, whose starched white blouse and long dark hair contrasted neatly with her brown skin. She spoke with distinct Mexican-accented English. "We shouldn't close the borders to immigration because we need people to come and work in the United States. Roxie said that immigrants don't pay taxes. They can file a tax form; they pay taxes to the government." She made the point with intensity and carried on, sounding slightly annoyed. "She's generalizing that every student that comes from Mexicali," she pronounces the name of the city in the Mexican manner, with the "x" sounding like an "h," "is coming to IVC just for the financial aid. I don't think that." And suddenly reality intruded into the academic exercise. "I study in the United States," she said. "I live in Mexicali. I cross the border every day. I pay for my books and for my classes. I don't get any financial aid." Hard to rebut the personal experience. But she wasn't finished. "We never see Chinese people or white people working in the fields at three in the morning after standing in long lines to cross the border for jobs that they get paid just minimum wages, and sometimes less than that. They don't have any benefits for their family, for their kids."

Are you listening, Lou Dobbs et al.?

"These people are just coming for the American Dream, just to get better jobs, a better education for their kids. These immigrants are seeking a better life." She had a more critical point. "It would take a lot of money and time to build a wall." She shuffled her notes and fired off a conclusion to deal with the eleven million illegal aliens Roxie suggested did not pay taxes. "Our alternative plan is to use amnesty and put them on probation while they are checked to see if they are eligible to become resident aliens and citizens."

Again, applause. The atmosphere was extraordinarily positive. Dr. Guinn sat in the back of the room making notes, flashing another contented smile.

The debate continued. An intense young woman held forth with a smooth litany of familiar arguments. Close the border so that U.S. citizens enjoy the opportunity to fill the jobs currently worked by Mexicans. Fine businesses that violate the law by hiring illegal immigrants; close them down if they don't cease the practice. Use the income from the fines to hire more Border Patrol agents. But then the starkly personal again intrudes. "Enforcing the border with more agents would prevent more Mexican casualties from happening out in the desert." Just how does she know? She knows. "My dad is on the Border Patrol. Every day he comes home telling me stories about how he finds lots and lots of illegal immigrants who try to cross through the desert. Sometimes they do catch them while they are still alive, but they die on the way over to the station." A tragedy for the Mexicans, of course. But she's worried about her father and his fellow agents. "Once that happens, they're held accountable for the deaths. We don't want that to happen anymore." She too argued the social services expense; enforce the borders, she argued, and "put more money in our pockets that's rightfully ours as U.S. citizens."

The debater preceding her may not abuse the financial aid system, she insisted, but "a lot of students do take advantage of financial aid." Again, these were not just talking points gleaned from reference works, the TV talking heads, or former congressman Tom Tancredo's speeches. "I have a lot of friends that get financial aid, and then they drop their classes. Then they use the money to pay for their car or their rent, or they go out shopping."

She took a challenge from a young man in the audience. "Do you know that in order to get financial aid you need to have at least a green card? So your friends," he said about the abusers she cited, "are probably U.S. citizens, not illegal immigrants taking advantage of financial aid."

She didn't dispute his point but responded with a mere, polite "Thank you" and looked back at her notes.

"We're not trying to build a big fence. We're trying to keep out the illegal immigrants, not the ones that have proper documentation for work or for permanent residence. We're trying to enforce our borders. Thank you."

Applause.

Next up to speak against a closed border was a forceful woman who insisted that the status quo requires employing more Border Patrol agents and that is good news for the Valley. It provides employment, which injects cash into the local economy. She attacked the charge that illegal immigrants do not pay taxes. "You know why they don't pay taxes? They don't pay taxes because you're not allowing them to be here and work. They work very hard." Again, personal opinion based on harsh observation backed up the argument. "They have jobs that we would not, in a million years, think of doing. I would never go and pick things out of a field with my back bent all the way down for hours." She attacked the idea that immigrants take advantage of social services. "How are they taking advantage if they're coming here for a better life? We are taking advantage of the system, because the system is given to us for free." Her voice rose with emotion, and she spoke ever more rapidly. "They have to work for it. They have to hide for it. They have to support their families. We, what? Go and apply for welfare to pay for our monthly bills. How are they going to take your job? I don't see any of you working in the fields." Again, the personal. "Here we are, enjoying this AC in here. It's nice and fresh, and you have people out there picking onions in the fields. I'm not taking their job. I don't want their job. I don't see how these poor, innocent people, who are trying to make a better life, are a threat to national security. They aren't." She is on a roll. "These people are running barefoot with hardly anything on their backs except maybe a thing of water. What are they going to do? Hit you on the head with a bottle of water?" Laughter from the audience. She finished with a flourish, recommending foreign aid to Mexico to help develop an economy there that provides adequate work to keep Mexicans from wanting to "jump the border."

Clapping.

The final debater was the lone young man in the day's competition. Self-assured in a black T-shirt and sporting a buzz cut, he opened with a cordial, "Good afternoon, fellow classmates." He immediately took issue with earlier suggestions that processes are in place to allow Mexican immigrants, with relative ease, to work and live in the United States legally. Again, his points were buttressed with the intimately personal. "I know this for a fact," he said in precise, unaccented California English, "because I myself was an illegal immigrant. My mom brought me here when I was two years old, and it took until age ten to finally get my green card. I just want to say that it's a struggle. A lot of people, if they could, they would do it," he said about gaining legal papers. "But it's not easy. A lot of people want to come to this country because it was founded by immigrants. I think people should have the right to come over here if they want to improve themselves and they want to work." He addressed the lead debater. "Roxie, you said they are taking our jobs. For sure, a lot of U.S. American citizens don't want those jobs."

This was a linguistic construction I heard repeatedly in the Valley: U.S. American citizens. It serves as a euphemism for Anglos or whites or other non-Mexicans. Take your pick.

"I don't see anybody busting their ass and going and applying. I have a lot of friends who are U.S. American citizens and have all the privileges. They have more opportunities than me. And I see myself doing better than them each year. It's not because . . ." He interrupted himself and spit out, "The fact is, they're lazy." Again the Valley turns the stereotype inside out: the Mexican calling the gringo lazy. "The society here is becoming lazy. You can't really get mad or bitter and say that the immigrants are not contributing to the United States. The fact is, they are. They're providing for you. Every day, when you eat lettuce or whatever, the house you live in, they're providing for us." He pointed out the purchasing power of the migrant. "They buy clothes, they buy cars." He called for an Immigrant Appreciation Day. "César Chávez fought for our rights, especially the people working in the fields."

He stopped, after reiterating that the border should not be closed.

"Okay," cheered Dr. Guinn, "let's open it up for comments." The classmates dissected each other's debating skills. I gave them straight A's: the arguments of the national debate over immigration summed up with the passion of participants in the ongoing story.

I looked up the poet Juan Felipe Herrera on the occasion of the publication of his book from City Lights, *187 Reasons Mexicanos Can't Cross the Border*. I was especially intrigued by the first line in the epic list of 187 answers: "Because Lou Dobbs has been misusing the subjunctive again."

The number 187 comes from the vile referendum put before California voters in 1994 and known by its banal official title, Proposition 187.

Stroll to Mexico, but be prepared to wait in a long line if you wish to come back to the north side of the border.

It was designed to deny health care and other social services, including public schooling, to those residing in California without proper government documentation. It passed with a stunning majority of almost 60 percent but was struck down in federal court as unconstitutional—not because of the heinous idea of denying such services to American residents, but instead because it was determined that the law improperly allowed California to intrude into immigration affairs, a domain of the federal government.

Hence, the first line of Herrera's piece. "I decided to respond to the xenophobia, paranoia, and all the bad policies that were affecting immigrants and migrants in the United States," he told me, "especially in California. So I responded to that. I updated it because the list keeps on growing." He laughed. "I decided to use that title for the collection of work that I've been doing for the last thirty-eight years plus."

Herrera holds the Tomás Rivera Chair in Creative Writing at the University of California at Riverside, and he is the son of Mexican immigrants. He grew up in the migrant fields of California, like the Imperial Valley. So we talked, sons of immigrants, about how we—not the Lou Dobbs warped nativist vision—are the real America. Like it or not. Love it or leave it.

"That's it," Herrera agreed. "That's where we're at. And it's actually the whole world. It's actually the entire globe. The migrant and immigrant experience is at the heart and soul of all our experiences. And yet our deep core experiences are not really understood and not seen clearly. That's why I put this book together, so that there's a little bit more clarity, a little bit more dialogue, as you continue to do so well."

Ah, always nice to hear a compliment, especially from an esteemed colleague. Herrera's analysis again brings to mind the line from the British cultural studies pioneer Paul Gilroy: "It ain't where you're from, it's where you're at."

Juan Felipe Herrera expressed frustration and irritation that the nativist rants continue to avoid—or at least to dismiss—the fact that Mexican and other Latinos contribute to almost every sector of the U.S. economy.

"I don't know why that is not mentioned. César Chávez and Dolores Huerta at the United Farm Workers union showed the world that agribusiness depends on the farm worker more than we all knew, and they showed the power of the farm worker to stop that machine. The migrant experiences contribute, whether it's your hamburgers you're eating, or the lettuce in the burger, or the wine in the glass at any party, or the Christmas tree during the holidays, or tobacco, you know? You name it."

But then he turned deadly serious. "The numbers are incredible and the situation is horrific," he recounted about the border. The children, the women, the men, the bodies lost. They're just simply lying on the desert, rotting away. The people being pulled and pushed in different directions and sent to detention centers throughout the Southwest and then sent to prison, and then some just walk back through the borderline." A phantasmagoria, he called it, and proceeded to tell a story.

"I used to live in Iowa City in the late eighties, and I used to visit this town seventeen miles northeast of Iowa City called West Liberty. Little tiny town. It's a poultry- and meat-processing town. Bologna and salami and all those things that are made from those meat products. There was maybe one Mexicano, maybe one. I probably saw one. I went back eleven, twelve years later. And it was like 100 percent Mexicano."

A typical story. And fuel for the Lou Dobbs–style paranoia express. We talked about how the borderlands now stretch through all fifty states.

"I think you hit it on the taco shell," Herrera said. "The Borderlands are everywhere. It's no longer what we used to think or what we started to think—that the borderlands are just San Diego–Tijuana or Calexico–Mexicali; the Borderlands really are extended."

Bowling Green, Kentucky, is a good example. Throughout the nineties, Mexicans came north to work and added Mexican restaurants, Mexican grocery stores, Mexican Saturday night dances, and the Spanish language to the city's cultural mix. I spent time there researching the Bowling Green–Mexico border for *Wetback Nation*. One of my sources was Western Kentucky University professor David Coffey, who said of the exponentially growing Kentucky Latino population, "They're working in tobacco, landscaping, horse farming, poultry processing, fruits and vegetables, and forestry." He tells anybody he can get to listen, "These are the people who roof our houses, mow our lawns, paint our houses, wash our dirty dishes in restaurants, and clean our dirty laundry in hotels."

Despite the creation of such borderlands far from the physical frontier that divides Mexico and the United States, is there a unique mélange, a specific culture, on the strip of the borderland?

"It's intense, creative, and militarized," said Herrera about that swath territory—what sociologist Arjun Appadurai calls an ethnoscape—directly adjacent to the line between the two nations. Its artificiality influences its reality. The line was drawn arbitrarily, on land that was first Indian, then Spanish, and finally Mexican. Gringo influences intensified after Mexico lost California, of course, but the history is impossible to erase, as are the relationships.

"It wasn't there before 1924," Herrera said about the international border. "My father didn't have to cross the border, he just traveled. He came up from Chihuahua in 1903. He was moving back and forth. Chihuahua–Colorado, Chihuahua–Wyoming, Texas, New Mexico. There was no line. There wasn't a legalized line." He mused about the border, calling it "definitely a very vital space, because of all its extremes. One side is quote/unquote free, and one side is alien."

"Which is which?" I asked.

"Hey, which is which?" he said. "Which is which? They trade places quite a bit, that's true."

It's a complicated equation that influences how and how much some Mexicans merge into the north of the border mainstream culture.

"In a sense it cannot happen, because of the historical roots the Mexicanos have in what is now called the United States. This was Mexico. This was an indigenous site as well. Mexicanos have indigenous and Mexican roots in the United States before it was the United States. Before it was California and Texas and Utah. Yes, we can be called immigrants. But we really are migrants with two homelands. One is in the United States, and one is in Mexico and/or Latin America, and it's simultaneous. For us it's a double homeland. That's hard to articulate in the times we live in."

It's very hard to deal with that on a legal basis as well. Where lie the loyalties for these transnationals?

"That's the one thing that we've attempted to address and literally have been blown back by tanks and military, when we attempted to organize and mobilize on that issue, that legal issue."

Tell that to the Lou Dobbs–Patrick J. Buchanan–Bill O'Reilly troika. I have engaged the three of them, interviewing them and being interviewed by them.

When Buchanan and I talked immigration, he looked longingly back at the fifties as a time of utopia for the America of his dreams. "I do believe this," he told me, "the America we grew up in up until 1965 had an ethnocultural core. Ah," he continued wistfully, "every nation does. And ours was by and large Western European and Christian. That did not mean everyone in the country was a Christian, nor could everyone in the country trace his ancestors to Europe or the West. But that was basically the core of the country, and it's one of the things that really held us together. Now I see the masses of immigration coming from the third world, and in such huge numbers, illegally, as presenting a tremendously more difficult problem of assimilation."

Assimilation to what? Buchanan had his answer ready.

"When you have 90 percent of the country basically of European descent, and you have 90 percent of the country Christian, is this the enthnocultural core of the nation, or is it not?"

Oh, Pat, your dreamy 1950s are long gone, I told him.

He came back with a response that ought to motivate every eligible American voter to cast a ballot.

"I believe that the country is united far more by culture and patriotism than by any abstract ideas. And abstract ideas like democracy don't mean, excuse me, a whole hell of a lot to me."

Whew.

"The point I'm saying is the melting pot is broken," Buchanan insisted from his Washington, D.C., hideout, far from Carroll Buckley's multicultural Imperial Valley. "I mean, you can bring in a hundred million Chinese from China into the West Coast, and after a certain period they will probably all be employed in some venture or another. But I'm not sure that would be California as I understand it or America as I know it."

Why must California be a California as you understand it, Pat?

"I'm not sure what I would have in common with those folks," he said about those millions of hypothetical Chinese, and the millions of Mexicans living in our midst without proper U.S. documents. "Those folks coming here are not Americans, and many of them don't want to be American. You're going to have over a hundred million Hispanics in this country at mid-century. I believe almost all of whom, because the cohort is so large, will retain their Spanish language and culture and newspapers and radios and TVs."

So?

"Look, we are an English-speaking country."

It was a variation on the theme when I talked with Lou Dobbs. He cited undocumented migration from Mexico into the United States as a "continued assault on our middle class. At the same time that corporate America has outsourced three million American jobs over the course of the past five years—and most of those are middle-class jobs, we've lost three and a half million manufacturing jobs—we brought in an estimated ten million illegal aliens, which further depresses wages and raises taxpayer costs for social services and health care in this country."

He said he was worried about the very survival of the United States as he knew it and wanted it. "Oh, I think there's no question that the empire is in decline, but I also have great faith that we can reverse that decline."

When I debated Bill O'Reilly it was more of the same, he saw a threat from the south whether it was from Mexicans coming across the border without proper paperwork or with a visa.

"Most Mexicans who want to live here and work here," O'Reilly insisted about even those who travel to the United States legally, "are just going to overstay the visa." He wanted a militarized border to stop those without visas. "The solution to the problem is to put the National Guard on the border to seal it down so that people can't run across."

And who would be doing his cooking and cleaning? O'Reilly supported a guest worker program, the old "come here, work cheap, go home" idea that failed postwar Germany and was a disaster when it existed for Mexicans in the United States as the now-abandoned bracero system, the guest worker policy that took advantage of Mexican workers from the late forties through the early sixties.

Was it a ratings-grabber or reality when Geraldo Rivera verbally slapped his Fox News colleague Bill O'Reilly live on the air over O'Reilly's demagogic hatemongering, goading and encouraging his viewers to be prejudiced against Mexicans living in the United States without proper paperwork? After reading Rivera's autobiographical book *His Panic: Why Americans Fear Hispanics in the U.S.*, I was convinced of his sincerity and invited him to talk more about the O'Reilly types and their immigration paranoia.

"The fear is so real, it's ripe," he said. "It's an almost tangible thing. I've never really experienced anything like it in almost four decades in public life. I feel this almost visceral resentment bordering on hysteria in much of the country, and much of it is directed at the Hispanic community."

I told him about the migration of my father from Hungary. Hispanics, I suggested, are the Hungarians of our current era.

"Nativism," he agreed, "which I define as half racism and half nationalism, has greeted every successive wave of immigrants. The Irish certainly got bashed in the mid-nineteenth century with the 'Irish Need Not Apply.' In that case it was anti-Catholic, a perception that somehow they were less white than the majority culture that was already established in this country. And yes, it happened again to the Germans, and later in the nineteenth century the whole crowd that came in through Ellis Island, especially the Italians, got beat up pretty good. There's this maddening tendency that I write about—once your particular group gets over the bridge, you want to burn the bridge behind you. One of the most bitter ironies is that so many sons and grandsons of immigrants are among the leaders in this virulent largely anti-Hispanic anti-immigrant movement of today."

Rivera walked me through his personal history and suggested that it helped explain why he believes there is growing discrimination in the United States against all Hispanics, no matter their origin or immigration status.

"Every Puerto Rican after the Jones Act of 1917, including my dad, was made a citizen of the United States. Puerto Rico is a territory of the United States. We are not personally affected by the immigration issue. But there is a growing feeling, and I'm sensing it in all parts of the country, that we're all in this together." Ever the showman, Rivera told a story from his act.

"I ran into Mitt Romney after I did the O'Reilly show. I went into the green room, and Governor Romney was there. I said, 'Governor, I'm glad that I ran into you, because I have to tell you how parents are complaining to me that their citizen children are being made fun of at school, being called border-jumpers, and people are being carded for proof of citizenship, and there's discrimination in the workplace, and landlords are afraid to rent to Hispanics, because they don't know if they're going to get burned by some anti-immigration legislation.' He said, 'I'm only directing my wrath at the illegal immigrants.' I said, 'Governor, the language is so extreme, the rhetoric is so radical that it's lapping over and it's affecting all of us and it's going to cost you in Florida.' This was when Romney was still the Republican frontrunner for the presidential nomination. He said, 'I have forty-five Hispanics on my advisory committee.' I said, 'Governor, it's not going to be enough.' Romney did everything that every other politician in Florida seeking the Cuban vote does; he wore a guayabera shirt, he drank café con leche, he said, 'Cuba sí, Castro, no.' And the Cubans voted against him five to one. They voted for McCain five to one."

Geraldo Rivera particularly fires his literary salvos at fellow television personality Lou Dobbs and Dobbs's decision to join former Colorado representative Tom Tancredo as an anti-immigration absolutist.

"Lou Dobbs is certainly a demagogue," said Rivera, "and what he has done is resurrect a failed career as a business journalist on the back of this most vulnerable segment of our population. Lou Dobbs knows that when he puts that same shot of that same Mexican kid climbing that damn wall every time he's talking about this issue, that whatever his words are, the impression is that we're being swamped by this tidal wave of dark-skinned, again Catholic, immigrants. It's the latest wave, and they're going to ruin whatever our precious country is and bring in leprosy, which was a false charge. Bring in violent crime, another demonstrably false charge. Destroy our economy, another false charge. The rhetoric night after night after night is what has whipped up this anti-immigrant frenzy." Long after Lou Dobbs left his anchor slot at

CNN, his name remained all but synonymous with anti-immigration nativism, his influence on demagogic news-media types personified by Michael Savage and Glenn Beck.

Another paranoid worry I heard all along the border, and that I've heard throughout the United States, is the bizarre fear of the Spanish language. With English the dominant lingua franca worldwide, how any monolingual American can take offense when he calls his credit card company and hears, "Para español, marque el numero dos," is difficult to understand. If you cannot understand the guy delivering your pizza or weeding your garden, learn some Spanish, gringo. When I talked with Pat Buchanan about Spanish versus English, he became apoplectic, insisting that the United States is identified by being monolingual. It brings to mind a joke that I heard repeatedly working in Europe, and I tried it out on Geraldo.

What do you call somebody who speaks three languages? Trilingual. What do you call somebody who speaks two languages? Bilingual. What do you call somebody who speaks one language? Pause. American.

Rivera, while calling his own Spanish sometimes more *menos* than *más,* laughed.

"We're unique in the world in that we extol the virtue of ignorance." His worry is not that Spanish is dominating, but rather is getting lost in the face of the English monolith.

"The problem isn't that we cling to Spanish; the problem is the second generation is forgetting Spanish. Then the third generation, our children, if we have the resources, are learning it in an academic setting, not in a communal setting. Every study shows, proves, that current immigrants are learning English at a faster rate than previous waves of immigrants, including the Mexicans, despite the fact that the Mexicans are exceptional because not only did the part of the country that they're trespassing on once belong to their great-grandparents, but also Mexico remains so close, and cross-border or transborder life so fluid, up until now, with this ridiculous wall. I don't know a single second-generation Latino immigrant who doesn't speak English, and I know thousands of them."

Calexico, and other border cities, presents a different story than the America north of The Eight. Spanish is a natural default language for much of Calexico. But as Rivera correctly observed, "Even in Calexico, English is still the language of the real estate developers and the high-enders, and everyone who's coming across and who hopes to make a life on the northern side of the frontier knows he has to speak English."

"*Correcto,*" I said.

"Well, you don't sound very fearful of the invasion."

"On the contrary," I told him. "Embracement seems like so much more fun."

"What makes America great," said patriot Rivera, "is that we have harnessed the immigrant vigor. We have harnessed this hybrid energy of diversity."

What, then, brings out our dark, nativist, anti-immigrant American side in today's world? Geraldo Rivera pointed me back to broadcast-news media colleagues, the Lou Dobbs Brigade.

"I really believe that the savage right-wing talk-radio campaign, talk radio and cable news, is what is driving it. It is far worse than even the Bill Clinton blowjob lie that got morphed into impeachment by some of these same people. Now it's more egregious, it's more raw, it's more flamboyant in its ignorance of the facts or intentional avoidance of the facts, and they are drumming up a mob sentimentality."

It was time to say good-bye; I told Rivera I hoped to continue the conversation.

"I look forward to running into you somewhere and bashing Lou Dobbs together," I said.

"You got a date."

I enjoyed a cordial conversation with Tom Tancredo while he was still in Congress, a politician who made his national name synonymous with opposition to immigration.

"Yeah, who would have thought it?" he told me. "I must admit to you that years ago, when I came into the Congress and started this discussion, it really was a monologue. There was no one in the Congress of the United States that would pay much attention to it, for fear that it would cost them politically. It wasn't necessarily because they all disagreed, but they all were frightened of the political ramifications."

I asked Tancredo why he thought it was that the entire Congress didn't join him in his absolutist stance against migrants in the United States without proper documentation.

"Fear of the political fallout that they believe may occur," he said without hesitation. "We have reached a point in this country, because the numbers are very large—twelve to twenty million people, we're not sure exactly how many are here illegally—that there is significant political pressure, not just because of their presence here, but by the market that they create and the number of people that are benefiting financially from their existence in this country. It's not just the employer who exploits these folks and benefits financially; it's the market that they create. It's the Bank of America, recognizing that market and making it possible to open up an account without a Social Security number."

Tancredo famously cut up his Bank of America credit card to protest the bank's opportunistic policy change. He became the poster boy for intolerance, a pariah for those seeking a compromise solution—and a hero to nativists and others opposed to the presence of undocumented migrants in their midst. When I talked with him, he was using the bully pulpit of presidential politics to draw attention to illegal immigration.

"I automatically provide people with some sort of space to get into where they can say, 'Look, I'm not that guy, because that guy is a racist, demagogue,' pick your epithet, but I believe nonetheless we can move towards securing a border. I am farther out than most of the folks that run for president when I say things like, 'We need a time out on immigration,' not just stopping illegal immigration. It gives them room and what they then like to do is say this guy is so far out, so crazy, that we can take a more moderate stance here. To tell you the truth, that's okay with me. It is not the worst thing in the world to have changed the debate so significantly in this country, especially at least among the Republicans running for office, that they are willing to say things like, 'We will secure the border and we will go after employers.' That's the moderate position now, and that's fine, and I wish I could tell you that it was exactly what I had planned, but it's pretty close."

No matter where Americans sit on the immigration fence, they express not just an opinion, but a strong stance on the issue. All 350 million-plus of us are not just concerned about it, we want a policy other than the dysfunctional status quo. I asked the congressman if he could appreciate the other side of the story.

"I can tell you what I hear all the time, the nostalgic aspect of it that we are 'a nation of immigrants,' and it has made us great. That the diversity that we achieve through massive immigration is a positive and healthy thing. That the economy is dependent upon massive numbers of low-income, low-wage people to sustain it. That these people are escaping dire poverty, the same thing that my grandparents did, and yours. They came looking for a better life. Why should we try to shut the door on them? What makes them different? Is it because they're Mexicans? Is it because you have some sort of a racist attitude toward people of color? Would you feel the same way if we had massive immigration from Scandinavia or the European continent? That's the kind of stuff that I hear most often."

Good arguments. But they didn't sway Tom Tancredo. I asked him if he truly feared that the United States was facing the destruction of its culture—that our nation was at a crisis point.

"I believe we really are at the proverbial tipping point. I do believe it is that serious. I'm not just saying this. It's not some political smoke I'm blowing at anybody. I believe with all my heart that we are in a cultural crisis that's created by what I call the 'cult of multiculturalism' inside this country. Massive immigration simply exacerbates the problem, and that is immigration of people who do not have a desire to assimilate, and on our side we do not have a desire for them to assimilate. That's very dangerous."

Hey, who says we don't have a desire for them to assimilate, and to assimilate, again, to what?

"I'm really talking about this radical multiculturalism philosophy that permeates so much of our society until there's nothing of value in the United States or the West in general, and why would anybody want to connect to it? There are a lot of folks that look at America in a different way than I do."

"If, as you self-identified," I said to him, "you are out on the fringe yourself, and we are a country that's built on compromise and trying to find points of consensus, how do we come together on this? How do those of us who disagree with you—and that includes me—come to find a point where we can find a way to solve what is a crisis: the openness of that southern border, our lack of control of that border?" I asked Tancredo if he had a blueprint for uniting us.

"I don't want to sound trite. But I do not for the life of me understand why we could not accomplish just exactly what you've said by simply saying we will enforce the law. The law is the common element here. We call ourselves a nation of law. We believe that that is one of the founding principles of the country. We have a law, it says you can't come into the country illegally. We have another law that says that you cannot obtain a job if you are here illegally. If you enforced those laws, then, of course, you have solved the problem. So the compromise is this: You don't move to the position of a 'time out,' which is what Tom

Tancredo wants. You don't move that far. But you do move at least to the point of enforcing the law. And you will see that we will begin to get control of the situation. People who have come here illegally will return home because the thing for which they come here is not available. Why isn't that a compromise? Why not just enforce the law?"

"You know, Congressman," was my honest response, "as onerous as some of your rhetoric is, it's an irritatingly difficult point to contradict."

He laughed. "Well, that's made my day just hearing that."

I offered a compromise back to him. Enforce the immigration laws until we change them, but in the meantime figure out some device to regularize those Mexicans living in the United States without proper government authorization. He blinked.

"Of course, I understand the situation and the world in which I operate, the world of politics. I have a friend who many years ago when I was in the state legislature was an editorial writer for the *Denver Post*. I think he still is. He once told me his dad worked for a union for a long time. He said you would go in and scream for red revolution and settle for an increase in the pension plan." We laughed. "Of course, to a large extent that is what is happening. I have to set the bar as far as I can. I'm being completely candid with you. I recognize fully well what position my argument puts me in and the difficulties that you would have politically to achieve a goal. If I had actually set out to become president, then, of course, it would be ludicrous for me to do it in the way I'm doing it. I don't have that as my goal. I never have. I have the luxury of being completely and totally candid about what it is I want to accomplish and saying to you, 'You bet, I will set the goalposts as far as I can down the field,' because then I will have a better chance of getting at least the game played on my side."

Who are we as Americans, and what do we think? One of the contemporary devices we use to answer those questions is the opinion poll, and Sergio Bendixen, who is the president of Bendixen & Associates, is a pollster who specializes in answering those questions regarding Latinos.

He told me that he is proud of the track record of his company. "It has proven to be fairly accurate, at least up till now." His hesitation related to a trend he was spotting, a trend dangerous to the pollster who goes door-to-door with a clipboard full of questions. Americans, perhaps because of the post-9/11 paranoia, aren't as ready to answer questions about their behavior and opinions as they were in the recent past. "We'll see whether the new habit in America of people being uncomfortable speaking to strangers at home continues to increase. If that happens, maybe the polling industry will have to change in a meaningful way. Up until now, meaning 2008, we're seeing that about 40 to 50 percent of Americans are willing to talk to pollsters."

I've spent a lot of time working outside of the United States as a journalist: behind the Iron Curtain when the Iron Curtain was there, in the Middle East, in places where a knock on the door or a ring of the telephone often creates a reflexive action of avoidance or certainly not a candid response. Such concerns must be problematic for the polling business.

"I think there's some of that," Bendixen said. "I have polled all over the world, including in Russia. You do have to take into consideration the culture and, obviously, the environment of whatever is going on politically in terms of the concerns of people. But usually, if you approach things in a professional way and you utilize professional interviewers that are well trained, you can achieve accurate and representative samples, and you can get fairly good answers to your questions."

Sergio Bendixen's clients include the International Development Bank (IDB); it studies the cash remittances sent home by migrants and migration patterns, from Latin America to the United States, and the United States to Latin America. Bendixen's pollsters must find a representative sample of Latin Americans in the United States, which means, by definition, identifying those without proper documentation for being in the United States. Hence, he and his team must figure out how to convince people in the United States illegally to identify themselves as such and agree to be interviewed.

"A few years ago I would have thought that impossible," he told me. "But we have come up with the proper methodology, the proper questions, the proper approach to make people feel comfortable. For example, in a recent study that we put out for the IDB, 50 percent of the five thousand people interviewed acknowledged over the phone to a stranger and to an interviewer that they were undocumented immigrants."

I asked him if it was a trade secret or if he would share his methodology with me. How did he get such cooperation, and how could he be sure that he was hearing the truth?

"Yeah." He was gracious and agreeable. "Let me tell you how we do it. First of all, you begin by speaking Spanish, so that makes them feel very, very comfortable. Then you let them know that the poll is being sponsored by friends, by people at the Inter-American Development Bank or by people at a company that they would know, or a newspaper that they happen to read, or an organization that they happen to be familiar with. That this is being done to understand their point of view better. And then the question that we put to them goes something like this: Many Latin American immigrants have come to the United States and have been able to complete their paperwork and are now considered legal residents. Other people, many others, are still working on getting their papers ready, and they are considered undocumented immigrants. What are you? And half of them say they're still working on it and they're undocumented."

Fascinating. The spin is positive, suggesting that those who are undocumented are merely in transition for legal status, not illegal aliens.

"In that culture people do tend to get to become friends, even over a short phone conversation."

"But how," I asked him, "can you build that trust in a society where there is so much paranoia by using the anonymity of the phone call? Why would they believe what you are saying?"

"They do. The combination of language rapport between the interviewer and the interviewee, *and* asking the question in a way that does not make them feel that they're answering a question in a way that's going to make them look bad. In other words, we give them the choice between: Is everything now okay? Or are you still working on it? They feel that a comfortable way to answer the question."

Not all of Bendixen's questions are as dry as legal or illegal immigration.

"A few years ago *Reader's Digest* in Spanish hired us to find out the percentage of the Latin American immigrant-population males who were cheating on their wives. And 18 percent told us over the phone that they were. So, it's amazing what people will tell you. I have a feeling that that number kind of underestimated the real percentage."

Another Bendixen poll reported that Latin American economies were on the brink, in 2008, of suffering hard times because of a reduction in remittances from migrants working in the States.

"Two years ago we learned that about three-quarters of all Latin American immigrants were sending money home on a regular basis. That number had grown from about 55 percent in the earlier part of this decade. There was a bonanza of money arriving not only in Mexico but all over Central America, South America, the Caribbean. The IDB estimated it at sixty billion dollars-plus in 2007. But in 2008, in the most recent study that we just released, we found that that number, the 73 percent of Latin American immigrants who were sending money regularly to their families, had dropped to 50 percent. Now we see a very strong trend away from people in the United States—Latin Americans, obviously, we're talking about—sending money home."

Why?

"A fear about their futures; the fact that they don't know what's going to happen to them here in the United States. They don't know whether they're going to have to return home. They don't know whether they're going to have a job. They don't know whether they're going to have a place to live. The economic downturn was the other big part of it, which has made life difficult not only for immigrants, but for all Americans. This is going to have a tremendous impact. In some countries, like the Dominican Republic and Honduras, it could create national economic crisis. In other countries, like Mexico and Peru and Ecuador, it will just mean the millions of families that had been able to get over the poverty line will be back living in conditions where they could not afford the basic needs of everyday life."

That could mean greater pressure on the Calexicos of the borderlands, because when there is an economic downturn south of the border, it often translates into increasing immigration into the United States for jobs.

"Many of the pressures, the dynamics, that have created the situation where fewer and fewer people are sending money home, have to do with the anti-immigrant movement in the United States, which has become very powerful. As you know, hundreds and hundreds of laws are being approved every day at different legislatures, city councils, county commissions, against immigrants, making life a lot more difficult, especially for the undocumented. Many of them no longer are sending money, and, as you said, that is only going to result in the creation of a lot more pressure back home for people to immigrate to the north, because they are not going to be able to take care of themselves in their own countries without the help of their families that have come to the United States."

Sergio Bendixen, so sensitive to cultural issues as a critical element of his business success, seemed like an ideal source to check on labels. How does he refer to those who are Spanish speakers living in the United States? Geraldo Rivera uses *Hispanic*. But the list—diminutives and derogatory slurs excluded—includes *Hispanics, Chicanos, Mexican-* (or other hyphenated) Americans. *Latinos.*

"*Latinos* is the safest one," Bendixen weighed in. "Let me give you the official answer. If you ask them straight out, all forty-five million Hispanics in the United States, or Latinos, what do they prefer to be called, 55 percent say *Hispanic.* Twenty-eight percent say *Latino.* The rest say something different: Mexican American, or just plain American, or whatever. But two-to-one *Hispanic.*" That, despite the fact that by definition *Hispanic* refers to the Iberian peninsula, not necessarily a factor in the lives of New World Spanish-speakers. "The people that do not like being called Hispanic do get offended. If, for example, you call someone with Mexican heritage Hispanic, they feel that the Hispanics are the ones that killed all the Mexicans, all the Aztecs, all his ancestors. They don't like to be called Hispanics. So *Latino,* even though it's not the preferred term, it's the safer one."

I'm a troublemaker, so I felt it mandatory to ask, "If one wishes to be offensive, what's the most dangerous term?"

Bendixen shot right back, "I won't say it."

All these subcategories.

"I think this new generation, the people that you poll that are eighteen to twenty-nine, they no longer see themselves in racial or ethnic terms. They actually define themselves much more by their music and the fashion that they prefer."

One more question for the pollster Sergio Bendixen before I said good-bye, a critical one, and one he ought to be able to answer.

"Are you ready?"

"Go ahead."

"Are you sitting down?"

"Yeah."

"Of those thirty-one flavors at Baskin-Robbins, what's your favorite?

"I like vanilla cherry," he said without hesitation.

"Vanilla cherry?"

"Or it's cherry vanilla. Sorry."

"Cherry vanilla, right. Vanilla cherry, that's backwards," I objected.

"In Spanish it would be vanilla cherry."

Of course. Get used to it, Dobbs Lou, O'Reilly Bill, and Buchanan Pat.

Adrian Martínez is a fast-talking Hollywood producer. Literally fast-talking. When I found him to talk about the pilot television show he was working on, I was forced to ask him to slow down; it was hard to understand him. The show carried the intentionally provocative title *Who Wants to Marry a U.S. Citizen?*

"You talk really fast, Adrian," I said.

"Right, right, right, right," was his response. "I tend to do everything fast. I'm always on the rush."

Who Wants to Marry a U.S. Citizen? was patterned on *The Dating Game.* A panel of three contestants who are in the United States legally are on the set. Eventually, their visas will expire, and they wish to stay. A U.S. citizen interviews them to decide which one he or she wishes to go out on a date with and, presumably, potentially marry; consequently, if the marriage is legitimate, that contestant could become a U.S. citizen.

"We don't know the outcome of courtship," Adrian explained. "Obviously, people fall in love, sometimes they marry, sometimes they don't. We're not promising anybody a marriage, and we're not encouraging people to get married should they make a connection. All we want to do is play the role of a matchmaker in a fun way. We're not out to encourage immigrants to marry U.S. citizens or vice versa."

Nonetheless, the not-so-hidden subtext was that the game show could be an avenue to citizenship, and just the announcement of the pilot drew further attention to the ongoing immigration crises.

"We're all immigrants, right?" Adrian said. "This country is founded and based on immigration. We've been getting e-mails, a flooding of e-mails, from people who want to be on the show, saying, 'I am the perfect U.S. citizen to marry a foreigner.'" And if a marriage occurred, would it be legit? "That's not for us to decide. That's the Immigration's job to do. Some people think immigrants are going to start flooding our show and use this as an opportunity to circumvent the immigration process, and that's not at all the case."

However, Adrian was pleased to draw attention to the problems he saw with the border: "Our system is in trouble." He quickly added that a game show was not the remedy. "I mean, wow, we can't fix that! It's just a tough issue."

The Mexican Consul General's office sits just a few blocks from the border in Calexico, in an elegant *pequeño* building adjacent to the campus of San Diego State University. Officious-looking in his dark suit, its flashy brass buttons contrasting sharply with his equally dark shirt, which was offset by a radiant tie that shone yellow, Consul Ecce Iei

Mendoza Machado offered a forgiving, fatherly smile to a barrage of questions and later stood adjacent to the red, white, and green Mexican flag for a formal portrait. His answers were, well, diplomatic. For example, in response to a query about the Mexicali–Calexico relationship came this: "The Calexico city council and the municipal government in Mexicali have an excellent relationship and get along well." What more could you ask for, what else would you expect?

But of course he acknowledged the post-9/11 changes.

"People who used to cross the border to Mexicali to have something to eat or to visit relatives have to restrain themselves a little bit, since the waiting times are more than two hours, and the temperature's going up to fifty degrees." Celsius! He was candid about the adverse effects on commerce and study, pointing out that because of the extensive border waits, fewer Mexicans were coming north to take advantage of shopping and school opportunities.

But the most serious problem for the consulate continued to be dealing with the tragedy and debris of immigration. He talked about the rescues in the desert: migrants all but dead. The failed rescues: bodies and sometimes just skeletons discovered littering the desert. The trauma unique to Calexico: drownings in the All-American Canal, the irrigation ditch with a lining so slippery that migrants who use it as a crossing point find it difficult—and too often impossible—to haul themselves out of the water.

"Another problem that's been increasing since the post-9/11 strengthening of the border is violence on both sides." He blames people-smugglers for creating new types of crimes. "Since the immigrants sometimes cannot afford their fees, some get involved in drug smuggling. Others get raped. They get battered, assaulted."

Ecce Iei Mendoza Machado sympathized with his American colleagues. He repeated the stories of violence perpetrated against the Border Patrol, not just thrown rocks but also Molotov cocktails. He cited high-speed chases on the U.S. side as migrants and their *coyotes* tried to evade the Border Patrol and the Highway Patrol to avoid capture. He had a ready example: "Last Sunday a woman died, the consequence of the rollover of a van full of immigrants. Twenty more people were injured." I knew the story; it was the Suburban. He looked fatigued by the continuing trauma and his inability to do much more than pick up the pieces of failed policy.

The migration mess, he said "has increased the operational costs of law enforcement on both sides of the border. They have gone up many millions of dollars and Mexican pesos. This money," he said with sadness in his voice, "could be used for other economic issues in each border city, and it's regrettable."

He called for reform of the U.S. immigration laws to regularize the status of those Mexicans already living north of the border and to allow for further legal migration of workers whose labors and incomes are critical to the economies of both countries. Meanwhile, he and his staff must deal with the day-to-day realities of the border mess, and it's not just trying to identify the bodies that pile up in the morgues ("We ship their bodies back to Mexico, to places all over the country").

"We try to get back belongings to people held in detention centers. We go and interview people at the state prisons." Human rights of detainees are a concern. "Sometimes human rights are not observed by the immigration officers or other law enforcement officers. We try to enforce labor rights."

When the obligatory photograph with the consul in front of the Mexican flag was snapped, he said good-bye with a reminder that the "wall," as he calls what the United States insists is a "fence," is separating generations of Mexican families.

Back in the Mazda. Crank up KXO. Sounds like a talk show. It's an announcer debriefing Sylvia of the local Red Cross chapter about the upcoming fundraiser called Rhapsody in Red.

"We always have fantastic prizes," said an excited Sylvia. "We have a golf set that's worth almost $1,500. This year, because of a very generous anonymous donor, we have a time-share for Acapulco. A retired fire chief and his gorgeous wife donated a chocolate Lab, a puppy, and it's AKC-registered. The reason we're going to have that little guy as an auction item is because we want someone that really wants him or her to take the puppy home. We have a cooking lesson at a very popular restaurant. It's going to be fun. It's a fun evening and very low-key, classy, but it's our Imperial Valley. We all love it and we all fit in. It's just a great way to support your American Red Cross."

"Most of these funds will stay right here, won't they?" asked the KXO announcer.

"They stay in the Imperial Valley. Everything raised that evening stays in the Imperial Valley."

"We all know that if a disaster hits, you guys are always there. Now it's our turn to be there for you."

Stately Ecce lei Mendoza Machado, the elegant Mexican consul general, in his Calexico offices.

"Oh, thank you. Yes, we hope to see you. We do encourage advance ticket sales, of course. We do have them at the office."

It does sound like Mayberry RFD.

I met with San Diego State University professor Juan Carlos Ramírez-Pimienta at the Carrows restaurant in Calexico. If you like Denny's, you'll love Carrows. He teaches in the Spanish department of the university's tidy campus in Calexico adjacent to the Mexican consulate, a collection of Mission Style architecture just north of the border. Latin American culture is his specialty, and he loves working in the borderlands, because "all my students are experts. For someone like me who does research on Mexican popular culture, my students are a great resource. Things go much faster, because I don't have to explain what a mariachi is. If I were teaching in Montana, I would have to act it out. Here, everybody knows. To me that's a great advantage."

He sat down, relaxed, at this favorite Calexico haunt of his, enthusiastic to debrief me about his studies of the borderlands. "It's a central location," he said of his choice to meet at Carrows, "and I don't like Denny's. It was an un-Denny's thing!" His somewhat wild, shiny black hair hung over his collar, and one lock persistently fell over his forehead. On the wall of the Carrows dining room, as we discussed migration, a plaque offered advice to Calexicans all: "Bloom Where You Are Planted."

I asked him to define Caló, the language—or dialect—that organizers of the Imperial Valley College poetry reading included in their call for entries.

"The connotation is crime-associated, lowlife," he told me, "associated in the Mexican-American community with the lowrider or *cholo* phenomenon, or gang phenomenon. Every generation has a way of inventing their own words, their own language, to be able to talk among themselves. Immediately, the next generation, the old generation, starts wondering: What is it they're saying? They associate some low capital to that dialect, while forgetting that they did the same in the sixties, seventies, and eighties."

Ay te watcho for "watch out" was a Caló example from the professor. How did he characterize the difference between Spanglish and Caló?

"Spanglish is the mix of the two languages," he said, with a linguistic order. Usually the noun is in English, not the verb. For instance, people would say, "Voy al carwash." In Spanglish, he theorized, one cannot change any word. Rules exist. He is convinced Spanglish comes out of necessity. For example, new terminology for technology is coined in English and would sound unnatural were it converted to Spanish. In the mélange of cultures and languages on the border, Professor Ramírez listens to the pragmatic development of communication techniques. He told me he loves how Spanish-speakers incorporate useful words from English into their daily lexicon. *Carwash* is one of his favorite examples. "*Carwash,*" he says it as one word. "*Carwash* is such a nice, neat word." He dismisses Spanish-language equivalents such as *túnel de lavado.* "You could say it, but languages are about all mechanisms of communication. So if in the process it is easier in the borderlands to say, 'Vamos al carwash,' let's go to a car wash, then people will use it. It's so much nicer than the Spanish equivalent, which doesn't have a nice ring to it. If there's some fragment of a language that people would find useful, they will use it. Then that fragment will be incorporated, first unofficially but then maybe officially, into the new language."

So as a Spanish professor, does he frown on this bastardization of the mother tongue or embrace the fluid creativity?

"I don't consider it anything bad. It is just an evolution of languages, and that phenomenon has been happening for centuries and centuries. That's how Spanish and French and Italian and Portuguese got to be. They were bastards, quote/unquote, of Latin. As Latin dispersed, it became more and more specialized, and that's how the language is developed. This is a natural phenomenon, and it shouldn't threaten anybody."

Are you paying attention, English-only advocates?

Language and food relate to the physical border and senses of identity. "Border, by definition, is a place where space and identity begin to lose their relationship," instructed Professor Ramírez. "As you get closer to the 'Other,' that space is becoming less United States or less Mexico, and more into something else." Yes, more into what we've been calling the borderlands. "That creates fear in people, on both sides of the border," said Ramírez. At least in some people. Others thrive in the mix. I asked him why the fear?

"I would say because people fear what is not them. They fear that they might get contaminated or change. When something else comes along, we become uncomfortable because we perceive that we might have to change the way we act, or the way we think, or the language we speak. I know why I'd be afraid; I'm afraid when I go into unknown circumstances."

When I traveled through Europe as the Berlin Wall fell, through countries as they changed very rapidly in '88 and '89, it was a thrill to see the flux. But perhaps it was because I was convinced that I could always go home that I rarely felt fear, and certainly no fear of that "Other."

Or, as the professor put it, "What happens when your home is the one in turmoil? I would be more afraid if I perceived my home to be changing into something else. There are some people who are uncomfortable with valid reasons. Can we as a country assimilate x number of immigrants? I think that's a valid question." But he laughs at the idea that Americans need fear Mexicans are taking over north of the border.

Such fear arises more readily among those who are distant from the border, because there's no familiarity with what it is that exists immediately a few feet away across the line. Where Calexico and Mexicali abut, neighbors on both sides of the line share a social, ethnic, cultural, and linguistic base. Changes can exist within just a few miles of the border. Interstate 8, for example, creates a distinct demarcation. South of The Eight, influences are distinctly Mexican; while north of The Eight, gringo influences dominate.

"Calexico is perceived as a town where you can actually live and survive in Spanish with no problem," said the professor. "I believe there might be some fear of Calexification of Imperial County." Great term: Calexification. "There are some biological metaphors, I think. As a disease maybe. As a color that is spreading. Calexico is becoming an almost totally Mexican town. That might make people uncomfortable. I believe this."

The professor studies *narcocorridos,* the news report–like ballads that often romanticize the lives and work of narcotics traffickers. I welcomed his history lesson.

"Mexico is one of the very few countries in which the ballad tradition has continued. In Europe it was very prominent in the Middle Ages, but it stopped. Ballads are called *corridos* in Mexico. A corrido is a narrative song, and there's a subgenre, as you mentioned, that deals with drug trafficking and drug traffickers. This is a very old subgenre. The oldest song I've been able to trace is either from the late twenties or from the early thirties."

As the drug wars intensified between traffickers just south of the border—resulting in bloody, fatal shootouts in the streets of Tijuana and Juárez—performers of narcocorridos were becoming targets themselves. But the professor debunked the suggestion that they were being targeted because of their music. "It is not really true that they're being specifically targeted," he insisted, saying he knew of only one case, in Sonora, where a singer was killed for his songs. "Now, having said this, there's a lot of violence in Mexico related to drug trafficking."

Of course.

"That's not a secret. So in the midst of all this violence, musicians are also bound to get killed, but not at a higher rate than any other profession."

Professor Ramírez grew up directly on the border in Tijuana. His brother Marcos is an artist headquartered in Tijuana, who created an installation on the border in the late 1990s: a huge, two-headed horse suggesting the Trojan horse and its relationship to the Mexican migrants secreting themselves into America. "The fact is," the artist told the *New York Times*, "that man migrates. We all have to keep moving, and we will continue to keep moving."

Such confrontations of the migration reality run in the Ramírez family. The professor referred to his familial home in Tijuana as an embassy, because so many migrants stopped off there en route—clandestinely—north of the border. His mother would send them off to the frontier at nightfall with a box lunch for the crossing. No wonder that he grew up to become a scholar of border studies.

"Relatives would ask for shelter for a couple of days and then try to get into the United States. My mother would, of course, bless them and give them a few burritos, a few tacos, for their adventure."

Hours later he would see some of them at the embassy's door again.

"Sometimes they would come back, and they would be beaten up, usually by robbers on the border. Sometimes they were deported immediately. If we didn't hear from them in a few days, we would assume they were okay. But often we would find a box of strawberries, a box with grapes, at our door. We wouldn't even know who left them there. No thank-you note or anything. But we would assume, oh, somebody's going back to their hometown, and this is a thank-you."

The U.S. government can come up with some bizarre-sounding job titles. Tomas Torres, for example, is the Border Team Coordinator Region Nine, San Diego Border 2012 Program, EPA Office. But Torres laughed it off when I contacted him. "The bureaucracy often gives us these funny titles, but all I really am is someone who coordinates with federal, state, and local governments to get projects done along the U.S.–Mexico border."

That's why I wanted to talk with Torres; he is the Environmental Protection Agency's point man for the filth on the border. Imperial

San Diego State University professor Juan Carlos Ramírez-Pimienta tutors the author on the finer points of Calexico Spanglish.

County is *last* in the rank of counties in California for decent air quality. It suffers other unwanted environmental superlatives. Its New River is one of the foulest streams in the United States. I stood on the banks of the New River alongside a border patrolman. It was the middle of the night, and he had the headlights of his squad car shining on the water and the filth suspended in it, and shining on the sign announcing that the river is toxic. If he did find any of the migrants coming across illegally at that spot, he sure wasn't going to jump in and arrest them, because the water is simply too dangerous to touch; it's that polluted. I saw that Calexico is an environmental disaster, and the EPA specialist unfortunately agreed: filth from Mexico comes north in the New River and with the wind; agricultural wastes from the Valley's growers foul the landscape. The wind stirs the desert soil into the air between plantings.

"Calexico and Mexicali definitely are the sister cities that have probably the toughest challenges along the U.S.–Mexico border, both in air quality and in water quality," Torres told me, "as you very much witnessed."

What to do? The EPA created the Border 2012 Program in response to what must be called a crisis. The goal is to clean up the air, water, and land by the year 2012. Based on what I saw in the borderlands, the challenge seems all but insurmountable. Torres expressed some guarded optimism, because the planning for remediation is supposed to go from local to national instead of being imposed from Washington and Mexico City on Calexico and Mexicali.

"We have local task forces that identify the high-priority issues, the problems on the ground, and raise those to the local, state, and federal level so that we can put in the resources and efforts to take care of those problems. In the case of Calexico and Mexicali, funny you should mention the New River, because we just constructed a brand-new wastewater treatment plant south of the city, which essentially has eliminated the fifteen million gallons of sewage that was entering the New River and into Calexico."

The United States and Mexico both funded the project, because it is in their combined interests. The sewage is generated by Mexico, but it flows with the river into California. We Americans tend to think of ourselves as the first world and Mexico as the third world. Mexico is the dirty side of the border. "Don't drink the water" is a cliché, but also a truism. There's *basura* in the streets down there, because garbage is just tossed out the window. Those are the stereotypes. I asked Tomás

Torres if those generalizations are based in fact. No so fast, gringo, he seemed to say.

"On the U.S. side of the border in California, the region is actually one of the poorer parts of the United States. On the Mexican side, however, it is one of the wealthier parts of the country, if you can believe it. So when we sit down with Mexico to negotiate some of the projects, some of the priorities, we think the sky's falling, and Mexico says, 'Well, we've got much worse problems in the interior of Mexico. The border for us is a much wealthier part of the nation.' But the reality is that there are significant needs along the border that have not been met. People along the border do not have sufficient drinking water. Not everyone enjoys drinking water or wastewater services still, today."

An amazing statistic. Don't drink the water on both sides of the border.

Torres affirmed the conclusion: "On both sides of the border."

Wow.

"Yeah, and the air pollution problem. Mexicali air pollution does not know borders. We need to work together collaboratively to address the severe pollution problems there."

Again we find a parallel with Germany. One of the first significant areas of cooperation between East and West Berlin was to try to deal with environmental issues: pollution and garbage disposal. Talks over smog and trash helped create a dialogue that led to other political issues. But there were some first world and second world—East Germany was arguably in the second world—power plays. East Germany became the garbage dump in many respects for West Germany. There was even an opening in the Berlin Wall that was specifically for garbage trucks to come across from West Berlin with the consumer trash. Some of the same sorts of inequities exist today in the California–Mexico relationship, although Tomás Torres does not see the borderlands in as much of an imbalance as Germany in the Iron Curtain days.

"I just gave you the example of the water and wastewater infrastructure needs. We still don't have all communities hooked up to water and wastewater. Similarly, Mexico only has one hazardous-waste landfill in the entire country. We're working to develop those kinds of infrastructure systems so that Mexico doesn't become the dumping ground, so that there are adequate places to put trash, to put hazardous waste, and to have recycling capabilities. We do have the expertise in-house to be able to provide this kind of training, this kind of technical expertise, and that's what we're doing."

The poisonous New River flowing north into California.

John Hood is a graphic artist who labors at the California Department of Transportation—Caltrans—the state outfit that builds our freeways and tries to keep traffic moving. Among other assignments, John Hood designs road signs. When I talked with him, he told me his favorite signs are the yellow, diamond-shaped caution signs with the silhouettes of animals on them—cows standing around grazing and deer gracefully jumping.

As with any segment of society, there is a highway-sign subculture. Those Caltrans signs are stolen, not just for souvenirs, but for their value as scrap aluminum. In San Francisco we have the block numbers above the names of the streets, and when the street comes to an end, in that last block up above the name of the street is the word *end*. I can only imagine that the sign on Bush Street in the final block, "End Bush," must have been swiped constantly until Barack Obama finally did the job.

John Hood's work is unsigned, anonymous, but extremely well known in Southern California, because he designed the iconic image of an immigrant family running north, a silhouette image posted on Interstate 5 in a Caltrans effort to reduce the number of migrants being run over as they ran across the freeway. I asked Hood to describe his work.

"It depicts a family just running. We had an influx of pedestrians on the freeway down by the border here on I-5 and near a checkpoint just a little further up north. People were getting slaughtered on the freeways. The California Highway Patrol showed us really graphic photos of pedestrians getting killed on the freeway."

Initially, Caltrans proposed a fence down the middle of the freeway, but the worry was more people would be threatened, because they would be trapped. The sign seemed the best Caltrans strategy. It shows a father, a mother, and a child running—the little girl with pigtails flying behind her.

As he worked on the design, Hood said he considered his own past. "I'm from the Navajo tribe from New Mexico, and we have maybe sixteen million acres and well over two hundred thousand in population. It's the largest Indian reservation in the United States." That heritage, he said, influenced his work, "because when the government started rounding up our people—it was Kit Carson that rounded up the Navajos—they had to weaken the economic system, which was the crops and livestock. They had to destroy that and their homes, and the Navajo finally decided, okay, let's go see what they have to offer us. The government captured about nine thousand Navajos and marched them three hundred miles to Fort Sumner. A lot of the people died on the way, close to four hundred women and children."

Hood found himself emotionally involved in the sign design, and not only because of his Navajo past.

"As the point man for my squad in Vietnam, I saw people running—kids, you know—and the destruction of life in a combat zone. When you think about things like that, it touches you and it opens up your heart. It's just like you open a window, and you have to close it sometime. That was hard for me to do when I came back from 'Nam. All the visions of the past kept coming back to me." John Hood learned that he was suffering from posttraumatic stress syndrome because of his Vietnam War experiences. "Internally and spiritually I just started healing myself, and I did. For a while I was entombed with all my past, and I couldn't share it with anybody else except somebody of similar background, with combat experience. Every time I hear a chopper I know what kind of chopper it is, and all my senses bring back memories. For me, part of the sign design was influenced by those experiences. I think the tenderness of your heart kind of tells you a lot of things."

I thought about all the times I'd sped past those warning signs on Interstate 5, oblivious to their background. How potent to connect—via the designer—America's history with its indigenous natives and its history promulgating a disastrous war with its current failed immigration policies. John Hood continued to reveal himself and his creative process.

"You have to feel with your heart rather than your mind. Your heart tells you how to speak. Those are some of the things I was taught when I was a young kid by my mom, a traditional Navajo. I was raised by my paternal grandmother since I was three years old. So I had a dual type of a mother, you know, my biological mom and my grandma."

This was not just some assignment from Caltrans for Hood; this sign was something much more.

"Our target was safety and we tried to address the situation because it was getting worse. It was monumental to see people die like that, helplessly. There is a reason for what they're doing, and I think a lot of times they don't have a choice."

The now-famous image is an official part of America's immigrant heritage: it is on display in the Smithsonian's National Museum of American History in Washington, D.C.

I parked the car on First Street in Calexico, and Markos and I strode into Mexicali. No guards, no border formalities, no visas, nothing but hawkers selling sodas and candies. We walked along the south side of the wall, peering through the gaps into the dreary streets of poor Calexico from a gracious city park on the Mexicali side. I recalled the viewing platforms in old West Berlin; tourists would climb above the Wall's top and peer into the Communist east. A business opportunity for Mexicans! Build viewing platforms on the south side of Homeland Security's wall and charge a few pesos to look at Gringolandia. Music was blaring in the park, vendors were hawking junk we didn't want or need. We strolled; it felt comfortable on the other side. Of course, we could pat the security of a U.S. passport in our pockets, no need to scale that wall to get home. We planned to go home, and not to follow in the journalistic footsteps of our colleague Ambrose Bierce, who was last seen heading south of the border to cover the Mexican Revolution and left with the words, "If you hear of my being stood up against a Mexican stone wall and shot to rags please know that I think that a pretty good way to depart this life. It beats old age, disease, or falling down the cellar stairs. To be a Gringo in Mexico—ah, that is euthanasia!"

We would be satisfied to be gringos in Mexico just for a late-night dinner and a couple of bottles of something other than Bud Light.

The Mexicali crooner whose band members offered the author friendly, local
female companionship.

We were early at El Sarape, well past the diner closing time of eight
o'clock across the border in Calexico. But there on the Mexican side,
at eight o'clock most of the tables in the place were empty. The maria-
chis were hanging out stage left, taking care of business. One player
approached us and offered us a good time with a girl he knew. We
declined. He went back to his chair, sat for a while longer while we
nursed our drinks waiting for dinner, and then came back and asked if
we were sure we weren't interested in some fine and exciting company.

Finally, the ensemble took to the stage, a stage festooned with mir-
rors reflecting the neon glowing behind the violin, trumpets, and guitar-
rón. The singer—complete with pencil-thin moustache—looked as if he
were sleep-deprived or just sad as he sang those sentimental Mexican
songs that always feature *alma, corazón,* and *amor.* He belted out the
standards, horns blasted, and we definitely were in Mexico.

≥ ≥ ≥

Thursday

Efficiency Is Security

Virginia Munger's father was from Germany, her mother was born in Española, New Mexico, and that's where they married. He was a mechanic and was infected with the California dream. He set up shop as an Imperial Valley pioneer and fetched his wife and daughter. They came across the Old Plank Road, an experience Mrs. Munger recollected for me when we met for lunch at the Barbara Worth Resort. Mrs. Munger was in her nineties then, almost as old as Calexico. That first trip west was in the late 1920s, as best as she can remember, when she was about seven years old. The Valley was still settling. She shared some fleeting memories of those days, back when her father worked at the CM Ranch, just east of Calexico.

"We lived on Second Street, and the block that we lived on had about ten small houses. Each house had a living room, a bedroom, the kitchen, and a porch. They were all screened porches for the summertime. Most of them had a bathroom, but it was on the outside. There was water, but it was on the outside. At that time everybody was poor. But nobody felt poor, because we all had the same thing. We didn't have welfare, and people did well. Most of the men, with the exception of my father, worked in the fields. Most of our neighbors were Mexican people, but my Dad was German, so we cooked differently from them. We always had bread and made sandwiches, and we'd go over to the next-door neighbor, and they had tortillas and chili." She laughed. "We'd exchange." She stopped and then mused, "We didn't have air conditioners."

No air conditioners? One hundred seventeen in the summers?

"We didn't know the difference. That's what I was telling my daughter the other day, because she had her air conditioner on in the car, and I get cold. I said to her, 'I can't figure out why we were all so happy.' We didn't have air-conditioning and we didn't have a fan.

At the library—I was a reader, still am—they had a big tub of water and a fan that would hit the water to cool things out. But I can't remember ever really being uncomfortable. We slept outdoors at night, and nobody locked the doors. We were right next to the border, and we didn't have any people who would come over and try to hurt us, or anything."

She smiles a sweet, knowing smile. Her short white hair is neatly combed back from a forehead remarkably smooth, given all those desert years. Her short-sleeved tailored blouse is crisp, freshly ironed for this lunch at the resort, her regular spot for the weekly bridge-playing sessions she shares with her Valley girlfriends.

George's wife, Maria, joined us for the lunch. Mrs. Munger was her friend, and she had arranged for me to meet with her. As an Imperial Valley girl, Maria had her own stories and memories of the bygone days. "I remember my dad saying they would wet a sheet and wrap it around them to fall asleep at night. And, like, in ten minutes it would be dry." She and Mrs. Munger laughed.

We stayed in the late 1920s with her, soaking up those old days, and I asked her if she just walked across the street to Mexicali when she had something to do in Mexico.

"We didn't walk across. There was a ditch and we would get in the ditch and bathe in it or just play in the water. The Mexican kids would come to this side, and we'd go to their side. We didn't go that far, just across it to play with them. We didn't try to go to their homes, and they didn't come to our homes either. But we played out there."

Mrs. Munger went to grammar school and high school in Calexico just a few blocks north of her house, close enough to walk home for lunch. During her schooldays, the Depression hit America, but not her life. "We didn't know about the Depression. We didn't have anything to start with, you know." But they were surrounded by farms; food was plentiful. Fresh out of high school, she married young and moved with her husband east out of Calexico a few miles to a ranch. Two years later he installed a flush toilet, "and boy, we were in heaven." More laughs at the memory. "I had a washing machine before, but I had to go to the ditch to get water. People talk about hard times. They weren't hard. I guess because we didn't know any better. We never went hungry. We didn't have everything we wanted, but we had just about everything we needed."

After years of working on others' ranches, Mrs. Munger and her husband bought their own place. They farmed, they raised their children,

Calexico pioneer Mrs. Munger punctuates a story about the good old days.

and she dreamed of far away. "My husband was from Arkansas, and I always wanted to move to Arkansas. I won't tell you what he said." Another laugh. "He refused. We used to go to Arkansas quite often. It was so green and beautiful. I loved Arkansas. But not him. He said he picked all the cotton he ever wanted to pick. He loved it here in the Valley. I loved my husband, so I stayed."

That says it all.

But she expressed no regrets and told me she loves the Valley, too.

"My only son is in Yuma, and he didn't care about farming, so we sold the farm. My girls are in San Diego." The girls tried to convince her to move to the coast, but she insisted on staying put at home, in the old homestead, surrounded by the farmland she sold to Maria and George, and close to her bridge-playing friends.

"We play bridge here in the summertime because our clubhouse closes for the summer. We have lunch and play every Thursday."

I asked her if she recalled the story of Barbara Worth.

"No, no."

Did she ever meet the author of *The Winning of Barbara Worth*, Harold Bell Wright? He lived just a few miles from Mrs. Munger's home.

"No," she answered again. "After I married my husband, bless his heart, I loved him and all that, but a woman's place was in the home. I was a stay-at-home wife, and I didn't get too much news. You raised the children and he took care of the rest of it. I had four kids. I did all the cooking and did my washing and laundry. For a long, long time that road where we lived wasn't paved, it was just dirt. If it rained, you didn't go anywhere, because it was just too muddy. Calexico was a long, long ways off." A long ways off in effort; in distance, it was just a few miles. "That's where I did most of my shopping. I didn't join anything until he passed away. I didn't know the difference, so it didn't bother me staying at home. It would now but it didn't then. I didn't know any better. After he died, oh, about two years later, I was asked to work at the school, and I thought why not? I loved it. I worked there for nine years, and boy, I'll tell you I would have paid them to just let me work there. I was so thrilled when I got to work. Gee, that was really something. I could speak Spanish and English, so that was a help. I love kids."

The Depression? Not a problem, there was plenty of food in the Valley. World War II? With Mexicali across the street, consumer goods and food rationed in the States were easily available.

"We all had ration coupons, and in fact I still have some. But we still were able to get the gas for the tractors. My husband smoked and they were hard to get, and sugar was hard to get. But we just went across the line and got brown sugar. It wasn't as refined as ours, but it was sugar. You could just walk across there then. You didn't even have to show your passport; nobody had one anyhow. I can't remember ever being hungry. They had the meat," she said about Mexicali markets. "You could get all you wanted, well, all you could carry."

Fast-forward to the future, and Mrs. Munger expressed worry for her grandchildren based on the changing ethnicity of the Valley.

"When you go to town now," this Spanish-speaker complained, "in some of the stores, in some of the restaurants, how many American people do you see waiting on you?"

I told her that during my first day in Calexico this trip, the only English I heard involved my conversations with Markos. That news triggered a torrent of tempered and graceful, but seriously annoyed, examples of linguistic frustrations from Mrs. Munger, despite her history of playing in the ditch with the *niños* from the other side of the line.

"We had a meeting several months ago at our club—we had things for sale there—and one of my friends came up to me, and she said,

'Why don't you go over there and talk to that lady? She can't speak English and you can speak Spanish.' I said a bad word. Then I said, 'She can go and learn English. She's in the United States.' That's exactly how I feel, you know? It makes me mad when you go to stores and they speak Spanish. Speak English!"

Why does it make her mad? Especially when she speaks Spanish.

"They're here. Why do I have to speak Spanish? When I go to Mexicali, they don't make an effort to get somebody that speaks English. All over the Valley now, we almost have to learn to speak Spanish in order to communicate with people here." She recalled for me her days as a teacher's aide, helping Spanish-speaking students learn English, and then she launched back into her attack. "But now it's getting to the point where they don't want to learn English, you can learn Spanish."

Virginia Munger barely touched her lunch. It wasn't just that we had kept her talking; she confessed to a late big breakfast. Waitress Bonnie Peterson cleared the dishes, and I asked Mrs. Munger if she could explain to strangers what is so attractive to her about the harsh and dirty Imperial Valley and her childhood hometown, Calexico. She could, in fact, with a quick story.

"My son was born here, and he says to me, 'How can you stand that hellhole?' He hates it. He moved to Yuma." She thought for a second. "I don't know. I think it's the people. I was deathly sick about three years ago and was in the hospital in San Diego and stayed with my daughter for three weeks. When they brought me home, coming over the mountain I saw that valley, and I thought, 'Oh, thank God, I'm home!' Over there it's just buildings, buildings, buildings."

"We live in paradise," Maria agreed.

"Yeah," said Mrs. Munger. "That's it. I just love it here. Home."

The house next door to Maria and George's place fell into disrepair. One day Maria found a package of letters that had fallen from the attic. They were the correspondence of Chrystle Spear, her longtime neighbor. She sent the package off to Chrystle's children, who were gracious enough to share them with me. The excerpts I include here offer a glimpse of that different era, as the Valley pioneers prospered.

"She was such a nice lady," said Maria about Chrystle. "She'd come over and I'd be dusting and she'd say, 'Why do you do that? It'll just be dusty again tomorrow.'"

The abandoned house where Maria Mainas found the stash of love letters from John Gorman to Chrystle Spear.

It was August 13, 1937. John Gorman was living in Somerton, Arizona, judging from his stationery, and he sat down at his typewriter to continue his courtship of Chrystle Spear.

"Dearest Chris," he wrote. "After reading your super-sweet letter over, I am very much surprised and grateful to know that all you want from me is a senior picture. When will you return from Valley Center, and where the heck is Valley Center, California at? Anyway, I hope you have a very good time and do not make too many boys fall in love with you, because I would not like to have to beat too many guys sock-silly in order to get my two-cents in the game."

Charming. Sock-silly!

"Sometime," he continued, "if I ever manage to get over there to see you, or you steer that Pontiac of yours thisaway, I should like to see one of your annuals, with your photos, what and all, in it. By the way, don't you s'pose that I should rate somewhat of a small photo or so of you, just to remember you by, at least? I am just going to ask you in plain words, but if you insist, I can tell you how sweet you are and call you darlin' and honey, like you did me. And I would probably be meaning such sweet nothings a lot more than you did when you typed them at me."

(!)

"Or maybe that's why you used the typewriter, so I couldn't come back at you with a breach of promise suit—or somethin'. You didn't do at all bad with the typewriter, but if I could write as well, or as legibly, to be high falutin', as you, I would not type at all."

John's typing isn't so hot, either. Plenty of backspaces, where he corrects errors by striking the needed letter on top of the mistake, fill the sweet page.

"However," he crooned on, "if I write letters by hand, people will think I'm a foreigner because they would not be able to read what I call good old American writing."

The closing line is a showstopper; Johnny is one funny guy.

"You know, Chris, what with your new car and your ability to make money, as that four bits in two hours, manicuring that lady's hair and giving her nails a facial, and your looks and my—well, I can't think of anything good about me right now—anyway, we should get along swell. You see, it has been my ambition and lifelong contention that I will marry a good looking girl, if she has a car and money. LOVE AND KISSES, AND ——. (You might match that but you can't beat it.)"

And then, despite his protestations, he signs it "Johnny" in an elegant script, underlined with a flourish line that extends from the graceful "J" to the deep, swept tail of the "Y."

Unfortunately, Chrystle did not keep copies of what she wrote back to Johnny. But July 27, 1938, Johnny is still writing on Somerton letterhead, and still typing sweet nothings under the salutation "Dearest Chris."

"According to your letter I don't know whether you're mad because I wasn't there when I said I MIGHT be, glad because I wasn't there, or whether you ever give a hoot whether I ever ankle around down by your ranch."

Give a hoot! Ankle around down!

"And, secondly, since I intend to be in Holtville, or more exactly, the Spear home, this coming Friday evening, I am trusting the big, bad dog won't be loose and the gates and doors locked—and you gone."

Johnny wrote that he was going to see the Somerton Firemen's soft ball team play at Brawley and that he was traveling to the Valley with a friend.

"Chris, can you arrange a 'date' for Ralph, please? I will guarantee Ralph as one of the finest boys I know. Why I think he is even a nicer boy than I am, and you know that's saying quite a bit. So, in short, will you and another comely Holtville Honey be ready and waiting for us somewhere around 6 (California time) this Friday?"

Jump to October 31, 1938, and Johnny is writing on letterhead from the *Yuma Star* ("Covers Yuma Valley like the sunshine"), and there's a hint of why John Gorman writes from Somerton, just a few miles south of Yuma. Under the slogan "Yuma County's Leading Weekly Newspaper," is the announcement: Joseph B. Gorman, editor and publisher.

Johnny wrote to "Chrissie, dear" on that date, saying that the last letter from her "was a 'dream letter' from my dream girl." He refers to a couple of photographs she stuck in the envelope. "The one in which I gently edged my innocent fingers around your lovely waist. The other one is rather cute, especially the dress you have on in the picture. I have that particular photo framed in a beautiful blue-hued mirror-glass picture frame on my dresser."

August 5, 1940. Johnny moved, the stationery marked simply Los Angeles, California.

"Dear Chris," he wrote in longhand, and a quite legible longhand. "I realize you more or less 'bequeathed' me, as your boyfriend, to Evelyn. And, inasmuch as I have preferred to 'free-lance' a great deal with regard to girls and romance, that did not disturb me too much—just a little. Naturally I would prefer dating you and I really think it's a dirty shame that you had to up and fall in love or is it just 'going steady' without the love? You were such a nice girl, too. Thank you for everything, Chris, and maybe I can do something nice for you sometime." And it was signed, "Just one of the boys, Johnny."

Earl Roberts Jr. is the president of the Calexico Chamber of Commerce. When I arrived in town, I immediately wanted to talk to him, in part because of a sign in front of the chamber's downtown office. It was a message I spotted not just there, but all over town: Efficiency Is Security. When one doesn't have the background to know the details of local lore and shows up in a place such as Calexico, a place so different from my hometown San Francisco, for example, and sees a sign such as Efficiency Is Security, it's puzzling, confusing, even off-putting. It sounded to me at first fascistic, even reminiscent of the infamous *Arbeit Macht Frei* over the gate into Auschwitz. It didn't make any sense. I tried and

The Calexico Chamber of Commerce found a haunting slogan to use in its struggle with post-9/11 Homeland Security rules and regulations.

failed to put the legend into some sort of context. So I connected with Earl Roberts to find out what it was supposed to mean, to learn the genesis of Efficiency Is Security.

Calexico wants more efficient border crossing.

"Customs has the resources to be able to process vehicles and pedestrians more efficiently," Roberts explained to me. "They have the knowledge, they have the ability, and they keep holding up traffic because they seem to think that the longer the wait is, the more secure the country is. We get these comments on the news saying, 'Well the wait at the border is two or three hours, and oh, those guys must be doing their jobs.'"

I had been listening to KXO and hearing more traffic reports, almost all detailing those border wait times. Calexico, Mexicali's tiny market town to the north and gateway to the United States of America, relies on that border traffic being efficient for its economic security.

"For generations it's relied on it," Roberts agreed. "For generations the border wait's been five, ten, fifteen minutes. People on the Mexican side count on coming across the border and purchasing their groceries

The protest slogan is posted by Calexico businesses to make clear their distaste for the long waits border travelers heading north suffer since September 11, 2001.

on the U.S. side. Our families here that have had these businesses have depended on that business. Now, all of a sudden, customs is keeping lines at a couple hours, and people don't come over any more. It's breaking with tradition, it's breaking with habits. Even if we made those lines back to ten, fifteen minutes, we've broken a lot of the habits."

A lot of the relationships originating on the north side going south were also broken. George, I knew, used to just spontaneously take Maria down to Lucerna, their favorite restaurant in Mexicali, for a nice dinner. But the couple stopped those Mexican dinner dates because of the border wait. Earl Roberts was convinced that an hour and a half, two hours' delay while searches take place or paperwork is checked does not equal security.

"No, because it's not an hour and half or two hours to search a particular vehicle, it's an hour and a half, two hours that you spend in line waiting for everybody else to get searched. If I'm a customs inspector and I've been working at this port for thirty years, I get a memo from Washington—from somebody who has never been down here before—that says I must ask all these questions to every single person that comes up to my lane. They've got a list of seven or eight questions that they have to ask. Here I am, I come up to the line, and this gentleman might be my neighbor for who knows how long, and I say, 'Hey Joe, how's it going?' And the inspector must say, 'Well, Mr. Roberts, let me ask you your name first. Let me ask you' the next question, the next question, the next question, and we'll spend two, three minutes on me when they could be checking somebody that is unknown to them, that is nervous, that they're trained to look for. People who are doing illegal things. But they're not allowed to, because Washington gives them orders on how they have to do things."

Earl Roberts Jr., as president of the Calexico Chamber of Commerce, is in an intriguing and odd position right now as he brings the dysfunctionality of the post-9/11 border to life with his role-playing story. Of course he joins most Americans in wanting his country to be secure, and he recognizes the authority of Washington, D.C., but from his perspective in Calexico he sees a complete disconnect: Washington doesn't understand the needs and problems of the town where he lives and works, and the citizens that he serves in his capacity at the chamber of commerce.

"What we'd like is for Washington to allow their people, their federal agents, to do their work the way they were trained to do, and not hold them to a certain standard of making them ask things that are just holding up the line."

Hence, Efficiency Is Security?

"I'm doing everything I can to try to get these guys to process traffic faster. We've sent a group of businessmen and local political leaders up to Washington twice now, to talk to our congressmen, to talk to our senators, to talk to the people at Customs Border Protection, to try to get them to emphasize efficiency at the border." Roberts felt Washington was listening. "It's been quite positive. The truth is we have an excellent port director here that is trying to work with the community. He meets with us quite often. They've been changing things and making them better. Lines are not as bad as they were last year, for example."

An example of hyperlocal politics moving the machine.

"Yeah. A little bit, but not as much as we'd like. We'd like to go to the old days before 9/11, where we have ten-, fifteen-minutes wait times at peak hours."

Earl Roberts served as both the president of the Calexico Chamber of Commerce and the owner of an import/export business. He was in an ideal position to give me some examples of how the border waits have negatively affected business on the American side.

"The examples are clear to see." He escorted me toward what I noticed the minute I set foot on the Calexico sidewalks. "You just drive through downtown Calexico and see all the storefronts closed. That's directly a result of these new policies and these long border waits. We had a business here called Western Auto, been here for forty years, right downtown, it was where everybody went. They closed down about three months ago. They specifically say that they cannot do business with two-hour wait times. The local community can't support that business; we're a small community. We need the business from Mexico. As the president of the chamber of commerce, I'm here to represent the local businesses, and it's been very, very difficult."

His speech seems so odd, it's almost a reverse of the stereotype. Calexico is basically just a small town, officially a city, but it's only thirty thousand people or so, not a metropolis, and its merchants are dependent on the trade from the south. Gringos dependent on Mexicans, gringos whose own government is keeping customers from coming north efficiently to patronize their stores. President Bush told Americans to go shopping after 9/11 and keep the economy humming. Then his administration's policies battered the sales of stores in Calexicos from San Diego to Brownsville.

It's a sad story Roberts knows well from sharing it with his colleagues. "Every single border town along the United States–Mexico border depends on the Mexican side. And you know what?" He was just warming up, pleased for the receptive audience I provided for his heartfelt business sermon. "To a certain degree the Mexican side depends on the U.S. side. Along the north side of Mexico are the populated areas. We have all these people that we can do business with, and over years and years and generations we have been doing business with them." He was frustrated, baffled, and upset as he announced the obvious. "I mean, Mexico's not our enemy. Mexico's our friend. Sometimes we treat them as though they're our enemy. You know how many billions we are wasting on setting up a Berlin Wall with Mexico? For what purpose?"

I made it clear I agreed with his assessment, and I kept listening to this astute Calexico businessman tell me what is so obvious and logical that it defies imagination that it still needed explaining.

"You don't want these people to come work over here? Then take 10 percent of those inspectors that you're hiring, and use them to give fines to the people that are harboring these people, giving these people jobs." He walked us through the reality. "They wouldn't come over if there weren't any jobs. They wouldn't be coming over. Why do we spend billions on something when we could be using that money for infrastructure or for helping the needy or . . ." He was exasperated and just said, "et cetera."

I told him about looking at the so-called fence and how it immediately conjured up memories for me of the Berlin Wall and my experiences living in Germany before the Iron Curtain became history.

"God, that's great that you say that. I've said that to everybody, and this is the first time I get a positive from it." He laughed for a second but stopped when I asked him for his emotional response to the slice the wall cuts between his two cities. It was clear to me that he thinks of Mexicali as his city, too. Or at least as a familial extension of his Calexico.

"It's hard for me to understand why we want to alienate ourselves from Mexico. Mexico's a great country. I've lived in this border city all my life. My friends live down there, and they live up here. A lot of us have dual nationalities. We're very intermingled. All of a sudden the people up north want to separate us. It's hard to swallow. Because the power comes from Washington, it's hard for us to fight the giant. But there's no need to do what Washington is doing."

He cited our recent history accurately as he made clear once again that Mexico and Mexicans are not our enemies. "Nine-eleven happens. None of the terrorists came through Mexico. They came through airports and the Canadian border. But all of a sudden it's like every single one of those trucks coming across from Mexico is a terrorist. The truck driver is being treated like a terrorist, and it's really holding up commerce, and it's affecting relationships and people's lives." He feels alienated and separated from those making decisions that radically changed his life, probably for the rest of his life. "People up north don't understand it."

Markos and I felt we understood Earl Roberts, from our experiences living and working along the Iron Curtain. "As hard as you try to believe that there is no parallel between cold war Berlin and contemporary California," Markos mused, "it is nearly impossible not to be struck by the physical similarities and separation. The contrasts

An ominous threat or intriguing promise from alongside the highway.

between the two sides are equally stunning as they used to be in pre-1989 Eastern Europe."

Washington is just about as blind to local needs and realities as it looks to the Other coming down from the north as it is when it succumbs to fears about the masses coming up from the south. I checked in with Mike Bradley, the mayor of Sarnia in Ontario, for a taste of how post-9/11 U.S. policies affect the day-to-day lives of Americans and Canadians living in the northern borderlands. Outside the immediate orbit of capital cities—whether they be Mexico City, Washington, D.C., or Ottawa—grassroots leaders such as chamber of commerce president Earl Roberts and the mayor struggle with local problems and see things with a different perspective than those cloistered inside the Ottawa beltway, or its equivalent.

"Oh, there's no question," agreed Mayor Bradley. "The disease is the same on both sides of the border where there's amnesia about how the rest of the country functions when you move away from the capital. We deal with it all the time, particularly as a border city. Obviously, the border relationship goes back a long time, and it's always been a very strong and good working relationship. But particularly since 2001, the ideas brought forward from both Ottawa and Washington have been very damaging to the relationship and also to the local economies." Sounds like Calexico all over again. One of the ways that damage manifests itself is with the increasing difficulty of making the physical crossing—whether it be from Mexico to the United States or from Canada to the United States—for those who are engaged in friendly tourism or important commerce.

"The relationship between Canada and the United States used to be all about trade and tourism," the mayor said, but no more. "It's now all about security, and the trade and tourism are on the back burner." Mayor Bradley pointed out the error of this strategy, given that the biggest trading partner of the United States is not China or Japan, but Canada. "I understand the need for security, but what we're seeing is just pure overkill, which is crippling the economy of not just border cities." Given Canada's role in U.S. trade, he said, he considered every Canadian city essentially a border city.

The mayor traced the deterioration to September 11, 2001.

"Canadians obviously share the horror of what happened that day. But we saw an opportunity for the United States to lead the world and to build a coalition of partners that would deal with the tragedy, how it occurred, and with the people that brought it about. Since then it's been a squandered opportunity, in my view. We've seen things like the American Coast Guard wanting to use the Great Lakes as a free-fire military zone. Myself and other Canadian and American mayors were able to fight that off."

A free-fire zone on the Great Lakes? Who knew, except those who lived on the lakes or were otherwise intimately involved in these policy plans. This nightmarish scenario was another example of the types of radical executive decisions the Bush administration made or tried to make under the smokescreen of fear it capitalized on and generated following the attacks on the World Trade Center and the Pentagon.

"We're seeing all sorts of new restrictions on how people can travel," complained Mayor Bradley. "The tone and attitude at the land borders," he sounded sadly resigned, "it's just extremely negative. There's not even an attempt to welcome people to the country," he said about the U.S. authorities. "And God forbid if you're from another country and immigrated to Canada, you're going to have major problems." This change of attitude and policies directly affects Sarnia. "What's happened is that it discourages people from travel. We understand," he said about national caution, the need to police the nation's frontiers. "We do the same with our borders. You try to protect your own interests and not allow people in that you don't want there."

But border controls have changed from the pragmatic to the dysfunctional. Mayor Bradley turned his gaze to his office window. "I'm looking at Port Huron, Michigan. We're used to traveling back and forth and doing it in a secure manner and in a timely manner. But now people need photo I.D. to cross. I'm not opposed to that." What he failed to embrace was the pending U.S. law requiring Canadians and Americans to show a passport to get into the States, not just a driver's license or other form of government-issued identification. "It will have a very destructive impact on the Canadian border cities and provinces, but also on American border cities. They're going to have a very difficult time coping with the fact that Canadians won't be coming across, and Americans won't be coming across to Canada because they're going to require a passport to return home."

Homeland Security secretary during the George W. Bush era, Michael Chertoff, had strong words for the mayor and other critics of the new U.S. policy who labeled the new northern border controls excessive and inconvenient. "It's time to grow up and recognize that if we're serious about this threat [presumably his opened-ended use of the word *threat* meant terrorism], we've got to take reasonable, measured, but nevertheless determined, steps to getting better security." Among those intimately familiar with the border and irritated with Chertoff's remarks at the time was Republican congressman Tom Reynolds, who represented Buffalo. Representative Reynolds pointed to delayed and changing laws and rules for Americans and Canadians traveling from one country to the other and said that Chertoff "frankly has as much credibility on telling people to 'grow up' as Geoffrey the Giraffe."

"So what's wrong with just staying home?" I asked the mayor. "What's so important about Port Huron to you? You've got everything you need in Sarnia: restaurants, theaters, your home is there. You're looking across to Port Huron. What is it about the other side that is intriguing? You can get everything you need in Sarnia. Why bother trekking across to Port Huron?"

The mayor understood borders and their place in our lives from an up-close-and-personal perspective.

"I was born and raised in Australia. I came to Canada with my family as immigrants and have been here now for nineteen years, in this community. I've always treasured the relationship with Port Huron, and I've tried to develop it. In fact, in 1994, much to my surprise, the Port Huron paper endorsed my reelection campaign."

A distinct example of the artificiality of political borders.

"It's an example of trying to build relationship and build bridges." Since 9/11, the immigrant mayor told me, such constructive relationships have become much more difficult. "I really admire the American political system in the sense of how democratic it can be," he said. "I also like the initiative that I see: it's not what we can't do, it's what we can do. That is not really part of the Canadian psychology. It's good to mix those two worlds together. I always viewed it that we had the best of both worlds. That American attitude and the Canadian reserve. The balance was just wonderful."

But it wasn't just a psychological loss. The mayor quantified the changes in a dramatic manner.

"We have a major casino and a racetrack here that has slot machines. As a border city, a great majority of that traffic is American. In the last quarter we took a severe hit at both facilities. We understand what the reason is; it's simply the American tourist and gambler is not traveling here because they think they might need a passport or they're concerned about the security delays." Seventy-five percent of the casino's revenue was generated pre-9/11 by American tourist dollars.

Mayor Mike Bradley is a cosmopolitan by definition. He was uprooted from Australia, started a new life in Sarnia ("In the middle of a Canadian winter I question why my parents moved from Australia!"), and watches from the New World as Europe tears down artificial borders, while the U.S.–Canadian frontier is increasingly fortified.

"The border between Canada and the United States was advertised as the world's friendliest border. That has totally changed. Borders are very artificial. We saw, unfortunately, on September eleventh that if someone really wants to accomplish a goal, they will accomplish it and a border is really incidental to that."

As the mayor looked out of his office window at the Michigan side of the line, I asked him if it wasn't true that if I traveled east or west of Sarnia just a few miles I would get to places where the border is simply unprotected and one could cross unnoticed.

His response was truly Canadian droll. "I'm scared to say that, in case Lou Dobbs is listening." But he confirmed the impossibility of securing the line. "In the summertime here on the St. Clair River, there are thousands of boats going back and forth. That's the reality. And that's true of any border."

Not that the mayor wanted his border to be equated with the Mexican–American line at Calexico.

"We get beat up quite a bit by the right wing in the United States who look at this porous Canadian border." We were back in Lou Dobbs Land. Amazing the potency of his self-serving careerist demagoguery. "We get linked together with the Mexican border and the illegal immigration. That's not the issue on the northern border; this is not the same as the Mexican border as it relates to illegal immigration."

I told the mayor that if things get too bleak for him in Sarnia, he could escape across the border and come to San Francisco, that we would harbor him. It was an offer he said plenty of his political opponents in Canada would endorse.

One Canadian who knows firsthand that the United States government can be as twisted in its relationships with those north of the border as it can be with those south of the border is the author Farley Mowat. I caught up with him via telephone from his rural redoubt in one of the Canadian Maritime Provinces and told him I was pleased to talk with him, that his legendary life dealing with U.S. border controls provided an intriguing historical perspective to current border crises.

"Happy to be with you." He paused and added, "I think." It was clear I was in for a curmudgeonly ride.

I told Mowat that I wanted to check in with him because of the relatively famous incident during the era of President Ronald Reagan when he was invited south to California to speak at Chico State University. He was stopped at the border and turned back home, refused entry as a visiting dignitary. I wanted to hear that old story from his point of view in the face of ever-increasing restrictions on the American–Canadian border, restrictions prompted both by the attacks of September 11, 2001, and by the attempts of migrants without proper U.S. documents seeking to enter the States via alternative routes as the Mexican border was hardened.

Mowat's books have sold millions in dozens of languages. *Never Cry Wolf* is his classic defense of wolves, and *My Discovery of America* tells the story of his tête-à-tête with the Reagan administration.

"I wouldn't have a hope in hell of getting across that border now," he said, but added that worry about such a trip was not a factor in his life. "I think I'm secure; I'm not endangered by any further invitations."

I offered to provide the challenge by inviting him to come join me in San Francisco at his earliest convenience.

"What kind of vodka have you got?"

I informed him that we had access to the best vodka, that the populous Russian community in San Francisco means that our shelves are stocked.

"Ah, sounds good."

But aside from the vodka opportunities, I wanted Mowat's particular point of view regarding the relationship between the United States and its neighbors, his take on the reality about this mythically long unpatrolled and unfenced border that he came up against in a severe manner.

"I offended against the dignity of that central tenet of American belief," he explained, "the military. I was accused actually of being a threat to the U.S. Armed Services. I have to tell you, I've received a number of honors in my time, including the Order of Canada, but nothing approaches the magnitude of this honor that I, mere little Farley Mowat, was considered a threat to the U.S. Armed Forces! Holy cow! How could you better that one, eh?"

It is an amazing story, punctuated nicely with his stereotypical Canadian "eh" at the end of his speeches. The story defies belief: Mowat was denied the opportunity to speak at Chico State because he threatened to aim his hunting rifle at an American B-52 bomber flying five miles high—and pull the trigger.

"I had offended one of the biggest lobbies in the United States, the National Wildlife League or Organization, whatever they call themselves. You know the gunners and the hookers who run the conservation movement in much of the U.S. of A. I wrote a book called *Sea of Slaughter*, which details the destruction of animate creation in the eastern seaboard of North America over the period since the Europeans first got here. It was about to be published in the States, and the National Wildlife, what?—I can't remember their last name—the National Wildlife assholes didn't want it published. They found allies who said, 'Oh yeah, well, we've been keeping this guy under observation for years. You know he's actually friendly with some Russians.' They had a file on me in Washington, and they said, 'We'll get him because he once threatened to shoot at B-52 bombers that were flying over his home in Newfoundland on fail-safe missions armed with nuclear weapons pointed at the Soviet Union. He said that he would shoot them down if they continued to go over his house, because they were invading his private property without permission.' "

It was a great publicity gimmick at the time, designed to draw attention to the mutually assured destruction tactics of the Americans and the Soviets. What an image: a wild writer out in the middle-of-nowhere Canada pointing his lone rifle at a ludicrously out-of-range target flying over him with impunity.

"The problem is," he pointed out, "and it's very simple—it's not a problem but it's a characteristic of all bureaucracies everywhere in every nation—they have no sense of humor. Not the vaguest trace. If they had, they wouldn't be in politics, would they?"

Few politicians seem able to laugh at themselves. There are too few laughs in general among those practicing statecraft. That's certainly true of border politics. Cheech Marin did a bang-up job of mocking the border realities in his send-up *Born in East L.A.*, and the tragicomedy mockumentary *A Day without a Mexican* brought the theme up-to-date for the twenty-first century. There's a terrific scene in *The Day after Tomorrow* when the Mexican authorities grant refugee status to gringos fleeing south from climate change. But that's Hollywood. Farley Mowat was dealing with Washington.

"Probably the only mitigating factor in the survival of the human animal is that some of us have a sense of humor. Without that, we would long since have become extinct."

Not that Mowat fails to recognize the role that a state plays and that governance plays in modern society. With his lifelong interest in conservation and natural habitats, he acknowledges that there's a role for government.

"Yeah, there's a role, but they don't play it. It's a role that they adopt, in order to control us, to do as they damn well please. I have never submitted myself to it, not even during the Second World War when I was an infantry soldier for a good many years. It's a contradiction in terms to think that we can be governed by any large organization. We can be only governed by our own will and that only can be exercised effectively within the tribal zone, as it were, within a group of maybe two or three hundred people. Then the individual can be an effective leader. Beyond that, we lose effectiveness and the whole thing turns into rat shit, actually, as you can see. Look," he told me from his luxury of a hideaway out in the countryside, "I am, I guess, a primitive anarchist. I believe in government but not government of the many, by the few."

So then what do we do with a metropolis like Toronto or San Francisco?

Farley Mowat laughed and acknowledged, "That's right. I don't know." And he laughed again. Before we said good-bye, Mowat concurred with my conclusion that being turned back at the border served him well, added to his personal legend.

"I was quite pleased actually when I was forbidden to come down. I issued a counter-ultimatum: I said I would come again if I were invited by the president of the United States, personally. And if he sent Air Force One to pick me up. For a while there were some people around here where I live who kept peering up in the sky when they heard a jet go by. They said, 'Could that be him or could that be a B-52 looking for you?' He never sent his jet. I never got my apology. However, some senator—I've forgotten who he was now—managed to persuade somebody in government to withdraw my name from the blacklist. I was quietly told that anytime I wanted to come across I could do so if I would blacken my face and wear a suitable disguise. I don't have a suitable disguise and I didn't want to come, so I have never come."

Blackface or no blackface, Farley Mowat has not returned to the United States, and he insisted my vodka offer was not enough of a lure.

"To be quite frank with you, until you get your problems straightened away down there, I feel safer on my side of the border."

We talked before Barack Obama was elected president, and I told him I may well feel safer on his side of the border too, but that I felt an obligation to stay in the States and work for change, that I hoped to be able to foment some positive response to the hysteria in the borderlands. He laughed again.

"You better hurry up and cross, because the way things are going it's going to be an impermeable border before too long." His sardonic pessimism continued as he told me about his memoir *Otherwise*. "What it's about is the other inhabitants of this planet, who I consider are probably a lot wiser than the human species. At my state of antiquity, I'm looking forward to a peaceful end, and I'm not willing to sacrifice what little time I've got left in any attempt to resolve the problems of the human race. As far as I'm concerned, the human race is doomed, and probably the sooner it goes, the better."

I met up with Dr. Melani Guinn and her husband, Chris, the former Border Patrol agent, for dinner in El Centro. They picked the place,

The Virgin of Guadalupe, peeling but still keeping watch on the Imperial Valley.

a glorified taquería called Zarape, and Markos and I arrived early, eager
to just relax for a few minutes and digest the kaleidoscope of images
I was collecting. We sat in the shade at a table out front. It was late
afternoon (I was getting accustomed to the early dinner hour in the
Valley), and the hot, dry air was pushed past my face by a cooling wind.
It felt good. I waited for a drink.

After quite some time a jolly waitress came out for my order. "It's
nice out here!" she said, surprised to find me. Locals head inside, seeking the cooled air from the droning air conditioner. Melani and Chris
brought along a friend and colleague, the former editor of the *Imperial Valley News,* Bret Kofford. I asked them about the Valley pecking
order: Calexico south of The Eight, El Centro haughty as the county
seat, Holtville struggling to hold on to its small-town identity.

"If you live in Paris," Chris said, "you look down on New York."
He was relaxed, his mountain bike parked by the restaurant. He likes
to exercise in the heat. Crazy. "And if you live in New York, you look
down on Los Angeles."

Okay.

"If you live in Los Angeles," he continued with his explanation, "you look down on San Diego. If you live in San Diego, you look down on El Cajon. If you live in El Cajon, you look down on El Centro. If you live in El Centro, you look down on . . ." He paused and Melani yelped, "You look down on Niland!"

Bret agreed, "If you live in Niland, well, it's getting pretty rough."

What's wrong with Niland?

"Oh, man," said Melani. Her academic language relaxed in the informal atmosphere of the taquería.

"It's poor," Bret began the explanation.

"It's the apocalypse," voted Chris.

"Yeah. Exactly," added Melani.

"Rough town," said Bret. He went to graduate school in the South and took a job at the *Savannah Morning News*. He wanted to return to California and signed on as managing editor at the *Imperial Valley News*. He left the newspaper to teach; it afforded him more time to work on his screenplays. He liked the heat, and the Valley. "My wife is from Mexicali. I have a good job teaching English at San Diego State in Calexico. Aside from grading papers all the time, it's great to be a college English teacher."

"Those are the top two reasons people live here," Chris said. "Jobs and wife. Yeah, spouse. Usually it seems like a wife. The guy comes here and marries a girl from here, and her whole family is here." So they stay.

But Melani said she saw something more at play for migrants into the Valley, a chance to reinvent a life. "It's sort of the land where you can repair past mistakes." She pointed to herself as an example and laughed. "I mean, I get to be chair of the Humanities Division after I threw away my academic career at Berkeley. I thought, 'I don't want to be an academic. I'm moving to New York. I'm going to do something totally different.' I chose not to publish. I didn't really like that part of academia. I just got the doctorate and said I'm going to New York. I'm going to be an actress. I just tossed it, didn't even try. They were saying, 'Your dissertation is good, it's marketable. Turn it into a book.' It was about the abortion debate. It was very timely, all that stuff. I was like, 'Nah. I hate it. I hate teaching. I hate all this stuff, bye-bye.'"

I had watched her closely in the classroom. She was a natural teacher, obviously loving the work and loved by the students.

In New York she met Chris; he was hired by the Border Patrol and they moved to the Valley. "Here's so much opportunity," she said.

"Esthetically it may not be the most beautiful place in the world," said Chris.

"Sometimes," Bret said, "you can be driving out in the country and go, wow, it's beautiful. You see the farms and then you get these purple, orange sunsets. But the really good thing is that the people in the Valley are nice."

"I agree. I totally agree," said Melani. "People are very genuine. There's not like a lot of pretense, and I don't think it's true of all small towns. You can get real phony people in a small town, because there's a lot more need to protect your reputation."

What makes Valley residents different than those phonies?

"People don't give a crap about their reputations here," suggested Bret. "There's sort of a general acceptance of each other. As Melani was saying, people don't really judge you."

"I think it's partly isolation, that we're kind of isolated," offered Melani, when we kept seeking an explanation for what makes the Valley unique. "But I think it's the heat, too."

The harshness of the environment?

"Yeah, because you can be thinking you're the shit. You know, a woman with all the perfect stuff going on. Then you get out in 120, and you melt. You got a bit o' pit stains . . ."

"Pit stains are generally accepted here," Bret chimed in. "No one would ever condemn you for them."

"You cannot be looking good in this heat," said Melani. "You can barely wear shoes."

"It's the nice mix of cultures, I think," said Bret. I kept pushing for more explanations of what makes the Valley special. "This place was settled by people from Oklahoma, Arkansas, Texas."

Chris interrupted Bret's rhapsody: "We're doomed!"

"Poor people," Bret specified.

"The dust bowl," moaned Chris.

"You couldn't go past Yuma if you didn't have two hundred dollars," Melanie said. "So all those Super Dust Bowl people got stuck there."

"And poor people from Mexico and poor people from China," added Bret.

"I would say there's no upper class, and that's part of the reason it's special," said Melani. "The farmers are rich but they're not upper-class."

"They're like the ruling class," said Chris.

"But they don't have cultural capital," said Melani. "They just have money. They don't really have anything to kick anyone out of. Everyone can go to the Barbara Worth."

"Our dog shits in their fields," Chris offered; he is a natural troublemaker.

"Oh, maybe they have a condo in San Diego," said Melani. "Big deal. People here make fun of pretentious people."

We were all leaving clean plates; it was typical Cal-Mex eats. Nothing—to use the word of the afternoon—pretentious. But tasty and filling. And cheap. Bret got up to go home, dreaming of one of his screenplays, the one that some producers in Hollywood were considering. Chris headed for his bike. Melani was driving home. A car alarm went off. Nobody looked up at it.

That evening I slipped into my seat in the San Diego State University Calexico campus Rodney Auditorium for the candidates' debate. The

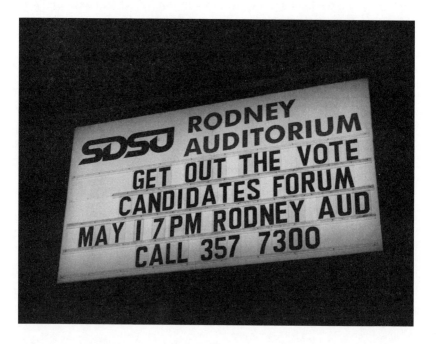

The San Diego State University Calexico auditorium, site of electioneering by Calexico politicians anxious to win border-town government offices.

political elite of Calexico were assembled, the movers and shakers of South of The Eight.

John Pierre Menvielle, running for the Imperial Irrigation District Division 2. Nothing much more powerful than the IID in a valley that would dry up without irrigation from the Colorado River. Think he might be related to Menvielle Road, the route to the new Calexico East border crossing? Perez, Gutierrez, and Gonzalez were signed up to explain why they should go to Sacramento representing the Eightieth Assembly District. Ramirez was running for the Fifty-first congressional seat. And eight candidates were vying for seats on the Calexico city council.

The language for the speeches and for the questions and answers was English. But in Calexico, where the language of day-to-day activities so often is Spanish, a simultaneous interpreter sat under headphones, with a microphone, performing a Spanish translation for those in the audience who preferred español. One of the candidates scheduled to speak did not show up, and I was told he skipped the evening's campaigning because he knew that his English wasn't adequate for the public event.

Mayor Lewis Pacheco, assailed in the *Imperial Valley News* for practicing compadrismo, took the stage. He was greeted with applause. "Thank you," he said and came right to his first point. "I just want to take a couple of minutes to explain what is happening with the newspaper. I was not given a chance to comment or make any kind of response to that report." He paused, and then with a deliberate voice in a slow cadence he announced, "Do not believe what you read in the newspaper. This," he said about the charges of nepotism, "is not true. What was in the newspaper was incorrect and untrue. A letter to the editor will be sent out tomorrow with the true facts." He directed the audience to the city's website, suggesting the minutes of the meetings in question would vindicate him. "Thank you. I just needed to state that, because I have my family to think of—I see them every morning and every night."

His body language turned apologetic as he faced neighbors about the state of the city, reminding them of his credentials: he has been an elementary school principal for twenty-three years and served four years on the city council, with one term as mayor. He looked tired as he explained the city's miserable financial condition and his efforts to combat the problems.

"We always look at ways of finding jobs. We've hired a young man to work on economic development. He's searching to bring in work and industry." The mayor's voice was weary, heartfelt, and sad. "He's meeting with Mexicali. I know people are saying, 'What's being done?'" He answered with an explanation that sounded like a plea for understanding. "It's just hard to compete with the *maquiladoras mexicanas*. How can we compete with people earning eight dollars a day?"

Here was the grassroots reality of globalization for the borderlands.

"It's impossible to compete with that type of labor force that we have in Mexico."

Each candidate was allowed only three minutes for an opening statement, with more time later for questions. Mayor Pacheco used his to offer a State of the City message. He explained the increase in water rates. Old pipes were cracking, the infrastructure was rebuilt. "Little by little, we're trying to make Calexico a better place."

"Thank you, Mr. Pacheco," announced the moderator. "Your time is up."

"Thank you very much." He almost seemed relieved as he added, to renewed applause, "June third, vote for Lewis Pacheco." He moved off the stage, stooped and with a gait that made it look as if he felt that his political time was indeed up. (After the June election he was again boldly smiling out from the homepage of the Calexico website, reelected.)

As the candidates mingled with their families and supporters following the Great Calexico Debate, Mayor Lewis Pacheco joined his wife and daughter for their congratulations. Daughter Roxanne was a familiar face. She had been the lead debater in Dr. Guinn's class the day before, arguing for tighter border controls in Calexico.

"Your daughter was magnificent," I told Mr. and Mrs. Pacheco. We chatted for a few minutes before I asked him about the vicious editorial in the *Imperial Valley News*. He again dismissed the charges of nepotism as old news.

"Oh that, that goes back to the early sixties and late fifties. You get your compadre in. Don't fill out the application, just come on in and you've got the job. The old compadre system. Those days are gone. You've got people who are going to fight for their rights, and women have just as much opportunity as a man does for a position now. You can't pull a fast one."

But the newspaper really does seem to have it out for Calexico.

Pacheco dismissed the newspaper, too, as being irrelevant to the fast-growing Calexico and its financial pains. The 2008 credit crisis and rapidly escalating fuel costs were stunting Calexico's projected growth. Mexico and Mexicans, he said, were pivotal to keeping his city in business.

"We've got a million people across the border that walk across and are buying milk, eggs, fresh chicken, bologna, bread, on a daily basis. We've got people crossing at two-thirty in the morning, three o'clock, four o'clock. Coming across to go to work over here, and they work in the fields. They go as far as Coachella, Blythe, and Yuma. It's an agricultural haven here. Folks on this side of the border are not going to work in the fields at four o'clock in the morning picking up watermelon and pitching cantaloupes, picking cotton and pulling out carrots." He makes it sound like poetry: picking up watermelon and pitching cantaloupes, picking cotton and pulling out carrots. "That's not for folks on this side of the border. So these people generate our economy. Hard workers walk across and labor in the fields; the haves come over in their cars, go to Walmart and fill up the parking lot with Mexicali plates and are buying American products." Walmart sends tax money to Calexico City Hall. Again, it's a role reversal. Americans used to go south to Mexico for the bargains.

For Calexicans, the pickings are lean.

"If you work for the school district, the phone company, or IID, you got it made. Everybody else is earning below $13,000, $15,000, $20,000. We don't have a lot of job offers. The kids leave to go to school, they go to San Diego and stay. There are no jobs here." Calexico must attract new industry, he told me. After hearing his laments from the stage just minutes before, I asked him if he remained optimistic.

"I am," he bravely answered, and he was standing straight again, poised and elegant in his dark business suit, "because I've been here all my life."

"You don't want to see it die."

"No." Again, he pointed south. "If it weren't for our neighbor, we'd shrivel up. We would shrivel up. No question about it. They're keeping the Valley moving. These people shop in El Centro. They shop in the mall. They shop. They have the money."

"So the harder we make it for them to come across, the more trouble you're in?"

"Yeah. Yeah."

"Do you figure that most of those who are jumping the fence are looking for work and not looking to sell drugs and cause problems?"

"Yeah. Yeah."

"They want to support their families?"

"Yeah, I agree. Once they jump that fence, they can go as far as Chicago and New York. They're everywhere. They're doing gardening. When I see those how-to-do-it shows about gardening and they show the working crew, they're Hispanic. They're indigenous people from the interior of Yucatán or somewhere. Look at that guy. He's the guy who's selling chocolates and bubble gum on the border. They send their money home. He's here illegally, I'm sure."

"Is there a danger that Calexico could fall by the wayside and end up a ghost town?"

"I don't think so." He says it again: "I don't think so." His voice sounds positive and enthusiastic. The apologetic and resigned tone he used up on stage during the debate is gone. He's back to a Calexico booster role. "We're trying to generate work here. Families have been here all their lives; they don't want to move. People that come across stay here because they want to be close to their ties in Mexico. We see a lot of Hispanics that do it legally, correctly, by getting immigration papers. They live here in town. Then on the weekends, on Fridays, they go across and spend Saturday, Sunday at the ranch and help out, and they come back Sunday night. With the proximity of the border, they don't want to leave Calexico. The further away you get from this border, the less Spanish we'll speak. If you stay here, you've got to know two languages. My daughter," he says about Roxanne, "has a hard time getting a job, because she's not truly bilingual. A lot of people in El Centro and Brawley go to the Walmart in Calexico, and the employee will speak to them in Spanish, and they just get burned. It just infuriates them. Why doesn't this employee speak English? But if it weren't for the neighbors, we wouldn't be surviving."

I met with Calexico city councilwoman Carmen Durazo out on the street in front of the auditorium. It was late, but it was still warm. Her tailored suit was crimson on carmine, setting off her earnest look. She extended a hearty welcome to Calexico to me, and I told her I felt welcome and that I was trying to understand what was special about the Calexico borderlands that allowed me to feel so at home.

"The reason is we have a very warm climate." She wasn't joking. She believed the hot weather was a factor. "If you notice, we're already in the upper nineties." It was still spring. "I think the heat translates to the people that live here; they're very warm people. Some people have come to Calexico and said, 'It's too hot, I'm not staying.' But once you step foot here, everyone is friendly. It's a warm environment and so people stay. It's still a small town—even though we're growing into a city—where everyone knows everyone, and everyone is proud of our community, and we try to be helpful."

Lovely. But it is not just a warm climate. It is a harsh and hot climate. Downtown, as the councilwoman herself expressed from the podium during the debate, is in serious trouble; there's a sense of the place being passed by, of almost being a ghost town. Why would people be coming here? Why would they be staying here? Why would they be coming back after they go off to study elsewhere? Why would they want to return?

"It happened to me." She told me she went off to her university studies and came back. "The reason I came was the warmth of the people. This is home. You don't get that living someplace else, when you've been raised in a community." She worried that not enough Calexicans are returning home despite the affordable housing, because there are not enough challenging jobs. "My daughter just got her doctorate at the University of California in San Francisco, she just finished, and she can't get a job with her doctorate here in her particular specialty. It's hard. She would like to come home, because family is very important here. It's all about family. And when new people come, we treat you as family."

But family is important everywhere. There are small towns everywhere. Is Calexico just another small American town, or is it something else?

"We're 'border brats,'" she told me, insisting it was not a derogatory description. "We've gotten the best out of Mexico, and we've gotten the best out of America. We're bilingual, we're bicultural. We appreciate the rest of the world because of that. The majority of the population is Hispanic, so therefore no one knows that we are a minority. We grow up strong and proud. That makes a difference in how people feel about themselves. You have to feel good about yourself inside to welcome others."

Spoken like a true politician, a true American, a vibrant Calexican. What an appealing place she painted. Yet, I told her, I was hearing disparaging attacks on Calexico, reading them in the newspaper. Even the term "south of The Eight" seemed to suggest some aspersion of suggested inferiority.

The councilwoman paused and then told me, "Some people don't understand Calexico, because they live in the rest of the Valley. Imperial Valley is made up of fairly isolated communities. In San Francisco your communities are linked with each other. But we grew up quite differently as communities. We all have different passions and different interests. They," those Others north of The Eight, "see us, some of them see us, as different. But I think El Centro is different. Brawley is different. Holtville is different. And Calexico is different. It depends on who resided there, who were the immigrants that came. Everyone's very proud of their culture. So south of The Eight is a good thing."

Even with the post-9/11 security, about thirty thousand Mexicans cross into Calexico every day to work and shop. She called my attention to the place names: Mexicali and Calexico—combinations of California and Mexico, of course. "They're sister cities. They grew together. We didn't even know what the border was. We depend on each other. We communicate well with each other and work well with each other."

It's a relationship that transcends the frailties of their dysfunctional respective national capitals and governments.

"I've been to Washington a couple of times, because we have such a hard time crossing that border, and I get so many complaints from people in Mexico. Why do we have to wait two hours in 120-degree weather? It's dangerous. It's unhealthy. Smelling carbon monoxide. Even pedestrians have to wait that long. Washington doesn't understand the border region." She said she is convinced the lobbying is making progress. "They're going to open up more lanes on the eastside, and they're opening up a new port in Calexico in 2011." She said priorities are skewed toward addressing illegal border crossings. "I think we should have more of an emphasis on the people that are crossing legally. We're not supporting them."

I told her I had crossed over to Mexicali for dinner the night before, and that Markos and I had enjoyed a fine late-night restaurant with energetic mariachi music. Why would Mexicans wait in line to come north when there are spectacular restaurants over there? There's a Costco over there. There's a Walmart over there. There are fine local shops. What is the Calexico draw?

"We Americans have an international reputation for business. The American dream has fueled that. Some of the things they offer in Mexico are actually more expensive than they are in the United States. Same product. It's because of different tax bases." But she's convinced it's not just price. "There is a trust in an American business. Because they shopped here for years and years. It can be the same product at Walmart here that came from China that is in the Mexicali Walmart, and yet they will trust the product in the Calexico Walmart. We also have better exchange and refund policies. It's a different type of a business environment with much, much more clarity."

There's been a reversal. Instead of Americans going to Mexico for bargains, Mexicans are coming to America for bargains.

Not so fast, she said. "It works both ways. We're a border community. They come and go. We both cross back and forth. There's certain things you can purchase in Mexico, like you said, the fine dining at restaurants, that are much cheaper and a big choice, because it's over a million and a half people in Mexicali. A lot of them come to our parks, because they're not as congested as their parks."

I asked her if she went south frequently, when was the last time Councilwoman Durazo ate a Mexicali dinner?

"I was just down there last night. I didn't have dinner. Didn't have time. I had to come back to a meeting. I went to tape an interview on a television and radio program. For half an hour I was interviewed as a city council candidate. So you can see people here listen to Mexican channels." She emphasized it again: "We are a border town."

A border town separated by a border.

She corrected me from her point of view. "By a border fence." She drew my attention to the mural painted on the fence on the east side of Calexico and related its history. "If you go down Imperial Avenue and make a right-hand turn, there's a mile-and-a-half mural. I was a project manager for it about five years ago. It's the only mural of its kind in the world. It celebrates immigration." Before the fence was built, Mexicans would simply walk across the line and shop at the Vons market on the north side of the border. "They would cross. The Border Patrol would watch them, and then they'd go back. They'd cross and purchase from Vons and go back. They didn't have any papers." After the new barrier was built, making an undocumented border crossing much more difficult, the Vons went out of business.

When the old Vietnam War–era landing mats were jammed onto the line as a makeshift wall, they were immediately tagged by graffiti scrawls. No surprise, what an appealing blank canvas. Carmen Dorazo and her colleagues secured a California Arts Challenge Grant and city support for their mural project. Some 1,500 volunteers spent over a year painting the fence to celebrate immigrants, "because we like immigrants here. The United States was founded with immigrants, and we promote it. Calexico and Mexicali," she said again, "are border sister cities."

Send the Tom Tancredos and the Dobbs-Buchanan-O'Reilly bunch to Calexico and they would change their tunes, she said.

Campaigning that night for a chance to represent Calexico in the Sacramento statehouse as assemblyman for District 8, Dr. Richard Gutierrez and his handlers were passing out T-shirts, pencils, and smiles. He'd made Calexico his hometown a few years before, and I asked him why he picked a place Mrs. Munger's son dismissed as a hellhole.

"My first impression was really, 'Man, do I really want to move to a border town?' I grew up in Seeley and went to school in El Centro." His brothers and his sister went to universities in San Diego and came home with stories of Chulajuana, the derogatory localism for the Pacific coast border town Chula Vista, just across the line from Tijuana. "You know the connotation of being an impoverished border town: a really poor quality of life."

But when the parents of their children's friends put their home on the market, Dr. Gutierrez said he and his family fell in love with the place. But not just the home; again I heard tales of community. He waved at his neighbors before he moved to Calexico, but it was not "the heartfelt camaraderie and friendship" that he encountered soon after he moved to Calexico. "Most of my newer friends here, I treat them like my dear cousins. They're like first cousins to me. There's a real genuine care and support for one another."

Credit isolation?

"Oh, not so much the isolation. I think it's more of the cultural real heartfelt commitment of friendship." And the intimacy of a small town. "You see them at the same functions, you see them at gatherings, and there is really that sense of true heartfelt family. I think the real Hispanic-Mexican culture reveals itself in that fashion, and I just relish the fact that most of my colleagues and friends are successful businessmen, bilingual, and feel genuine friendship and caring for each other."

A great definition of Calexico.

Across the street from the auditorium where the candidates debated, the National Day of Prayer was well in progress. Gospel testimony was belted out from the Calexico Park gazebo, introduced in Spanish and crooned in English:

> We'll sing and shout it,
> And tell someone about it,
> Until every nation knows about Jesus!
> Until every nation knows about Jesus!
>
> We have a story, a message to share.
> And we are determined to speak about Jesus everywhere.
> We're not ashamed to tell of His goodness,
> Proclaiming His name.
>
> Until every nation hears the word,
> Just what the love of Jesus can do.
> Until each and every life can know,
> Just how it feels to walk in freedom.
>
> We'll sing and shout it,
> And tell someone about it,
> Until every nation knows about Jesus!
> Until every nation knows about Jesus!

The amplified singing wafted over the park and into the street, mixing with the loudspeakers mounted on a car parked in front of the auditorium beseeching passersby in Spanish, accompanied by recorded mariachi music about the *excellente* work of city councilwoman Carmen Durazo *para la gran familia de Calexico*.

Louie Wong welcomed me into his Yum Yum restaurant well after hours on the night of the debate. After just a few days in Calexico, the word was out: I was a journalist from out of town, trying to learn about the borderlands from a Valley perspective instead of the usual San Diego–Tijuana point of view. The result was a warm welcome. Presiding over the round table, the stocky power broker looked content, his black hair dropped over an intent forehead. He listened as each of us there, after the doors were closed to the public, analyzed the candidates' performances. We were sitting at a large round table—one of the candidates, his mother and father, and several other ad hoc pundits. Louie offered me dinner, but I was still stuffed full of beans and rice from Zerape.

Calexico revival meeting members singing a hymn.

Boy, did I misjudge Yum Yum when Markos and I cruised Imperial Avenue a few nights before, writing off the storefront restaurant as a greasy spoon. It's a gourmet restaurant and a focal point of Calexico political power. The day after the debate, Louie treated me to a spectacular lunch, preparing a special vegan meal, packed with fresh vegetables cooked to perfection, served over delicate steamed rice. What a gracious host! What a fantastic chef! He regaled me with stories: his upcoming trip to China to visit family and friends, the fact that he posts the placards of all candidates for public office and donates to all their campaigns, his family's new restaurant opening a few blocks south, the early Chinese Calexico settlers. Business was booming, and Yum Yum was a civic crossroads, Louie Wong's delicious meals greasing business and government deals days and night. He smiled, clearly loving his role of political and business crossroads, interrupting the lunch he shared with me to greet customer after customer by name and with a few words as choice for them as the bok choy was for me.

I met Angel Zavala at the Barbara Worth, where he manages the bar and teaches salsa to a growing clientele. I came back from a hot day out

The Yum Yum Chinese restaurant sports a very, very bilingual sign.

Yum Yum proprietor, Louie Wong, and his wife.

in the field reporting and decided I just needed a nightcap before I went to bed, and there in Angel's bar salsa music poured out of the speakers and encompassed me. I sat at the bar, and on the dance floor was one couple left over from the evening of salsa instruction Angel conducts on Thursday nights. It was a ballet; it was ethereal. The couple was gorgeous—the two of them moved as one, and it was a perfect coda to the evening, such an embracement of what I had experienced reporting: a warm, fluid welcome and a cosmopolitan embracement that morphed into the dancers I was watching.

"What you were looking at is a form of salsa called *mambo*," Angel told me later. "I, myself, even though I learned on the West Coast here, my teachers were from the East Coast. What I've been doing is trying to bring some of the different culture here back to the Imperial Valley where I grew up."

I told him it felt as if I were watching a ballet.

"Well, thank you." He took it as a compliment, and I meant it so. "Once you get into dancing you really have to not just dance *to* the music, but you learn to dance *in* the music. It just really comes from the heart, and of course a little bit of time and patience to learn the dance. But it is amazing. That's what happened the time when I first saw dancing. I walked to a nightclub in San Diego, and I just happened to see salsa, just like you did, and I was just amazed. I spent the whole night there just watching everybody. From that point on, I thought: that's something I've got to do."

But this mambo I saw really seemed like a hybridization of some other salsa moves with some of the traditional mambo moves, as if some new kind of dance form were evolving there in the Barbara Worth. Angel agreed with that interpretation, telling me, "When I started my own dance team, I called it Salsa Evolution, because salsa is always changing. I've been all over, from Hawaii to Italy, and I got to see and learn from some of the best dancers around the world. I try to get little pieces from Afro-Cuban, hip-hop, techno, all the different types of styles, and then you learn to make it your own."

Salsa Evolution it was, what I watched. Local Imperial Valley folk I was watching, and it was world-class dancing. I had a front row seat for a show you couldn't find on Broadway. Not yet, anyhow.

"The female that you saw me dancing with, Adrianna López, I've known her since I was fifteen, I was in her *quinceañera* way back when." Ah, that melding of cultures, the quinceañera as a natural coming-of-age for these Imperial Valley Yankees. "When I moved back to the Valley," Angel told me, "I found out that salsa in the Valley was something different down here, it's mostly *cumbias* and *norteño* type of dancing, and salsa has just really started to bud down here. Whereas in New York and other places, it's just really big."

And the Rudolph Valentino who was dancing with the girl? What was his story?

"His name is J. R. Real. He is a former student of mine, and an instructor here, and they're both in a group called Fuego Latino, which I just started getting involved with to help them with choreography and coaching."

Angel Zavala helped me articulate the visceral experience I enjoyed watching the two of them dance, listening to the music, far from the bright lights of Hawaii or Italy, in the all but empty bar out in the all but empty reclaimed desert of the Imperial Valley, just a few minutes north of the wall and Mexicali. What is it that is so compelling and makes it impossible to look away?

"Maybe it's just the way people seem to just flow and enjoy themselves dancing along with a partner. It's a connection that you learn to feel. When you start learning, a lot of people tend to feel awkward or self-conscious about how they look. You just really have to pretend like you're—when you're dancing—like no one's watching. Once you start getting the basics down, you start to learn a little bit more, make it your own, and at the club you just feel the energy, you just . . ." He halts his enthusiasm for a moment, remembering his own feelings when he first experienced what so enthralled me at his bar. "When I was first watching it, it seemed like everybody was a professional. But it's just the way the people flow. It's different than what normally people watch, like on *Dancing with the Stars*." Not that Angel objects to the other Latin dance forms; on the contrary, he calls them "fantastic, it's great, it's great training. I'm really happy that *Dancing with the Stars* has taken off, because it gives more people an idea of what Latin dancing is. But when you start to do it in the club, it just takes a little bit different form, because we're not always looking for the perfect step, or the perfect turn, just more about feeling your partner and enjoying the music, having fun."

What brought this internationally experienced dancer and teacher home to the Imperial Valley, so far from Honolulu, New York, and Rome? The answer, after my intimate stay in Calexico, was no surprise.

"My mother. My mother. She wasn't doing too well with her house, and I thought I'd be a good son and come and help her out."

A good son he obviously is, but he seems nowhere near disappointed to be a homeboy back home. He found that same international culture in his old hometown.

"Yes. Yes," he agrees. At least with the few stars he's been able to connect with at the Barbara Worth, such as the couple I watched. As he cares for his mother and works at the Barbara Worth, Angel's life is more relaxed than when he danced around the world. "I'm not a professional dancer any longer, that was a few years ago, and I was even in a movie with Denzel Washington, the Antwone Fisher story."

The couple I saw is an ambitious one, competing and winning.

"We had our own *Dancing with the Stars* here at the Barbara Worth Resort," Angel reported. "And the couple that you were watching were the two top contenders. Adrianna Lopez got best score."

Angel Zavala made my nightcap an evening to remember. If I had been in New York City and had spent too much money at a box office somewhere to see what I saw that night, it could not have been better.

Friday

You Can Make It Here

The mélange of cultures in Calexico and throughout the borderlands presents the opportunity for—and maybe the necessity to recruit—trained guides. Gustavo Arellano certainly fits the job description. He writes the syndicated column *Ask a Mexican* and is the author of an anthology of those columns, with the same title.

When I caught up with the Orange County, California–based Arellano, I asked him to describe his work—Dear Abby variants that I found both hysterically funny and spot-on as culture commentary.

"The column is exactly what it sounds like," he explained patiently, "Ask a Mexican. I'll answer any and all questions about Mexicans, from the racist to the sexist to questions involving etymology, history, midgets, food—whatever people ask me, I'll answer it."

His work is as irreverent as it sounds.

"Exactly," he agreed. "The purpose of the column specifically is to debunk stereotypes that people may have about Mexicans. I confront racism head on and do it in a manner that's very up-front, very aggressive, but most importantly based in facts and satire. I like to use the vehicle of satire to answer my questions because that allows me more leeway in exposing truths and more leeway in having a discussion about the role of Mexicans historically and economically, especially in these days in the United States."

"To inoculate all of us," I said, asking for his bone fides, "who the heck are you, and what are your credentials to do this? Are you just some white guy from Nebraska posing?"

He laughed "No, no, no. I am the child of Mexican immigrants. My dad was an illegal immigrant. He came to this country in the trunk of a Chevy in 1968 along with three other men. I was born in Anaheim, California. My first language was Spanish, and obviously I'm speaking English now, so I'm fully assimilated. But at the same time my parents are immigrants, they're citizens now. I grew up in Little Mexico here in California, in Anaheim, and I came out perfectly fine. That's the prism upon which I view this immigration debate. I always hear people talking about how Mexicans can't assimilate, how they're ruining this country. My family, all of us kids, our first language was Spanish, and now we're all professional. If that's not assimilation, I don't know what is."

The definition of assimilation into American culture is a difficult one to find. To what are we supposedly assimilating? To the America of Pat Buchanan, Lou Dobbs, and Bill O'Reilly? Eisenhower's 1950s? Tall-steepled, white churches at New England crossroads, or adobe houses in Santa Fe? Grazing land in the high Nevada desert where Basque sheep-herders speak Basque as they tend their flocks, or NASCAR racetracks in the Deep South? Such a comparative list is endless. To what are we assimilating?

"I think for me," Arellano said, "what assimilation is in this country is that you become someone who's productive, somebody who's law-abiding, somebody who is working, and most importantly somebody who cares about improving your community and others. Other people might define it more conservatively and say you have to have an abiding love for the Stars and Stripes. I think one of the great things with immigration is that you're always putting in a healthy dose of skepticism into the American fabric. You really wonder why is it if I come to this country, I'm supposed to be welcomed, yet at the same time people hate me, people hate my kind of people, and this is something that all immigrant groups have always asked themselves about."

I asked Gustavo Arellano for examples of some of his favorite "Ask a Mexican" questions.

"I have to say my all-time favorite question is one a gentleman asked me: 'Why don't Mexicans want to learn English? Is it because they're too stupid, are they too dumb, they can't learn two or three words a day, what exactly is the problem with them?' My response was very simple. I said the United States government shares your concern. It released a report saying that this new wave of immigrants, they're not like the old wave, they only come to this country to make money and send it back home. They don't want to learn English, and we should clamp down on these new immigrants. If that rhetoric sounds familiar, that's obviously what's being said right now in the halls of the Senate. It was also being said in the halls of the Senate in 1911, because this report was the Dillingham Commission, came out in 1911. Those idiot immigrants at the time were Hungarians, were Italians, were Poles, were Jews, were Czechs. So this myth that conservatives have, that previous immigrants learned English immediately, that they disconnected with the mother country, that's a crock of you-know-what. American racism is a carousel, and here we are again. This time, now it's the Mexicans who supposedly can't assimilate and are ruining this country."

His tirade resonated well with me, a first-generation immigrant whose father was born in Hungary.

Arellano related. "I think it was Henry Cabot Lodge, the esteemed senator from Massachusetts, who actually specifically trashed the Hungarians. He had this great quote basically equating Hungarians to dogs."

American history is full of similar rants and raves. A businessman who testified before Congress in the 1930s, one Fred H. Bixby, was representing agriculture and cattle operations, and he was trying to define his industry's need for Mexican workers at the time. He said, "If I do not get Mexicans to thin those beets and hoe those beets, I am through with the beet business. We have no Chinamen. We have not the Japs. The Hindu is worthless. The Filipino is nothing and the white man will not do the work."

"America," Arellano reminded me of our common nasty history, "always relied on cheap labor, and it's something that's happened from the inception of this republic. You first have slaves; then after that you have sharecroppers. After slavery you started getting these waves, these massive waves of immigrants."

He offered another question from his slush pile. "Somebody asked me, 'Whatever happened to the lazy Mexican, because now all I hear is that they're stealing our jobs?'"

And the answer?

"My answer was this is a great immigrant stereotype that America has for its immigrants, where it paints new waves of immigrants as either a threat to society because they're stealing jobs or a threat to society because they're lazy and docile. Examples include Chinese: they're either coolies or opium smokers. You had Italians, who were tenement slum dwellers or members of the Mafia, and it goes down the list. Today with Mexicans you still have that stereotype of the Mexican with the sombrero sleeping under a cactus, but now you hear they're ruining the economy, they're stealing all of our jobs, and let's just ship them back to Mexico."

Another sample from his mailbag exposes the venom in his audience. "I have no problem with immigrants," wrote a frustrated reader.

"What I can't stand are a bunch of fence-hopping, river-wading illegals telling me I owe them a free education, free health care, and free transportation and then making me speak Spanish at every restaurant, car wash, and public school."

Nice.

Despite his skilled and caustic attack on prejudice, Gustavo Arellano is not universally loved within the immigrant community.

"Conservatives absolutely despise me, because they think I'm an apologist for the *reconquista*. Their fevered theories are that Mexico is trying to take over the southwest United States." But the left side of the aisle is not always happy with him either. "I do get criticism from folks who don't appreciate my satire, who say that instead of reappropriating stereotypes, I'm actually perpetuating them. It's funny how both sides can hate me at the same time."

That means he's doing his job.

As I considered the border, I looked east to Texas and the attempts by Washington to change the lyrics to the old cowboy refrain "Don't fence me in." I connected with an extreme border resident, an ultimate border resident, Eloisa Tamez, the director of the nursing program at the University of Texas at Brownsville, Texas's southernmost college. But for my purposes, I was interested in her residence; her house sits directly north of the border, the Rio Grande.

"It certainly does," she affirmed my research. "In fact, it's pretty close to the river's edge. It is a property that's been in my family for generations."

As she looks out her window at her backyard, she sees the river, but her terra firma is American dirt. Her own dirt. Bought and paid for long ago. Now her government wanted to take that backyard from her, put a wall across it, and block her view of and access to the river.

So you'll be looking out your kitchen window, and you'll be seeing the Berlin Wall?" I asked her.

"Berlin-like wall, pretty much, yes."

I asked her to dismiss for a moment the questions of immigration policy, even the questions of property loss to eminent domain laws. "As a woman in her kitchen, how do you feel about that?"

"This is a devastating image," she said about the proposed barrier, "because of the symbolism of such a wall. Not only to us who will be experiencing it right in our backyard, but also the symbolism that this wall represents to other countries. By that I mean we are a democracy, and we propose to all the world that we are a democracy. We are those that like to tear down walls and build nations, nations based on the protection of human rights. When you see this wall, the rest of the world is going to say 'Well, here's the country that tells us they're a democracy and tears down walls, and now they're building walls in the backyards of their citizens.'"

It was an intense and passionate speech, spoken with the unassailable credibility of a woman looking out her kitchen window and seeing in the micro of her own backyard the macro of the world stage. That personal analysis was one of the reasons she joined with other homeowners to try to stop Washington from building the wall. I asked her if she thought she and her colleagues had a chance to stop the wall builders.

"From the evidence that we see, perhaps we as individuals may feel now that we might not have much of a chance. That is not going to stop us from continuing to exercise our American-given rights of protecting our property."

I tried to play the Homeland Security role with her, asking her how—aside from her personal backyard loss—she could rationalize opposing a wall that would increase that security and improve our border integrity.

"I'm not opposed to the concept of providing security to our country. That has been part of the American way for all the years that it's been America. I'm not opposed to that," she said again. "I am opposed to the method in which this is being proposed. We were initially told, when Congress and the rest of Washington were talking about a solution to providing safety to our country, that it was to keep the terrorists out." She's another border dweller who knows her recent history well. "The terrorists come to this country legally. We now know that keeping the terrorists out, and especially through the southern border, is not the real reason."

"There's that saying that we hear along the border: build a ten-foot wall, that's all right, we have an eleven-foot ladder." I wanted to lighten up the conversation for a minute. Eloisa Tamez laughed.

"Yes, we hear that a lot, too. There's a lot of joking around about that."

"What's another border joke? Do you know any other border jokes?"

"Another one is that because the American corporations continue to hire illegal immigrants, that probably illegals will be hired to build the wall." She laughed again. "That's one of the things we hear."

I asked this neighbor to the north what her alternative proposal would be if her fellow Texan George Bush had called her from the White House for advice, before his administration endorsed the wall.

"First of all, they need to be listening to our local leaders, whom we trust that they will use their skill and who have the expertise to think of alternatives to the wall that would in fact probably come out with the same outcome. That is, to protect the borders and to hold illegal immigration to a minimum. Washington is not listening to our elected leaders here."

She and others in Brownsville supported a plan to rebuild the river levee as a low-key barrier. Money earmarked for the wall could be used to control flooding, and if the levee were reinforced, it could support increased traffic from Border Patrol cars and trucks. This approach, she said, would allow the Border Patrol to keep the frontier under surveillance more effectively. And it would keep the wall out of her backyard and out of the sullied reputation of the United States government.

No question Eloisa Tamez is an expert analyst of border issues. "I've dealt with illegal immigration all my life. I mean, from the time I was a child. I was born and raised here. The only difference now with the illegal immigration is that it's not only the Mexicanos who are coming across, but we see people from many different countries coming through: Brazil, China, Russia. We get all this from our local news as to who is apprehended at our borders. It's not just the Mexicanos."

She rejected the idea that the migration has a net negative effect on her community.

"It's been happening so much for over all these years that we're almost, like, immune to it because it's so normal. I know that it may seem strange for me to say that, but I've grown up with this kind of activity going on all the time. What's different now is the numbers of countries that are coming through."

As we talked, Eloisa Tamez called the migrants *Mexicanos,* and she called them "illegal immigrants." I asked her about the terminology and its importance, because when she referred to them as "illegal immigrants" it seemed she almost stumbled over the words, as if they were difficult for her to say out loud, uncomfortable. What is the right term to call the people who are coming across the border without the benefit of government-provided paperwork?

"*Illegal immigrant* is the correct term," was her response. "I like to see that better than all the derogatory terms that have been used in the past, like *mojados,* wetbacks. To me, those were derogatory. These are human beings. The people that come from Mexico, for the most part, are the poor who are looking for a better life and trying to make a living."

My hometown San Francisco is hundreds of miles north of the border. Since I'm a California boy, I know the crises on the border affect California well north of The Eight. But the border, of course, is not just an issue in California. It's not just an issue in this and the other border states, New Mexico, Arizona, and Texas. The de facto border extends up into all fifty states, metaphorically at least, because of the immigration realities that are going into all fifty states.

Nonetheless, it is important to look at the crises at the point of the border, the focal point for the crossing. There are issues that go on in the borderlands entirely different from the kinds of immigration issues hundreds and thousands of miles distant. Eagle Pass, Texas, and its twin city on the other side of the border, Piedras Negras, are a variation on the Calexico–Mexicali theme.

Piedras Negras, Black Rocks, plural. Across from Black Rocks I found Chad Foster, mayor of Eagle Pass. When I checked in with him, the first thing he said to me was, "We appreciate the opportunity to spread the reality of the Texas border."

He agreed that the border is up to all fifty states now, but his city and Calexico, sitting directly on the border, have different issues than we do hundreds of miles north.

"Yes, sir. We're just on the front lines of the border."

Eagle Pass is another of the places were the federal government has decided to reinforce the border with a fence that the federal government at least claims to hope will be impregnable, and the mayor's office was not ready to sign on to the plan. In fact, Eagle Pass decided to fight Washington. Mayor Foster pointed out to me that well-informed federal authorities know that no fence can secure the borderline. He quoted David Aguilar, then head of Border Patrol, admitting that this fence would only slow down an illegal entry by three to four minutes.

How does Mayor Foster feel about the borderlands and Eagle Pass? Just look at the sign he's slapped on the wall over his desk: "Welcome to Paradise." The mayor's paradise and ours in San Francisco are related in relatively recent history. When the California gold rush hit in 1849, Eagle Pass was an important stop for the forty-niners heading west in the winter, seeking a route far from the cold and snow that closed the more direct northern paths to hoped-for riches. Gold was discovered just a year after the Treaty of Guadalupe Hidalgo was signed by Mexico City and Washington. The document made official the end of the Mexican-American War and set today's boundaries between the two countries. Fort Duncan was built in 1849 to enforce that land- and water-grabbing treaty, and Eagle Pass came next, finally incorporating as a city late in the 1800s.

The mayor made clear another factor missed by many casual observers of the border. The Texas border is unique compared to other border states, because in Texas they know exactly where the border is. It's not some arbitrary mark on a map. It was established in 1848 with the Treaty of Guadalupe Hidalgo as the midstream of the Rio Grande River. That physical line of water is much clearer than a line drawn in the sand.

When I talked with him, Mayor Chad Foster was laboring as chair of the Texas Border Coalition, representing all the elected officials from El Paso to Brownsville. As he made clear to me, using a good old cowboy boot analogy about the crises along the border, "One size does not fit all." But there is a common denominator among his peers. "The Texas Border Coalition, our priority is border security. We live and raise our families on the border. The reason that Eagle Pass, Texas, exists was after Texas was taken into the United States, a string of forts were formed along the Texas border. Eagle Pass grew up around Fort Duncan, which was established in 1849. We've been addressing border security since that date."

There's credibility with such a legacy. The chief executive of Eagle Pass is an expert worth consulting and paying attention to; the advice he offers makes sense.

"We're going to spend forty-nine billion dollars to build seven hundred miles of fence," he reported about the federal government's plan, "which is only one-third of the border, and maintain it for twenty years—they put a number of forty-nine billion on that." He was not convinced taxpayers would get their money's worth. "We want real security. We don't want to convey a false sense of security to the interior populace. We're concerned. We want sincere border security, not blowing or wasting forty-nine billion of the taxpayers' money on building a fence that David Aguilar, again, has said will only slow down entry by three to four minutes." He punctuated his worry with facts from the patrolling agents. "As we speak, there have been forty-two tunnels found to date under the physical barrier."

Again, that number is forty-nine billion dollars.

"The mayors along the Texas border, we have no political agenda. None of us have any desire to further our political aspirations. All of us border mayors, we're just passionate about our community. None of us have any aspiration to achieve higher elected office."

Right, I teased him. A politician with no ambition. A Texas politician with no ambition? Not just one, but every mayor from Brownsville to El Paso? That's a Texas tale no Californian could swallow, despite his protestations. "I have my hands full just being the mayor of the city of Eagle Pass."

But I didn't want to stop the interview. I asked him to stick around despite our skepticism, and he talked Texas back at me.

"I will stay till it thunders."

I love Texas, I told him. The sun has riz, the sun has set, and we ain't out of Texas yet. Eagle Pass was not trying to stop the fence. The mayor and his constituents were incensed about the path Washington decided to send it through his city. "We never inhibited the federal government from coming into the city of Eagle Pass. The Texas border is unique in that 95 percent of the property that abuts Mexico is in private hands. The city of Eagle Pass, as an example, we passed a resolution in 2005 in opposition to any forms of walls or fences in our community." For good reasons in addition to being good neighbors. The mayor walked me through an example of the problems faced at the actual grassroots level.

"We have two international bridges. Between our two bridges, we have our municipal golf course; it goes up the riverbank. Contiguous to that golf course to the north is a city park. We have a golf cart path that parallels the river. The Border Patrol wanted to reinforce it with a structure that would support their vehicles—that's an excellent idea. There's a creek that goes into the river just south of our northernmost bridge. They wanted to bridge it and continue that road into our city park along the banks of the river—wonderful idea. They want to eradicate over a mile of brush that would facilitate a line-of-site vision to the banks of the river. Great idea, because it would make it more aesthetically appealing for those on the golf course and the members of our community that enjoy the city park. They then wanted to put fifteen light towers on a bluff a quarter of a mile off the river."

That sounded like a terrible idea to me, but the mayor disagreed.

"Well, no, it would illuminate our golf course at night. It would illuminate our city park at nights; it wasn't that bad an idea." More Texas talk came next as the mayor explained the place where he broke with the federal authorities. "Where the wheels came off the cart is they wanted to put the fence along that same alignment."

A fence that would block access to their riverbank for the good citizens of Eagle Pass. From the mayor's perspective, a fence that would de facto give Texas dirt back to Mexico, what he calls "a fence that would in essence cede our golf course and our municipal park to Mexico. That's when we just said no, that changes the border."

Again he told me that the border in Texas is defined in the Treaty of Guadalupe Hidalgo of 1848 as midstream of the Rio Grande. In Texas no one is talking about a border fence, because that fence won't go midstream of the Rio Grande. In order for the fence to be built along the alignment that the Homeland Security Department considers practical, he figured that almost seventy miles of fence, 2,400 Texas acres—just in the Rio Grande Valley—would end up on the Mexico side of the fence, including thirty-four homes and the World Birding Center.

Hard to imagine such a Texas giveaway from a president who was once governor of the Lone Star State.

Mayor Foster blamed a renegade Homeland Security Department. "It appears that we have a government within a government. The Texas Border Coalition is focused on security, while Secretary Michael Chertoff is focused on building a fence. We tried on three occasions to meet with the secretary."

I asked him how he figured he would break through the roadblock, how he as the chief executive of Eagle Pass was to make the federal government listen to him?

"That is our challenge and we're just overwhelmed. Mayor Cortez in McAllen looked at this border fence as a speed bump, because for forty-nine billion dollars, if we're only going to slow down an illegal entry three minutes, I mean, that's a speed bump, that's not security."

That's an expensive speed bump. As for the mayor, I pointed out to him that every time he spoke a Spanish word—such as in *Treaty of Guadalupe Hidalgo*—his accent was flawless in both English and Spanish. I asked him if he was fully bilingual, and received another Texasism.

"Ah, to eat breakfast in Maverick County you better be bilingual. I was born in Canyon, Texas, within the Texas Panhandle. My family moved to Eagle Pass when I was five years old. One of the great opportunities of living on the border is enjoying the Mexican culture, being able to become bilingual. We just have a wonderful relationship with all our neighbors in Mexico. That's not to say that we are not American citizens living on the border first. I'm a freak about watching the History Channel. When the gold mining began in California, according to the History Channel, they were speaking nine languages in the mines. It's a wonderful opportunity to be multicultural and bilingual. When I was in school, I understood the United States to be a melting pot," he told me. "I'm an Ag major, you call that hybrid vigor."

"Hey, Mr. Mayor," I beckoned him before we parted, "you professed earlier in our conversation to not have political aspirations, but guys like you ought to be in Washington."

He took advantage of the bait to slam Washington one more time. "If we want to clean up immigration, let's start within the Beltway. Every time I go to a conference, the individuals that are serving the DHS their coffee are immigrants. If we want to clean up immigration, let's start it within the Beltway."

Eagle Pass lawyer Emily Rickers offered her services to homeowners along the fence area—such as Eloisa Tamez—who are fighting the federal government's attempt at using eminent domain to take their land to build the new, supposedly secure border fence.

Why shouldn't her clients give up their backyards and have searchlights and Berlin Walls instead of tennis courts and vegetable gardens? It's our nation's security at stake.

"Part of what our clients really want the rest of the country to know about this case is that it's not that they don't want to help out in the effort to secure the borders and increase national security; they just know from their experience and living in this area that a border fence is a really expensive mistake, and it's not going to be an effective way to go about fixing this problem."

Lawyer Rickers rejected the idea that Washington didn't understand her argument, an argument we heard all along the border.

"I'm not sure it's that they don't get it," she said about the federal policy makers. "I think that they just see it as an easy way to appear strong on national security and, frankly, to appear that they've had a big national security success. It's easy to build a wall, but the impact of building that wall might not be seen for a couple of years. People can think that they're leaving a legacy that's going to be really effective, and it won't be until sometime later that we figure out that it's really not working."

I recommended that she invite the inside-the-Beltway types to come to the Rio Grande Valley to stand in the backyards of her clients and see what the reality is. It was an idea under consideration, she told me; meanwhile, she and other local leaders had a specific message for Washington: "Look, let us help you save the country a whole lot of money. It's not that we don't want this in our backyards, it's that we know it's not going to work, and therefore we don't want it in our backyard."

Understood and understandable. I asked for an example.

"We were talking to some people last night about their neighborhood, which doesn't have a fence right now but is on the slate for a place where there will be a fence. They were talking about seeing people running through their land and calling Border Patrol and getting passed from one sector to another—being told, 'Well, that's not our territory, you have to call the other sector.' The Border Patrol doesn't show up when they're called. When they do, agents don't even bother to get out of their cars to chase people. Those kinds of problems with Border Patrol agents are huge. They also talked about individual yards that already have many feet of chain-link fence around them with razor wire around the top, and the ways that people get through those fences. The people who are trying to cross the border are resourceful. In fact, they're coming here because they're resourceful, and they want to work, and they don't have opportunities in their home countries. They're going to get here one way or another: canals, holes in the fence. There are holes in the fence right by the bridge where there's a lot of law enforcement around. People jump the fence there all the time. It's just not an effective structure."

I told Emily Rickers that I spoke with Chad Foster, her mayor, and he pointed out that in fact the border is in the middle of the Rio Grande. It runs right down the river. But her clients, at least some of them, lived far from the river. The proposed routing of the fence is, at times, far from the border, leaving U.S. property on the south side of the fence, a result that would create a no-man's-land in the backyards of good Texas citizens. Crazy. I asked her to explain the contorted logistics of the fence path.

"That's a good question," she answered, "and that's one of the things that we would like for the government to come here and explain to people. Why do those fences have to be where they are? When they've been asked that question, they just say, 'Well, this is what our people have identified as being tactically necessary.' There's no way, the way that the laws have been written, that we found any way for people to try to question any of that reasoning. This is pretty much an exclusive executive mandate of where this fence needs to go."

It's a modern David-and-Goliath tale, but things didn't look good in the post-9/11 environment for Emily Rickers in the role of David.

"We certainly haven't given up yet. But an important part of what we're trying to do right now is just explain to the American public why this is such a ridiculous idea and to explain to people that this is not that Texas doesn't want to cooperate with the federal government, because that's absolutely not the issue. The issue is this is a colossal mistake. We're hoping people will really understand why this is a mistake and that more of this dialogue can happen at that point."

The lawyer is a Texan, and she knows her Texas history. How about turning back the pages of that history and rejoining Mexico? She knew I was joking, but she answered with a serious response.

"We're not interested in that. We're Americans just like everyone else." She added another Lone Star complaint. "It's just kind of ironic from a president that came out of Texas." Not that the president or any of those Texans who may be able to influence him would tend to be sympathetic to the Borderlands. "Texas is a really big state and a very diverse place, and the Texas border is unique from a lot of the rest of the state, particularly the lower Rio Grande Valley, where I'm based and where I do most of my work, which is relatively close to the Gulf Coast along the river. Things that play well politically in Dallas don't make sense down here."

Again, even as far from Calexico as you can travel on the border, the story is the same: the Borderland is a place in and of itself. It's not Mexico, it's not the United States, it's the borderlands. Culturally unique.

I offered Emily Rickers a soapbox. What is her message to Washington?

"Talk to my clients and talk to local political leaders. Use technology more sensibly. Increase the force of the Border Patrol and their training."

But no border fences through American backyards.

A smiling Gustavo Yee welcomed me to Sereno on the eastern edge of expanding Calexico, a sparkling new housing development. He was selling new homes, what the company called their Hacienda Series. "Contemporary Architectural Style," announced the brochure. "Designer Specified

Malvina Reynolds's "Little Boxes" sprawl east from downtown Calexico.

Exterior Color Palette. Vaulted Ceilings. Plush Carpeting Throughout Living Area. Designer Light Fixtures." And, of course, air-conditioning!

The Hacienda Series was almost sold out, despite the subprime-mortgage mess assaulting sprawling California cities. The bargain prices combined with the growing Border Patrol–prison education economy were treating Yee's project well, especially since the builders had the foresight to respond to the changing housing market by downsizing their products. He was offering me a new home with up to 1,500 square feet for about $200,000. Such a deal, yet sales were slow.

"It's been selling because people are looking for something in this price range," he told me. "But definitely we are in that sales dip. It's slowed a lot. When we started we were closing fourteen homes a month. Now we close not even one a month. That was every month. Fourteen homes, every month."

Astounding.

The developer Gustavo Yee worked for San Diego–based McMillin Homes, with projects throughout California. He said Calexico served the company well because there wasn't much competition. "People are looking for something affordable, good quality, good location, where

A two-hour commute on The Eight from San Diego buys a bargain house in Calexico.

the property tax is not too high. This is one of the better locations. His customers are mostly locals, not brave new San Diego two-hour commuters.

"Yeah, everybody thought they were going to commute from San Diego, but it's just not practical, I guess." Other factors are dissuading San Diegans. "We don't have the infrastructure San Diego does, stores and things like that. The weather's another thing. I mean, we get here to 117 in the summer. Where are you guys from?"

San Francisco.

"San Francisco," he repeated; the words are always magic. He offered me a geography and logistics lesson. "Here there's no traffic. You can be in San Diego in an hour and a half. There's no traffic on this highway," he said about The Eight, comparing the Calexico commute to a job in San Diego to a commute within San Diego County that could take the same amount of time to a house costing twice the price. "A lot of people came from San Diego, looking." But not too many bought. Vanpools are operating, hauling commuters from the new Calexico housing projects to San Diego for a fare cheaper than buying gas.

Amazing, but Calexico isn't San Francisco or even San Diego.

"At least in San Diego and San Francisco you guys have things to show for your high prices. Infrastructure. Here, we don't have nothing to show. We don't have a city with stores, nice weather, scenery. Here we don't have nothing, you know?"

Nothing. That sounded a touch harsh. I offered up one of Calexico's unique aspects as an alternative to nothing: Mexicali. "You have Mexicali. You have a big city there."

"Yes, but a lot of people don't want to go over there. I'm not saying it's not safe. Just like any city. I'm sure in San Francisco and San Diego there are areas where you just don't go. It's the same thing in Mexicali. As long as you kind of know your way around so you don't get lost, you'll be fine." Gustavo Yee knew what he was talking about. "I was born in Mexicali, I grew up there, so I know the city. Spanish is my first language, I know. They have good restaurants, good food, places to go. It's a little bit cheaper than here. You can save a little bit of money. Gas is a dollar less per gallon over there.

"It's a small town but we have expensive gas, they have to bring it from somewhere else." He listed other small-town oddities: "The squash parade and 4-H are big. Future Farmers. But if you want to go to a big city, Mexicali is a million-plus. Lot of traffic. Bad drivers. Good food. Good people."

He's moved to el otro lado.

"I live here, but most of my family live over there. I go maybe five times a week. The lines can be a problem, but fortunately I have a SENTRI card; for me, maximum is twenty minutes versus an hour and a half, two hours on the weekends."

A SENTRI card? Welcome to our classless society here in the United States. Pay some money, and life changes. Homeland Security runs a background check. You show up at their offices with your identification. All your relevant personal data (and who knows what else) is on the SENTRI card and is read by a radio receiver as you edge up the line toward the U.S. guardhouse in a special traffic lane designed for those borderlands residents who cross with great frequency.

"You basically live in both cities," I suggested. "You are able to take advantage of the benefits of both."

"Exactly. Because my family and even the church that I go to are in Mexicali. Mexico recognizes my Mexican citizenship. I can still vote, own property, own a business—and I'm also a U.S. citizen. I became a U.S. citizen about three years ago. I have a dual citizenship, so I take advantage of both."

"The best of both possible worlds."

"Yes. I have nothing to lose."

"You have nothing to lose?"

"Nothing. I always joke that if I'm flying and the plane gets, like, kidnapped, I'll just throw away my U.S. passport and keep the Mexican, because they always take the U.S. citizens as hostages." He expects that Mexican passport to be advantageous when he tours Europe; he said that people from France told him, "Take the Mexican passport, they'll treat you better."

My home away from home at the Barbara Worth Resort was just north of The Eight, in Holtville. Unlike Calexico, Holtville does sport a main square and a few Hollywood-stage-set-looking Old West buildings. It's a perfect backdrop for the annual Carrot Festival. Big rigs hauling loads of carrots rumbled by while we prowled Holtville. And I found the ultimate Holtville booster to explain its attractions, and what differentiates Holtville from Calexico, just a few miles south.

"Oh, my God, it's awesome," bubbled former Carrot Queen Dana Hawk. "Everybody knows each other. If something happens to somebody . . ." She interrupted herself. "Omigod, you're taking my picture!" Her long blonde hair drapes down her shoulders, just as it should for a Carrot Queen in the early seventies. She's bouncy, with a wide, white Tom's of Maine smile. She glows.

"I can give you an example," she started again with her booster speech. "You probably don't want to hear about it, but my niece was murdered about thirteen years ago. This is a very small, small community. Everybody embraced my family. Not a lot of bad things happen. That is something that had never happened and hasn't happened since. It was just one of those freaky things. But this town is like a family. It really is. If you don't know what your kids are doing, somebody's going to tell you. It's safe to walk down the street."

Dana and Holtville are inseparable; she's lived her entire life in Holtville, over fifty years. She never went away to school, rarely travels. What holds her? What's the lure?

"I wouldn't leave Holtville. This is my town. This is where my family and my friends are, and my heart. My dad was born here. My grandmother was born here. Yeah. I just could never." She sounds like a cheerleader; she looks like a cheerleader. "When I met my fiancé I told him from the beginning I'm not leaving, because he didn't want to stay here. I said, I will never leave, you better make up your mind because don't try to get me to move. There are a lot of people who were born and raised here and stayed, and a lot of people who went away to school who have come back. We always say, it's a saying in Holtville, 'They always come back.' They do. They come back to raise their families."

It was back in 1974 when Dana reigned as the Carrot Queen. She was sweet seventeen and the Carrot Queen. Townsfolk voted for her by donating a dollar to charity in her name whenever they made a local purchase. "Kind of neat," remembered Dana, to be voted queen.

"I thought it was everything in the world. I loved it. I was a cheerleader. I've been the princess of this and princess of that, but yeah, Carrot Queen meant a lot to me."

Her speech is punctuated with "awesome" and charming Americanisms such as "gosh dang." Her smile is cheerleader white and wide as she talks about the annual festival, like the Día de la Familia cooking contest, recipes that require, natch, carrots. I asked her to tell me about the oddest concoction with carrots that she's seen in her years at the Carrot Festival. "Golly," was her response. Carrot ice cream? Of course, that's no big deal in Holtville. She gave me a Carrot Festival cookbook.

Her bubbling about Holtville was—if not infectious—astounding. Her job is ideal for her and Holtville: she fronts the chamber of commerce in their little office squat on the square. I chided her for lacking enthusiasm.

"I love my town, okay? Honest to God, I love my town. This is where my heart is." I pointed out the sparse occupancy of the buildings around the square. Blame it on The Eight. "There were businesses everywhere. In the seventies, when the freeway came in, people bypassed instead of driving through, businesses started closing." But her frown was transitory and turned right back into a smile. "You watch! In the next few years it's going to start booming, because the Valley's running out of room, and more and more people are moving to the Valley. We need more businesses and more homes." But not too many. "I would never want it to be like El Centro. I like to keep it quaint, the way it is.

Effervescent Dana Hawk at the Holtville Chamber of Commerce, ever the booster of the place that crowned her Carrot Queen back when she was a high school student.

But we do need to grow. We have to grow. I don't want to end up like Niland." Niland again as the end of the road. "And I don't think that we ever will end up like Niland. People tell me that and I tell them they're crazy. There is no way we will. We won't let that happen."

Whew. It's almost exhausting to listen to her, she's so excited!

Who are the new residents? Commuters from San Diego, prison workers and Border Patrol employees, what Dana calls prison families and Border Patrol families. "People want to raise their kids in a smaller, safer environment."

Not Niland.

"I don't want to end up like Niland. It never really was a booming town by any means. It's just got the crime; you can't even walk down the streets these days. It's really, really drug-infested. Niland is just dying. It's just dying."

Niland. Everybody's bad example. For Bonnie Peterson, Melani Guinn and her gang, and now the Carrot Queen. Niland is displayed in all its faded glory, on the north end of the Imperial Valley far from the Mexico border, in the fine documentary film that tells the sad story of the Salton Sea, *Plagues and Pleasures on the Salton Sea.* "Niland now barely hangs on," reports narrator John Waters, in his inimitable sardonic voice, as pictures of a closing restaurant, a shuttered gas station, and a for-sale derelict building fill the screen. A junk salesman, identified only as Flash, sums up Niland from his point of view: "It used to be a nice little town, but now they're trying to make something out of it. But they never will. You can't take nothing and make anything out of nothing."

I asked Dana to explain the north-of-The-Eight/south-of-The-Eight divide.

"When I got divorced, I lived out ten miles. We were all Holtvillites. Holtville is only a mile by a mile. But a lot of our people, Holtville people, are from farms and country homes and stuff." Holtville, she said, is ten miles in any direction from the square. And Calexico? "Calexico is another world. It's really like almost going down into Mexico. It really is."

Why? It's barely more than ten miles south.

"Because they're a border town. The majority of people speak Spanish. You go do your shopping, try to speak English. The people in the shops don't speak English. Even at Walmart, you know? I'm not saying that's bad or good; I'm just saying it's so close to the border that it's a border town. It's always going to be different."

The days of carrot supremacy are gone; Kern County has surpassed Holtville in carrot production. But Dana is unfazed. We browsed the recipes in the Holtville carrot cookbook: carrot casserole, garlic carrot pizza, carrot pie, scalloped carrots, savory carrot squares, cinnamon carrot sticks, chicken and carrots in wine. My favorite? Carrot soda cracker, provided back in 1976 (just a couple of years after Dana's reign) by Jimmy Dykes. Take a moment and check out the recipe.

    4 egg whites
    1/4 tsp cream of tartar
    1 cup sugar
    20 soda crackers crushed
    1/2 cup pecans
    1 tsp vanilla
    1 1/2 cups coarse grated carrots

And for the topping:
3/4 cup fine grated carrots
1/2 pint whipping cream
1 tbsp sugar

Beat egg whites until foamy, add cream of tartar and beat until stiff.
Add sugar a little at a time, beat well each time. Add crushed crack-
ers, nuts, vanilla, and the 1 1/2 cups coarse grated carrots, fold into
egg whites. Pour into well-greased pie plate. Bake at 350 degrees
30 to 40 minutes. Let pie cool.

Whip cream, 1 tbsp sugar until fluffy. Mix in 3/4 cup of fine
grated carrots, spread into pie. Let pie set overnight before serving.

"A different desert is extra nice," commented Jimmy, "because it is
made the night before."
Thanks, Jimmy.
"Carrots are our claim to fame," cooed Dana.
"Once the Carrot Capital . . . ," I prompted.
"Always the Carrot Capital," was her response, right on cue.

Across the Holtville main square from Dana's office is a bustling convenience store. I found Blanche Benavides out front with a friend, stopping passersby, soliciting for the Imperial Valley Ministries, an indication that not every teenage Holtvillite gets crowned Carrot Queen.
"We're asking for donations for our ministry," Blanche explained.
"It's a Christian ministry. We're dedicated to restoring the lives of drug
addicts and their families."
There is a big problem with drugs in the Valley?
"I'd say they're everywhere," she said, and it wasn't based on theory,
she was experienced. "I was a drug addict for seven years, but I believe
Jesus Christ set me free, and that's why I'm doing this. Raising money to
help others like me. So homes stay open and continue helping others."
What drugs plague the Valley?
"Various different drugs. A lot of kids are starting young, using
them. They start off with marijuana, and then they go to harder drugs.
Like crystal meth is a big drug right now. It's very bad. Families are
doing it, teachers, all kinds of people are doing it. That's what I was
doing. I lost my life." She hesitated. "Well, not my life, but I lost my
kids, I lost my apartment, the car, everything." She did not look dis-
tressed. "I believe God's going to bring it back to me in full."

Her organization is named Imperial Valley Ministries. It's head-quartered in El Centro, with affiliated churches across the States and Mexico dedicated to ministering to the needs of drug addicts and alcoholics. "You have nothing to lose," says her leaflet, "and a miracle to gain. Total recovery is possible. You can be set free from drugs, alcohol, depression and sickness." Blanche said she has dedicated her life to helping such people and to preaching the gospel, "to let them know what Jesus did in my life. A lot of times just giving our testimony helps people. It lets them see hope to change their life."

She shook her cup again.

"It's all for a good cause."

"Gotcha. Here you go."

"Thank you."

"Sure."

"God bless you."

"Thank you, Blanche. Good luck."

I left her working the customers in a Holtville convenience store parking lot.

Holtville is named for the Missouri banker W. F. Holt, a capitalist visionary who saw the Imperial Valley desert, noted the adjacent flows of the Colorado River, and figured out how to finance the politicking and engineering that turned the desert into the garden it still is over a hundred years later. He was the model for Barbara Worth's foster father, Jefferson Worth. Harold Bell Wright dedicated *The Winning of Barbara Worth* to Holt. Makes sense that there is a Holtville in the Valley.

What is in a place name? Some, of course, echo with drama and history. Paris comes immediately to mind. Athens, Crete. The hills of Buda, the Danube, and the Pest side of the city. Some simply ring with the sound of romance: Hong Kong, Rio de Janeiro, Dar es Salaam. Others are mundane to the point of cliché. There must be a Springfield in every state of the Union. The predictable are legion: Madison, Washington, Jefferson City. And then there are the hybrids. The Cal Neva Casino at Lake Tahoe. The Delmarva Peninsula, spanning Delaware, Maryland, and Virginia. Should it be Minneconsin or Winnesota? Texarkana!

Hence, Calexico (and Mexicali). It doesn't take long to figure out the toponymy.

Calexico doesn't make the news often outside of the Valley. Tunnels under la línea may rate the arrival of a CNN crew from San Diego.

Consequential drug busts and high-speed Border Patrol chases that end with deadly car crashes may make the headlines elsewhere. An earthquake hit Guadalupe Victoria in Mexico, and Calexico was used in news dispatches as a geographical reference, as in "it hit the Mexican town of Guadalupe Victoria, about 31 miles southeast of the California desert city of Calexico." Not much of a claim to fame: the California desert city of Calexico.

"California is the world's sixth-largest economy," Markos reminded us, as we talked about our Valley experiences, "and yet it is dusty and desolate, sleepy and sullen-looking when compared to the Mexican side of the border at Calexico. Mexicali life seems a public cacophony."

In fact, Google *Calexico* and the first hit isn't the struggling border city, it is the band named Calexico. It isn't until the fifth that you find the official City of Calexico site.

"Yeah, well, that's a good thing," Calexico percussionist John Convertino told me when I hooked up with him to learn about the connection between the popular group and the California desert city.

"When Joey [guitarist Joey Burns] and I were trying to think of a name for the band, he had mentioned Calexico because we'd passed the city on our way out to San Diego when we'd play gigs there. The first thing that came to my mind was, 'Oh, yeah.' I loved the blending of the two names: California and Mexico. My grandparents were first generation, came over from Italy through Ellis Island. I'm half Italian and half American, I guess. There's Irish and German and everything else in my other half. I did have that connection of being a "mixed-up" person, like that name. I think Joey related to it as well, because he was born and raised in California. He had roots in California and was around Mexican culture quite a bit through his parents listening to mariachi music, so there really was a connection to the name."

Visualize the boys blasting west on The Eight, going an easy eighty miles per hour across the desert, trying to come up with the name of their band, and suddenly on the horizon is the Caltrans exit sign offering, "Calexico Next Exit."

"That's right," Convertino authenticated the image. "It was pretty obvious and a really good fit. Originally, the band was called Spoke, and I liked that name too, because Joey was just starting to experiment with singing, and his singing style was very much like a spoken style. But there was a heavy metal band in Florida with that name."

Always annoying when somebody takes your name first. I asked him why Calexico and not Mexicali.

"I guess we were a little bit more to the California side, being on this side of it. But I think Mexicali is a great name, too. We were just absorbing what was going on around us, the culture that was around us." Mexican music influenced their own, wafting up over the border to their Tucson homes. "Musicians don't feel barriers. It's the classic statement that music is the universal language. It truly is." He paused and considered the fact that we were talking with each other in the context of borderlands research. "Talking to a musician about borders is a good idea, because most musicians would just say, 'What borders?' I want to relate to you through music, I can relate to you through music. You can play a musical statement, and I will respond to it. I think it's a really good metaphor for how you could deal with borders."

The band played Calexico, in the gracious auditorium on the San Diego State University Calexico campus—where the candidates debated.

"It was a great experience, really, really positive." The city declared it "Calexico Day" in honor of the band. "Some kids came up from Mexicali and said our music was being played on the radio in Mexico. It was really inspiring and it made us want to get down there and play. But it's really difficult to get gigs down in Mexico. I think at some point we're just going to have to throw our hands up and just drive down there and start playing."

But as John Convertino thought back a few years to the Calexico concert, the warm reception from the crowd was more than matched by his memories of the border itself.

"I think what struck me the most playing in Calexico and being in the city was the wall. Just walking around the town before we played and seeing the wall and feeling the wall and actually seeing the guards up there on the wall, I was immediately taken back to late 1988, the first time I went to Europe with Giant Sand and played Berlin, and I went to the Berlin Wall. It's the same." Convertino said the atmosphere was the same: "If I go over that wall, I'm going to get shot. Or if someone comes over this side, they're going to get in some serious trouble."

I did it, the chamber of commerce president did it, and Calexico's drummer did it. It is impossible not to compare the barrier the United States is building on the border with the Berlin Wall, despite the protestations from the Homeland Security Department that their Mexican wall is designed with concern for its architectural and psychological impact on the borderlands.

Convertino and his bandmates were not swayed by such suggestions. "If we're, as a race of somewhat intelligent human beings, to learn from history and historical mistakes, we have to understand that every wall that's ever been built has come down. It's a waste. After so many historical walls going up and coming down, we're building a brand-new fresh one. When you really sit down and start thinking about it, it's quite infuriating. It really brings up some anger in me to think about the amount of money, the amount of work, the amount of labor, and the amount of fear and trouble it's just going to cause."

Already has caused. It has fractured the Calexico–Mexicali community and all the communities along the border.

"It's just nuts," Convertino summed up the reality. "That's the only thing you can say." But he's an activist musician. We talked about a combined reading from this book with a Calexico concert at the border, and he suggested a performance literally on the border, on the physical line. "I think getting down there playing some music and writing about it sure helps. But ultimately it's going to be getting the right legislation and the right shift in thinking."

We talked as crews were extending the wall, fixing razor wire to its top, while the Department of Homeland Security was taking border property owners on the U.S. side to federal court to force landowners to turn over their properties as venues for the barrier.

"There's a huge cement wall in Calexico and Mexicali, but I still think there's a possibility to slow it down or halt it." Convertino was firm, and he had his assignment.

"Playing the music, blended music, and being open about where the music comes from and how it's created. Getting people to hear it and see how it is productive, it's positive. It makes you feel good. How art works is that it gets into our souls. I think that's a good way to spread the word."

The border permeates Calexico's music.

"You can get along with your neighboring country even if they have different money or language and culture. It can be done," said Convertino, pointing to Europe as an example. "You have to shake your head and ask, 'Why are we building such a huge barrier to our brothers down south?' You just shake your head."

He knows all the arguments: drug smuggling, Mexicans taking jobs. He rejects them.

"You can't go down those roads. They immediately dead-end. Because I would not be here unless my grandparents came over from Italy."

And I wouldn't be in California if my father hadn't made the crossing from Hungary. That's the story repeated well over 300 million times in America.

"Yeah. And so you can't all of a sudden just say, 'Hmmm, no. Nobody else can come in now.' And, 'Hmmm. Nobody else can speak anything but English.' You just can't do that. It's just not going to work."

Shortly after we talked, John Convertino and Calexico released their album titled *Carried to Dust*, and a line from one of the songs neatly sums up the Calexico–Mexicali dichotomy: Two silver trees/Two silver trees/Two worlds in need/Two silver trees.

≈ ≈ ≈

Saturday

Going Home

Markos and I headed out of the Valley, north out of Holtville on 115; we turned east onto 78 and cruised the black Mazda through lush crop-lands in the direction of another desert anomaly made possible with Colorado River water: we would fly home from Las Vegas. A few miles east of Alamorio on 78 we gained altitude and left the below-sea-level Imperial Valley behind. The Algodones Dunes glowed, their windblown peaks and valleys looking like our Pacific waves coming ashore at San Francisco's Ocean Beach (except where they were torn up by dune buggy tracks). It was a spectacular Lawrence of Arabia land, shimmering in the sunlight, punctuated with cartoon-perfect cacti. We were alone on the two-lane blacktop. Just us, the Mazda, and a gas gauge floating fast toward "E."

Up over another desert rise and a quick drop into an unexpected Border Patrol secondary checkpoint, far, far north of the border and impossible to detour around.

"Good morning. How you doing today?" queried the smiling bor-der patrolman Martino, according to his nameplate.

"Doing great," I said. "How about yourself?"

"Good, thanks," said Agent Martino, and he identified himself. "United States Border Patrol. You both U.S. citizens?"

"Yes," agreed the Greek American and the Hungarian American.

"Have a good day," Mr. Martino dismissed us.

"All right," I acknowledged. But I wanted to talk with him. There was zero traffic. He must have been lonely in this isolated post. A chat would do him good, and we might learn something.

"How about gasoline?" I asked. "When will we find gasoline?" It wasn't a fatuous question. We had mindlessly left the Valley with less than half a tank. And we were decidedly in the middle of bloody nowhere.

Good news. "Gasoline is exactly twenty miles straight ahead."

Time to get to work. "I just have one question, Mr. Martino," I said. "How do you ascertain that we are citizens? We are, in fact, citizens. But how do you make the determination that it's okay for us to keep going?"

"Based on the facts," he said. "Like I can look at you, I can look inside your car. You guys aren't nervous when I speak to you. I can pretty much tell you're not lying to me."

"Okay."

"People that aren't telling the truth, there's a lot of different signs that we're trained to look for."

"Yeah? Like what kinds of things would they do?"

"Ah, a lot of different things. A lot of people shake. A lot of people get nervous; they won't make eye contact with you."

"What happens then?"

"We run records checks and if they turn out to be illegal . . ."

I interrupted him. "But how do you determine that they are illegal?"

"Based on the facts."

"What types of facts?" I ask.

"If they're a U.S. citizen," Agent Martino explained, "they'll know they're born here or they're naturalized, they'll know the process. They'll know the date; they'll know the forms they had to fill out. They'll know everything. If they don't know those things, that's a pretty good indication for me to start asking more questions."

"But isn't it the case that we don't have to carry identification? We don't have to prove to you that we're U.S. citizens."

"Right. That's true. That's true. But if I didn't believe that you guys were U.S. citizens, I would ask you more questions. Where were you born? What was the name of the hospital? Where were your parents born?"

"Then what's a tipping point? People confess?"

"Usually. Usually if you keep asking questions, you'll get them to break."

I was surprised and impressed. "Really?" I asked.

"Yeah," he said. "They'll say yeah, I'm here illegally."

"Wow!"

"It's all about the questions that you ask."

"It's just this confrontation with the badge and the uniform and the questions that makes them break?" I asked him.

"That's part of it. A lot of times you ask the same question over and over again, in different ways."

"And you have the authority to not let them pass, so you are the power."

"We have the authority to detain them for a reasonable amount of time. I mean, I can't sit here and question you for six hours just because I have a suspicion that you're illegal, but I can keep you here for a substantive amount of time to develop my facts and everything else."

"If they don't break, how do you determine that you need to send them back?"

"Well if they don't break, there's nothing really we can do. If they stick to their guns, I can call and get records checks on anybody. If you do have some form of immigration history, if you've been arrested before, or even if you've done something that's not illegal, like you've applied for documents, I'll have that all in my records database. For example, if you've been deported before, obviously you were here illegally. Once you've been deported, you can't become a citizen."

"But theoretically, if they were clever, they could say the right things, and you'd say okay, and wave them past."

"They could say the right things, but this is a pretty intimidating place if you're here illegally."

"Sure. Okay. Well, that's fascinating. Thank you."

"All right," he said. "Yeah, have a good day."

"Thanks, Mr. Martino. You too."

≩ ≩ ≩

Epilogue

My Prescription: Swallow Hard and Say, "¡Bienvenidos!"

America must stop making the same mistakes on our southern border. Overdue is a simple and logical policy change: it is time to welcome our Mexican brothers and sisters to cross the border.

De facto, national borders are archaic, centuries-old artifacts. Yet de jure, they are relevant economic, political, social, and cultural barriers to needed human integration. In an efficiently operating free-market system, the flow of capital, goods, and labor must be regulated for quality control, but otherwise unimpeded. The counterproductive rants of the paranoid nativist dinosaurs paralyzing the U.S. political agenda continue to infect American policy. Those unemployed, bitter, Bible-thumping, gun-toting white guys Barack Obama (an ultimate border crosser) identified during the 2008 presidential campaign must either get over their fear and hate of the Other or get out of the path of reality. Migration fueled by economic need prevails over fear and hate. And such migration self-regulates. When the economy stumbled in late 2008, many unemployed Mexicans unable to find work in the north returned home, retracing their steps south and back across the border.

It's time to transcend national borders and breeze past them with dismissal. In the Internet-driven virtual world, where so many of us spend so much of our work and play time, we build new tribal relationships with those in our specific subcultures of interest. These tribes know no physical geography or statehood or border guards—they're barely policed. Back in the long-ago twentieth century, most of our important relationships were face-to-face. We enjoyed three-martini lunches and sometimes got soused instead of a signed contract. We met for conferences, not conference calls. We went out on dates instead of trying cybersex. Virtual versus physical: one's not necessarily better than the other under all circumstances. They are different experiences with different goals and results. Just as the borders in the Internet world are easy to cross, so should be the lines that separate us as nations, especially the line separating the United States and Mexico. The beauty of the borderlands is that the distant has come home, the Other has become us.

Calexico is the Lower East Side is the Silicon Valley (Bangalore by the Bay) is Miami (with its Little Havana more Havana than Habana). Twenty-first-century nomads, making use of the Internet and the jet, accelerate the Mixmaster of the proverbial melting pot, creating the world's Calexicos. If AIDS can spread from one flight attendant (if it really did) to the rest of the world, if the crack epidemic can grow out of the demand for cocaine from Wall Street bonus–fat thrill seekers, so do our American culture and value system make a viral spread worldwide. But it is a two-way street. Patrick J. Buchanan, the perennial pundit, conservative Republican presidential candidate, and Nixon speechwriter, told me that he believes "the America we grew up in until 1965 was a nation with an ethnocultural core. Ours was Western European and Christian. That did not mean everyone in the country was a Christian nor everyone in the country could trace his ancestors to Europe or the West. But that was basically the core of the country, and it's one of the things that really held us together. Now I see the masses of immigration coming from the third world—and huge numbers illegally—as presenting a tremendously more difficult problem of assimilation."

Assimilation to what? What are Mr. Buchanan and his followers so afraid of? That our values will be diluted or, worse, overwhelmed and ruined? What is it exactly about those pre–civil rights and pre–voting rights days of the early 1960s that they lament losing? Our America only grows stronger with exposure to the Other: their ideas, their labor, their entrepreneurial talents (and of course their cuisine!). Our America belongs to the world, and the world is welcome to it. ¡Bienvenidos! Our inclusive and egalitarian American values make us strong. Our legal system protects us; that's all the assimilation we need demand from immigrants: that they obey the laws of our land.

What about the worries of the Buchanans of the world that the values of the Others negatively infect us? First of all, it's a little late in the game, Brother Buchanan. Walk into your favorite Walmart and read the label. This is an old story: too much of the stuff we consume is from Over There. It's not just the goods, of course, it's the services. Nothing like eating sushi in Chicago and hearing the sushi-knife-wielding, Japanese-character-decorated-bandana-wearing sushi chef with the nametag José ask you, ¿Algo más?

External forces simply cannot destroy the idea and the actuality that is America. Only we Americans can do that. The methodology is simple: trash the Constitution, engage in war crimes, deny basic civil liberties, debate torture as a valid policy tool, and build a Maginot migration wall (our ludicrous attempts to wall off our southern border have been as effective as our French allies' similar efforts in World War I).

Calexicos are the grassroots reality of merging cultures, reality-based twenty-first-century hatcheries that have been incubating since the Industrial Revolution. They don't feel bound by treaties or directives from their national capitals. They figure out pragmatic workarounds. Their black-and-gray economies thrive and often dominate. Of course, radical societal change can exhibit problematic and destructive dark sides. But the misery is not caused by the Other coming to America. Go to our Rust Belt, or learn about it in Bruce Springsteen's "Hometown": They're closing down the textile mill across the railroad tracks/Foreman says these jobs are going boys and they ain't coming back to/Your hometown, your hometown, your hometown, your hometown.

The government on the north side of the border can continue to build its Berlin Wall along the Mexican border. But note that there is no effort to fence the entire borderlands, just some seven hundred miles of the two-thousand-mile frontier. Why is that? Can Washington not afford the whole wall? Or does America know, as the mockudrama movie title announces so accurately, that the U.S. economy cannot survive a day without a Mexican? Is the idea to create a gauntlet so tough that it winnows the migrants coming north to the best and, if not the brightest, at least the toughest?

Anthropologist Michael Kearney, at the University of California at Riverside, who has spent much of his career studying borders, suggests that the Border Patrol is not in the business of keeping all Mexicans out of the United States labor pool, but rather is on duty to remind those who manage to get north to work hard and accept low wages— an understandable conclusion for laborers who risk arrest and worse. "The frontier between the United States and Mexico is formally a line with no width," writes Kearney. "But it is also a social and cultural zone of indeterminate extent, and some might argue that it runs from deep in Mexico to Canada." Count me among those some so arguing. What I call the Thick Borderlands runs from Interstate 8 to the internationally recognized official Mexican–American line. But what I consider the Extended Borderlands do stretch from Chiapas in Mexico through these United States to the Canadian provinces hiring Mexican migrant workers.

National borders are fading fast. Millions of migrants ignore them. Others arrange for dual and more citizenships, carrying multiple passports, pulling them out at the world's ever-less-enforceable national borders based on pragmatism and convenience, much like shoppers at Macy's. Let's see, should I use my Visa or American Express card for this sweater? Hmmm, should I cross into Canada and show my Hong Kong Chinese passport or my European Community Hungarian passport? University of California at Berkeley anthropologist Aihwa Ong calls it "flexible citizenship." Most of us are becoming true transnationals: Where do we work and play? Where were our clothes made? Who controls our media, news and otherwise? What do we eat? The grip of the nation-state is waning. Get used to it, Lou Dobbs, while you double-check the lock on your community's gate. Multinational corporations began ignoring national borders long ago. They even abandoned the moniker "multinational"; it became archaic. Instead, they are "globalized." Look at those freighters docked at the Port of Oakland. Any of them flagged United States? Ha.

How about the North American Free Trade Agreement? Once Mexico signed that treaty, it could no longer keep Monsanto's genetically modified cheap corn out of its *tiendas,* and its *campesinos* could no longer grow corn and sell it for a price that could compete with Monsanto's. Nothing illegal about Monsanto's actions; read the NAFTA fine print. It guarantees free movement of capital and product across the border. But what about labor? That out-of-business campesino looks north and sees "help wanted" signs offering work to compensate for his loss of corn income. But he must achieve wetback status to take the gringo jobs on offer; he must sneak into the United States and work under the table.

The system is broken. But beefing up the border is no solution. In fact, other than the self-aggrandizing Lou Dobbs–types (along with his echo formerly in the Congress, Tom Tancredo, another otherwise pleasant fellow when he is not foaming at the mouth to demagogue immigration), few Americans want to keep Mexicans out of their gardens, kitchens, nurseries, and meatpacking plants. Sealing the border ("Just what part of 'illegal' don't you understand?") isn't an option. We have the money. We have the technology. We obviously just don't want it sealed—or the might of the world's only superpower would seal it.

The same goes for militarizing the border. Despite the temporary use of the National Guard, mobilized to back up the Border Patrol (and to trash the Barbara Worth Resort, according to Markos's friend George), the U.S. military cannot fight in Iraq and Afghanistan, stand by for Katrina-type disaster work, and post a sentry opposite every Mexican en route to a roofing job in Orange County. We don't have the political will, and we don't have the numbers in uniform.

There is a simple solution.

Open the border to the free passage of Mexicans who wish to come north. Regularize reality. The migrants will have to properly identify themselves with a document that the U.S. government finds acceptable, a birth certificate or a driver's license, or some sort of government paperwork. On the U.S. side, that identity will be entered into a database. The U.S. government will keep track of this incoming traffic. It will cross-check the names with Mexican authorities and reject those migrants obviously ill suited for U.S. entry: known criminals, for example. Will there be fraud and will some misfits slip through the gates? Of course. But at least there will be a semblance of control, the beginnings of some knowledge about who is in our national neighborhood. The status quo leaves the gates wide open. We've no idea who the twelve, fourteen, sixteen, eighteen million (or more?) who just strode in are, where they live, or what they're doing.

What do we do with those "illegal" millions already here? Well, Mr. Dobbs-Buchanan-O'Reilly, you surely cannot evict them. They are in your spare bedroom permanently. Process them, too. Get an idea who they are, where they live, and what they're up to by offering them a regularized status. Bring them in from the black and gray markets. Allow them to take their children to school without driving with one eye out for the Highway Patrol because the state where they live and pay taxes will not issue them driver's licenses. Especially in car-culture California, just how many undocumented aliens do you really think are taking the bus instead of the Chevy because they don't carry a license? They're in the country illegally; who really thinks the lack of a driver's license keeps them off the road? And just who suffers from motorists cruising the freeways without the benefit of learning the rules of the road? Of course, we all do.

Regularizing Mexican migration (which will self-regulate based on the supply and demand of jobs in El Norte) and regularizing the millions already in the States is the only reasonable and long-term solution.

End of the line?

These Mexicans are coming no matter what we do, and they are people the United States wants and needs. Otherwise, they wouldn't be here; there would be no magnet to pull them from their villages and families. Worried that the United States will fill up with unemployed Mexicans if such a policy were implemented? Don't be. If there's no work, they won't come.

What about Salvadorans and Chinese, Romanians and Sudanese? Do we swing the fence gate open for the world? Of course not. Mexico is exceptional. We share our contiguous border, our history (including multiple U.S. invasions of Mexico and a Manifest Destiny land grab that cost Mexico half its territory), and the de facto mélange of our cultures and peoples. We can worry about the rest of the world later. Let's fix the crises with Mexico now.

There is a spectacular fringe benefit to this radical policy shift. Once Mexicans who wish to come to the States to work or study, or even just to tour, can travel north freely, the real bad guys can no longer hide in the shadows of millions of Mexicans heading north clandestinely.

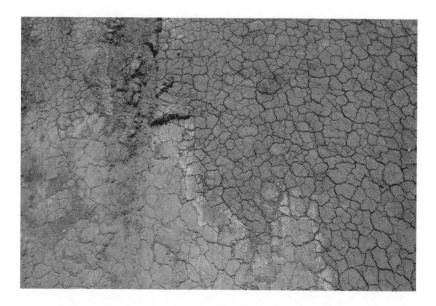

What the triple-digit temperatures do to Calexico earth without irrigation.

The dope smugglers, the terrorists, the types we really do not want in our midst will be exposed to the awesome manpower and technology of the Border Patrol. And that goes for the above-mentioned Salvadorans and Chinese, Romanians and Sudanese, and all the rest of the world's tired, poor, huddled masses yearning to breathe free, the wretched refuse. If we deal pragmatically with the Mexican migrants by letting them come and go as they please, with rigorous insistence on credible documentation of everyone who comes north, we *can* control the passage of the Salvadorans and Chinese, Romanians and Sudanese, et al.

Over time those Mexicans currently living a quasi-underground lifestyle around us will learn to blend and not collide with us. And we with them.

When Mexicans can again travel freely north (even after the U.S. Southwest was no longer Mexico, until relatively recently no paperwork was needed to traverse the border), the Border Patrol will know that plenty of those people in the tunnels and jumping the fences and running across the desert probably are worth chasing; there they can find criminals we need to keep out of our gated community/nation. Let's embrace the fuel of our economy, the immigrant seeking work.

This rational and practical policy can and should be put into practice now, saving us years of heartbreak and expense, or we can just wait until the reality of economic-driven migration erases the border. By our overt action or by the facts of borderlands life, the line in the sand marking the Mexico–U.S. border eventually will be as benign as the Arizona–California border: just a quick check, if that.

¿Why wait, amigos?

≋ ≋ ≋

Afterword

Calexico at the Intersection of Life and Death

Calexico, like every other place, is unique. But it is also strikingly similar to other U.S. border towns because the boundary with Mexico—simultaneously a divide and a bridge—significantly defines it. Calexico is thus caught between forces that necessitate the boundary serve as a gateway, and those that demand that it be a barrier. As such, Calexico is a bundle of contradictions. It embodies hope and despair, life and death, welcome and rejection. While one could make the same observation of any town, the contradictions are especially pronounced in places like Calexico—due to its southern limit born of conquest and exclusion and, at the same time, continuously remade through dynamic and intensifying socioeconomic ties.

Located on the front line of the ever-growing boundary-security apparatus, with thousands of federal agents and their dependents working and living in the area, Calexico is in some ways the ultimate American town. In others, it is its very antithesis—especially given the historical and contemporary equation of "American" with "Anglo," and given myriad demographic factors that help to blur the distinctions between Calexico and its cross-boundary cousin, Mexicali. An estimated 80 percent of Calexico's children, for example, enter the city's school system speaking Spanish, and approximately 95 percent of its residents are Latino. At the same time, while Calexico and the larger Imperial Valley are in many ways quite prosperous vis-à-vis their neighbors in Mexico, they are also home to significant socioeconomic hardship. As an April 27, 2009, *Los Angeles Times* article asserted, "Name the state statistic, and Imperial County (population: 172,000) is usually near the top or the bottom, whichever is worse: per capita income, welfare recipients, families below the poverty line, elderly living in poverty and so on." It went on to report that during the previous month the Imperial Valley had the highest official unemployment rate (which is always significantly lower than the actual one) in the United States for any area with a population of more than 50,000 people: 25.1 percent.

Like many such twin towns across the boundary, Calexico and Mexicali cooperate, and have long done so. The towns had such strong economic and social ties in the 1920s that their respective fire departments answered calls in either town. Still today, Calexico's fire department occasionally responds to emergencies in Mexicali. Meanwhile, many children from Mexicali cross the boundary on a daily basis to attend private schools in Calexico, as do about 60,000 middle-class Mexicans with U.S. government–issued border-crossing cards, in order to shop at Calexico businesses ranging from mom-and-pop stores to Walmart, providing a huge impetus to the local economy. At the same time, as Peter Laufer shows us during his intimate tour recounted here, many Imperial Valley residents cross into Mexicali on weekends to enjoy the city's restaurants or clubs.

This blurring of social boundaries leads to significant challenges for U.S. authorities policing the divide. Because Calexico's downtown abuts the international line, it is relatively easy for boundary jumpers to blend into the surroundings north of the border. At the same time, numerous residents feel sympathy for unauthorized crossers and provide them with food and water, or hide them in their homes. Others, drawn by the lucrative smuggling business, shelter migrants for a price. For such reasons, many Calexicans refuse to cooperate with the Border Patrol.

Despite binational interdependence, the relationship between Mexicali and the Imperial Valley is far from an equal or just one, an outcome facilitated by the very presence of the U.S.–Mexico divide. Reminiscent of apartheid South Africa's dependence on "homelands" for its workforce, the Imperial Valley draws much of its manual labor from across the boundary.

These laborers, who typically have work visas, usually arrive by four o'clock a.m. From there, labor contractors transport many of them to farms, some as far away as Yuma, Arizona—sixty miles to the east. And they return home to the Mexican side of the boundary at the end of the day. As the Valley's economy has diversified over the last decade and agriculture has declined in relative importance, many cross-boundary laborers now work in the service and construction sectors.

Given the history of the making of the U.S.–Mexico border region, and the Imperial Valley in particular, racism and overlapping class-based inequalities are deeply embedded in Calexico and its environs.

The much-touted novel *The Making of Barbara Worth* reflects this, while helping to explain the contemporary inner boundaries—the divide between El Centro and Calexico, for example—that Peter Laufer brings to light.

Harold Bell Wright, the best-selling book's author, described a process of civilizing the desolate area and its backward peoples, part of a chain of progress—a worldview embraced at the time by many of the Valley's elites. As Wright penned in 1911, "In the Southwest savage race succeeded savage race, until at last the slow-footed padres overtook the swift-footed Indian and the rude civilization made possible by the priests in turn ran down the priest."

Wright's notion of humanity was one with a steep hierarchy within—one made evident within his novel. The author, for example, described the population of Mexican origin with a combination of scorn and pity, and sometimes, a patronizing respect. Mexicans, Native Americans, and "Chinamen," among others, worked for Anglos in the book. Wright presented them throughout the novel, when they followed orders, as docile people of simplicity. But when they did not follow Anglo dictates, he depicted them as unreasonable, insufficiently patient, and quick to resort to violence. "If they were white men," one of the Anglo characters asserted when Mexican laborers rebelled because they had not received their pay, "it would be different." At other times, when they challenged the authority of local Anglo elites, the author characterized Mexicans as "cholos" and "greasers." Thus, there were good Mexicans—ones that did not challenge the status quo and the highly hierarchical social order—and bad ones. The same dichotomy presumably applied to non-Anglos more broadly.

Wright's characterizations surely resonated with many of the Anglos that began populating the Imperial Valley in the early twentieth century. By then, California already had a highly stratified racial order. Native Americans were at the bottom of the ranking, a product of a strict racial hierarchy that informed California's social structure from the time of its incorporation into the United States.

The institutionalized racism—especially toward the population of Mexican origin—persisted through much of the twentieth century. As a man from East Los Angeles, recalling the repeated humiliation his father endured as someone of Mexican descent living and working in southern California, recounted in a 1981 article in the *New Yorker* magazine, "In 1949, we were driving back from Mexicali, where my grandfather lived, and we tried to go into a restaurant in Westmorland [a town about thirty miles north of Calexico]. . . . There was a sign at the door: 'No Dogs or Mexicans Allowed.' "

Today's racial geography in the Imperial Valley is far more complicated, and less clear-cut, but people from Mexico and beyond, especially those of the "illegal" sort, continue to be racialized—treated as people as less worthy of rights due to where they are from—through the very existence of the international boundary as a line of exclusion and control. To overcome the deprivation and insecurity that exist in their homelands, they feel they must risk their lives trying to overcome ever-stronger U.S. boundary controls. And if they succeed in migrating, they must endure all the indignities and hazards associated with being "illegal"—from substandard wages to the threat of arrest and deportation and, with it, divided families.

While nature knows no boundaries, most of us continue to cling to hard territorial boundaries as necessary lines of protection against myriad threats, real and imagined. At the same time, however, it is clear that we cannot reduce human relations to bounded territories—as many Border Patrol agents themselves have shown. In late 2005, some agents in Douglas, Arizona, for instance, were caught dating the very migrants they are supposed to police. More problematic, from the perspective of U.S. authorities, are the numerous immigration agents who have succumbed to bribery and facilitated the smuggling of people and goods across the divide.

For many advocates of strict border controls, such phenomena are cause for more of the same in terms of strengthening enforcement. But in addition to denying the transboundary reality that makes such transgressions inevitable, hardening the boundaries only results in more violence and suffering. In a world of deep and growing inequality, insecurity, and instability, boundary regulation denies people the right to move to the places where there are resources to realize basic human needs—whether they be jobs at decent wages, sufficient food, refuge from repression, or love.

During the summer of 2006, I worked in southern Arizona with a group that provides humanitarian aid to migrants, called No More Deaths. During that time, there was a story in the local newspaper about Antonio Torres Jimenez, a long-time Tucson resident. Some friends from his hometown in Guanajuato, Mexico, who were then living in Tucson, had found his body in the Arizona desert in late June 2006. He had perished while trying to return to his Tucson home. He had been a permanent resident of the United States, but several years earlier U.S. authorities had stripped him of his legal status because of an administrative violation. He had had to return to Mexico after the death of his eldest daughter to be with his wife and other children. But he had stayed there too long and had thus lost his green card. Dependent on his construction job in Tucson, he continued to come back and forth. In the process, he had to take increasing risks to beat the ever-more-formidable enforcement apparatus that scars the borderlands, which ultimately brought about his death.

Such a tragedy is what we see increasingly in the border regions that divide and bring together rich and poor, the safe and the insecure, the first and third worlds, the white and nonwhite.

Since the mid-1990s, there have been approximately six thousand migrant bodies recovered in the U.S.–Mexico borderlands. Many of the deaths have taken place in the All-American Canal. According to a May 2, 2010, report on 60 Minutes, the television news show, over 550 people have perished in the Imperial Valley waterway over the years. A drowning expert interviewed on the show, John Fletemeyer, a professor at Florida International University, called it "probably the most dangerous body of water in the United States," due to a combination of the canal's very cold water and its swift-moving current.

As Peter Laufer notes, the death toll in the U.S.–Mexico borderlands is vastly greater than the number of East Germans who died trying to get across the Berlin Wall during the cold war. This is just one of the many manifestations of suffering and indignity that people must endure simply because they were born on the wrong side of the boundaries that make up the unjust world order in which we live.

On the same day that Antonio Torres Jimenez perished in the desert of southern Arizona, I attended a baptism of a healthy, beautiful, two-month-old girl at the Catholic cathedral in Tucson. She had been born in May 2006 in the same desert to a woman from Guatemala who was crossing with two other women. The two women stayed with the mother during and after the birth, helping her to cut the baby's umbilical cord with a nail clipper. Because they stayed with her, the Border Patrol was able to apprehend them and return them to their homeland.

It's important that we tell this story, and others like it. To overcome feelings of despair, we need to remind ourselves that border regions can and often do bring out the best in many: kindness, generosity, and solidarity. This is true in Tucson, just as it is Calexico and throughout the Imperial Valley. This is not to deny the cruelty and xenophobia that also reign there, but to highlight that what Calexico is, and what it becomes, is our collective choice. Whether the border embodies life or death, hope or despair, welcome or rejection is up to all of us.

Joseph Nevins
Vassar College geography professor and author of *Dying to Live: A Story of Immigration in an Age of Global Apartheid*

≈ ≈ ≈
About the Author

Peter Laufer, PhD, reports on borders, migration, and identity, and he often focuses on examples from his home state, California, for his studies. His book *Wetback Nation* calls for opening the Mexican–American border to most Mexicans wishing to travel north, a policy change, he argues, that will make the U.S. southern border more secure than the continuing failed attempts that rely on fences and guards to prevent unauthorized entry into the United States. He is the James Wallace Chair in Journalism at the University of Oregon School of Journalism and Communication, and the author of over a dozen books that deal with social and political issues, including *The Dangerous World of Butterflies* and *Mission Rejected: U.S. Soldiers Who Say No to Iraq*. More about his books, documentary films, and broadcasts, which have won the George Polk, Robert F. Kennedy, Edward R. Murrow, and other awards, can be found at peterlaufer.com.